Be
2copies
8.68

T5-BBB-230

The Semi-Professions
and
Their Organization

The Semi-Professions and Their Organization

▶

Teachers, Nurses, Social Workers

edited by *Amitai Etzioni*

DEPARTMENT OF SOCIOLOGY

COLUMBIA UNIVERSITY

The Free Press, New York

COLLIER-MACMILLAN LIMITED, LONDON

Preface

*T*HIS BOOK ATTEMPTS TO INCREASE sociological knowledge about the *professions* by focusing on a group of new professions whose claim to the status of doctors and lawyers is neither fully established nor fully desired. Lacking a better term, we shall refer to those professions as *semi*-professions. Their training is shorter, their status is less legitimated, their right to privileged communication less established, there is less of a specialized body of knowledge, and they have less autonomy from supervision or societal control than "the" professions.[1]* We use the term semi-professions without any derogatory implications. Other terms which have been suggested are either more derogatory in their connotations (e.g. sub-professions or pseudo-professions) or much less established and communicative (e.g., "heteronomous" professions, a concept used by Max Weber).[2]

By focusing on semi-professions, we also enter willy-nilly

* Notes to Preface begin on page xvii.

three other areas of sociological study: that of *organizations*, in which practically all semi-professionals are employed; that of *demography*, because the large majority of the labor force we deal with is female and its demographic attributes significantly affect our subject; and that of *conflict analysis*, because—as we shall see—the normative principles and cultural values of professions, organizations, and female employment are not compatible. Hence this may also be seen as a study of societal sources of tension, adaptations, and their limitations.

Members of the respective semi-professions may find here a sociological contribution to an analysis of their situation and its dynamics. Our position may initially arouse some resentment for we do not accept some of the claims and self-images these professions have fostered; hopefully, however, this resentment will be followed by greater self-analysis and understanding. The comparative dimension may, as it often does, serve to increase the scope of awareness, helping teachers, nurses and social workers to realize that what they consider "their" problem is shared by other semi-professions and is, in part, socially induced.[3]

An intriguing policy recommendation arises from the following analysis: as we see it, a significant segment of the semi-professions aspire to a full-fledged professional status and sustain a professional self-image, despite the fact that they themselves are often aware that they do not deserve such a status, and despite the fact that they objectively do not qualify for reasons that will be discussed. One reason, it seems, they aspire to professional status is because the only alternative status is that of the non-professional employee, specifically the white collar and blue collar worker. As semi-professionals see it, they obviously are "more" than secretaries, salesgirls, or office clerks. Unable to find a niche between these white collar statuses and the professions, and not wishing to be identified with the lower-status group, they cling to the higher aspiration of being a full professional.[4]

This unrealistic aspiration is not without cost. The costs are those typically associated with persons seeking to pass for what they are not: a guilty feeling for floating a status claim without sufficient base and a rejection by those who hold the status legitimately. The semi-professionals' efforts to change themselves, more fully to live up to the claim floated, generate a major source of tensions because there are several powerful societal limitations on the extent to which these occupations can be fully professionalized. Various rationalizations are provided to justify continued attempts to reach the unreachable; for example, semi-professional ideologues argue that, since the line marking professional from the semi-professional is a murky one, how is one to tell who is "in" and who is not? (The correct observation is that although the borderlines are not sharply delineated, the parties involved are not prevented from recognizing those who are manifestly, on several accounts, on one side or the other.) Finally, as in other such status groups, the desire to pass for a higher-status group produces pressures which split the group into those closer to the "passing" limit and those more remote, thus weakening both subgroupings in the societal give-and-take.

The policy recommendation which obviously emerges is for these middle-status groups to acknowledge their position, to seek to improve their status rather than to try to pass for another. They are semi-professionals; a public relations man may devise a better label ("servicing professions" has been suggested, but, as we see it, all professions serve). The main point is that the membership must realize that there is a distinct middle ground from which these groupings neither can nor need to break out. They may seek to promote a society in which status differences matter less in terms of income, prestige, and other rewards; but even in the best of all worlds there will still be differences resulting from the division of labor between those with no professional knowledge, those with highly specialized knowledge, and those who are in between. For instance, their title to self-control will and ought to vary. Once it is recognized that there is a middle ground, inauthentic aspirations and positions are more likely to be renounced and the dysfunctional consequences of attempts to pass will tend to disappear.[5] The semi-professions will be able to be themselves.

This book first discusses one semi-profession at a time. Lortie provides an overview of the teachers, drawing both on his own studies and on works of numerous others. Scott and Toren divide the labor in their study of the social workers: Scott's analysis is built around his own case study; Toren extends the theoretical analysis, drawing mainly on the work of others. Katz contributes a study of the nurses. All these studies deal extensively with the tension between the professionals' principles and the organizational ones, arising from the fact that the authority of knowledge and the authority of administrative hierarchy are basically incompatible, a point elaborated below.

Another tension is the subject of Ida and Richard Simpson's comparative work, a tension that is found in all the organizations employing these semi-professionals (schools, social work agencies, and hospitals). It is the tension between full-scale, especially semi-professional, employment and women's status in our society. This analysis provides a "control" over those of the other participants in this volume, as tensions that may seem a result of the clash between professional and organizational principles actually may be the result of the composition of the labor force. (Here the extension of our line of analysis to an organization which employs mainly *male* semi-professionals, e.g., engineers, should prove highly rewarding.)[6] This holds even more true for the various adaptations evolved. It is difficult to believe that many of the arrangements we found in the relations between doctors and nurses, social workers and their supervisors, teachers and principals, would work out if, let us say, 90 per cent of the nurses and of the supervised social workers were male, especially lower middle class, as are so many of the females employed in these positions. Such a statement may sound prejudiced against a most attractive minority. It must therefore be noted that we are not advocating that the tensions between professional and organizational principles be solved or even reduced at the cost of equality for female employees but merely observing a frequent actuality that the data presented by the Simpsons quite adequately demonstrate.

William J. Goode provides a deep dynamic perspective. Yesterday's non-professions may be tomorrow's professions; are the semi-professions just a stop, a transitional stage? The answer, he shows, differs for different occupations. In the process of establishing what the propelling factors are, Goode studies the various attributes of the key semi-professions and the directions they are taking.

* * *

This volume is the result of a somewhat uncommon form of teamwork which deserves a few comments. Once a subject spanning several areas of specialization had become the center of focus, a pooling of talents was called for. Of course, one of us could have studied social workers first, then nurses, and finally teachers, but each having worked previously in a particular area assured deeper anchoring in the respective fields than could have otherwise been hoped for. Teamwork requires a meeting of minds, at least to the extent of establishing a common definition of the subject and the dimensions to be covered and to allow comparisons. The obvious solution was a symposium or workshop. But experience suggests that such meetings, which are expensive, often do not generate the expected fertile communications (the resulting volumes are my witness). It may be that these meetings are too short, that the authors are not working on their papers when the symposium or workshop is convened, or that they have already written them and are already committed to their presented content.

We tried something else. The following memorandum was sent to all the authors and from that time forward they were on their own. We deliberately did not "edit out" the occasions in which they overlapped because divergent treatments of the same subject at this exploratory stage are called for. The product of our low-cost, maximum-autonomy approach is not satisfactory; there is much less meeting of minds and parallelism of treatment here than would be desirable. Some other mechanism that allows for more fertile communication among authors who share in such a joint enterprise seems necessary. We reproduce here the original memorandum both to record the way this volume was conceived and to introduce a theoretical issue that is explored in the following chapters.

Memo to Participants*

ADMINISTRATIVE VS. PROFESSIONAL AUTHORITY

Administration assumes a power hierarchy. Without a clear ordering of higher and lower in rank, in which the higher in rank have more power than the lower ones and hence can control and coordinate the latter's activities, the basic principle of administration is violated; the organization ceases to be a coordinated tool. However knowledge is largely an individual property; unlike other organizational means, it cannot be transferred from one person to another by decree. Creativity is basically individual and can only to a very limited degree be ordered and coordinated by the superior in rank. Even the application of knowledge is basically an individual act, at least in the sense that the individual professional has the ultimate responsibility for his professional decision. The surgeon has to decide whether or not to operate. Students of the professions have pointed out that the autonomy granted to professionals who are basically responsible to their consciences (though they may be censured by their peers and in extreme cases by the courts) is necessary for effective professional work. Only if immune from ordinary social pressures and free to innovate, to experiment, to take risks without the usual social repercussions of failure, can a professional carry out his work effectively. It is this highly individualized principle which is diametrically opposed to the very essence of the organizational principle of control and coordination by superiors— i.e., the principle of administrative authority. In other words, the ultimate justification for a professional act is that it is, to the best of the professional's knowledge, the right act. He might consult his colleagues before he acts

* The bulk of this memorandum is taken from Amitai Etzioni, *Modern Organizations*, pp. 76 ff., © 1964. Reprinted by permission of Prentice-Hall, Inc., Englewood Cliffs, N.J.

but the decision is his. If he errs, he still will be defended by his peers. The ultimate justification of an administrative act, however, is that it is in line with the organization's rules and regulations, and that it has been approved—directly or by implication—by a superior rank.

THE ORGANIZATION OF KNOWLEDGE

The question is how to create and use knowledge without undermining the organization. Some knowledge is formulated and applied in strictly private situations. In the traditional professions, medicine and law, much work is carried out in non-organizational contexts—in face-to-face interaction with clients. But as the need for costly resources and auxiliary staff has grown, even the traditional professions face mounting pressures to transfer their work to organizational structures such as the hospital and the law firm. Similarly, while most artistic work is still conducted in private contexts, often in specially segregated sectors of society in which an individual's autonomy is particularly high, much of the cognitive creativity, particularly in scientific research, has become embedded in organizational structures for reasons similar to those in medicine and law.

In addition there are several professions in which the amount of knowledge (as measured in years of training) and the degree of personal responsibility (as measured in the degree to which privileged communications—which the recipient is not bound to divulge—or questions of life and death are involved) are lower than in the older or highly creative, cognitive professions. Engineering and nursing are cases in point. These professions can be more easily integrated into organizational structures than can medicine or law, for example. Most professional work at this level is carried out within organizations rather than in private practice, and it is more given to supervision by persons higher in rank (who have more administrative authority but no more, or even less, professional competence) than the work of the professions discussed above.

To some degree, organizations circumvent the problem of knowledge by "buying" it from the outside, as when a corporation contracts for a market study from a research organization; i.e., it specifies the type of knowledge it needs and it agrees with the research group on price, but then it largely withdraws from control over the professional work. There are, however, sharp limitations on the extent to which knowledge can be recruited in this way particularly since organizations consume such large amounts of knowledge and they tend to need more reliable control on its nature and flow. There are three basic ways in which knowledge is handled within organizations:

1. Knowledge is produced, applied, preserved, or communicated in organizations especially established for these purposes. These are *professional organizations* which are characterized not only by the goals they pursue but also by the high proportion of professionals on their staff (at least 50 per cent) and by the authority relations between professionals and non-professionals which are so structured that professionals have superior authority over the major goal activities of the organization, a point which is explored below. Professional organizations include universities, colleges, most schools, research organizations, therapeutic mental hospitals, the larger general hospitals, and social-work agencies. For certain purposes it is useful to distinguish between those organizations employing professionals whose professional training is long (five years or more), and those employing professionals whose training is shorter, (less than five years). The former we call *full-fledged professional* organizations; the latter, *semi-professional* organizations. Generally associated with differences in training of the professionals in these two types of organizations are differences in goals, in privileges, and in concern with matters of life and death. "Pure" professional organizations are primarily devoted to the creation and application of knowledge; their professionals are usually protected in their work by the guarantee of privileged communication, and they are often concerned with matters of life and death. Semi-professional organizations are more concerned with the communication and, to a lesser extent, the application of knowledge, their professionals are less likely to be guaranteed the right of privileged communications, and they are rarely directly concerned with matters of life and death.

2. There are *service organizations* in which professionals are provided with the instruments, facilities, and auxiliary staff required for their work. The professionals, however, are not employed by the organization nor subordinated to its administrators.

3. Professionals may be employed by organizations whose goals are *non-professional,* such as industrial and military establishments. Here professionals are often assigned to special divisions or positions, which to one degree or another take into account their special needs.

We shall first discuss the relation between the two authority principles—that of knowledge and that of administration—in non-professional organizations, then in "full-fledged" professional organizations, in semi-professional organizations, and finally in service organizations.

THE SEMI-PROFESSIONAL ORGANIZATIONS

The basis of professional authority is knowledge, and the relationship between administrative and professional authority is largely affected by the amount and kind of knowledge the professional has. The relationship described above holds largely for organizations in which professional authority is based on long training (five years or more), when questions of life and death and/or privileged communication are involved, and when knowledge is created or applied rather than communicated. When professional authority is based on shorter training, involves values other than life or privacy, and covers the communication of knowledge, we find that it is related to administrative authority in a different way. First, professional work here has less autonomy; that is, it is more controlled by those higher in ranks and less subject to the discretion of the professional than in full-fledged professional organizations, though it is still characterized by greater autonomy than blue- or white-collar work. Second, the semi-professionals often have skills and personality traits more compatible with administration, especially since the qualities required for communication of knowledge are more like those needed for administration than those required for the creation, and to a degree, application of knowledge. Hence these organizations are run much more frequently by the semi-professionals themselves than by others.

The most typical semi-professional organization is the primary school. The social-work agency is the other major semi-professional organization. A semi-professional sector, rather than full-fledged organization, is found in the nursing service of hospitals.

The goal of the primary school is largely to communicate rather than to create or apply knowledge. The training of its professionals on the average falls well below five years of professional education. The social-work agency is less typical since it applies knowledge but is semi-professional in the fairly short training involved, in the fact that no questions of life and death are involved, and that privileged communication is not strictly maintained (e.g., vis-à-vis the courts). Among social workers, the longer the training and the more professional the orientation, the greater the tendency to orient to the social-work "profession" and not to the agency (the organization).

Nurses apply knowledge, but their training is much shorter than doctors, and the question of what therapy to administer is concentrated in the hands of the doctors; in this sense the nursing service is not directly related to professional decisions of life or death, although nurses have much more effect on it than teacher or social worker, and in this sense are less typical semi-professionals.

The work of these three groups has less autonomy than that of the professions discussed earlier. Their work day is tightly regulated by the cases where performance is not visible—e.g., in the case of social work because it is done in the field, or teaching because it is conducted in the classroom—detailed reporting on performance is required, and supervisors are allowed to make surprise visits to check on work being done. Nurses are directly observed and corrected by doctors and by superior nurses. Such supervision is not characteristic of the mechanisms of control found in the full-fledged professions. Inspectors are not widely used to drop in on a professor's classroom to check his teaching, especially not in the better universities. No doctor will be asked to report to an administrative superior on why he carried out his medical duties in the way he did or stand corrected by him. External examinations used in schools to check on teachers as well as students are very rare in universities.

Furthermore, much of the supervision is done by people who are themselves semi-professionals or professionals. Almost all school principals have been teachers; few have been recruited directly from training courses for school administration, and almost none are lay administrators. Virtually all social-work supervisors have been social workers. Few have assumed supervisory positions early in their careers and again almost none are lay administrators. The same is true of nursing. Thus while the semi-professionals are more supervised than the professionals, supervision is more often conducted by their own kind.

Some de-professionalization occurs in these organizations, as it does in full professional ones. Those teachers who are less committed to children, that is, the least "client-oriented," are more administration conscious, and more likely to become principals. Few principals, unless the school is particularly small, keep teaching other than in a very limited, ritualistic way. Similarly, the social-work supervisors tend to be more organization-oriented, less client-oriented even in their field-work days, and they see few cases, if any, once they move up in the hierarchy.

Not all the differences between professional and semi-professional organizations can be traced to the difference in the nature of the professional authority. Part of the problem is due to the fact that the typical professional is a male where the typical semi-professional is a female. Despite the effects of emancipation, women on the average are more amenable to administrative control than men. It seems that on the average, women are also less conscious of organizational status and more submissive in this context than men. They also, on the average, have fewer years of higher education than men, and their acceptance into the medical profession or university teaching is sharply limited. It is difficult to determine if the semi-professional organizations have taken the form they have because of the high percentage of female employees, or if they recruit females because of organizational reasons; in all likelihood these factors support each other.

Whatever the deeper reasons, the fact is that the professional and administrative authority are here related in a different way from professional organizations. Control through organization regulations and superiors is much more extensive, though not as extensive as that of blue- or white-collar workers, and it is done mainly by semi-professionals themselves. As in professional organizations, the articulation of the two modes of authority is not without strain. Here, the semi-professional subordinates tend to adopt the full-fledged professions as their reference group in the sense that they view themselves as full-fledged professionals and feel that they should be given more discretion and be less controlled. Teachers resent the "interference" of principals and many principals try to minimize it. Social workers rebel against their supervisors. Nurses often feel that they are more experienced than the young intern or more knowledgeable than the older supervisor, and hence should not be expected to submit themselves to the command of either.*

Here are some of the questions a study of semi-professionals might seek to answer. The frame of comparison, holding cultural and societal contexts constant, might be on the one hand full-fledged professionals, and on the other white-collar employees; or various sub-groups of the same semi-professional group, such as primary school teachers in better versus poorer school systems, or more versus less qualified nurses, etc.

1. What are the *sociological* characteristics of the group under study? That is, what social class and ethnic groups are they recruited from; at what level of education attained before employment; at what age did initial employment occur; what level of income, etc.

2. What *psychological* characteristics does the group display? That is, are they highly submissive, conformist, alienated, etc.

3. What typical *attitudes* to clientele, management, service ideology do they hold to?

4. *Organizational variables:* How close the supervision? By whom? What modes of rewards and punishments are

* End of reprinted material.

used? Is the service supervised visible? Are the employees members of professional associations and unions?

How effective are the mechanisms of supervision, and which are more effective than others in terms of "productivity" and employee satisfaction?

How "professional" is the self-image of the employees and how do they adjust this image to the reality of supervision from above?

*   *   *

Amitai Etzioni and Nina Toren benefited in their contributions to this volume from a grant from the Department of Health, Education and Welfare No. (WA) CRD 280-6-175. Special thanks are due to Fred Katz, who was willing to join the enterprise on short notice when the author originally slated to study the nurses was unable to complete his contribution. Elaine Klinker Hoiska assisted in preparing this book for the press. William J. Goode's study developed completely independently of the project that led to the editing of this book; at the same time his contribution is central to its theme. Maybe editorial coordination is unnecessary after all.

A. E.

Washington, D.C.
November, 1968

Notes

[1] On the relevant dimensions, see Ernest Greenwood, "Attributes of a Profession," in *Man, Work, and Society*, ed. Sigmund Nosow and William H. Form (New York: Basic Books, 1962), pp. 207–18, and William J. Goode, "Community Within a Community: the Professions," in *American Sociological Review*, 22 (1957), 194–200. On the dynamics involved, see Goode's "Encroachment, Charlatanism, and the Emerging Professions: Psychology, Sociology, and Medicine," in *American Sociological Review*, 25 (1960), 902–14; Harold L. Wilensky, "The Professionalization of Everyone?," in the *American Journal of*

Sociology, 70, No. 2 (September, 1964), 137–58; and Rue Bucher and Anselm Strauss, "Professions in Process," in the *American Journal of Sociology*, 66 (January, 1961), 325–34.

[2] Max Weber, *The Theory of Social and Economic Organization*, trans. A. M. Henderson and Talcott Parsons (New York: Free Press, 1947), p. 148. See also W. Richard Scott, "Reactions to Supervision in a Heteronomous Professional Organization," in *Administrative Science Quarterly* (June, 1965), 65–81.

[3] On this point, see Amitai Etzioni and Frederick L. DuBow (eds.), *The Comparative Perspective* (Boston: Little, Brown, 1969), editors' introduction.

[4] On this point, see Peter Leonard, "Social Workers and Bureaucracy," in *New Society* (June 2, 1966), 12–13, and Wilbur J. Cohen, "What Every Social Worker Should Know About Political Action," in *Social Work*, 11, No. 3 (July, 1966), 3–11.

[5] For additional discussion of this point, see Amitai Etzioni, *The Active Society: A Theory of Societal and Political Processes* (New York: The Free Press, 1968), Chapter 21.

[6] For a fine study, see Kenneth Prandy, *Professional Employees: A Study of Scientists and Engineers* (London: Faber and Faber, 1965).

Contents

The Semi-Professions
and
Their Organization

The Balance of Control and Autonomy in Elementary School Teaching ▲ Dan C. Lortie

DEPARTMENT OF EDUCATION
UNIVERSITY OF CHICAGO

CONTROL OVER PEOPLE AT WORK VARIES in scope and in the sources from which it comes.[1]* Certain entrepreneurial occupations permit relative freedom from external control; one thinks, for example, of the owners of independent retail establishments. As more and more work is carried on within organizations, however, the trend is toward greater control over work behavior. Yet the growth of organization does not mean that such controls emanate solely or primarily from hierarchical sources of authority. There are occupations carried on within organizations whose members claim professional status and who declare allegiance to a specialized colleague group which transcends any single organization. In this instance, the several strands of hierarchical control, collegial control, and autonomy become tangled and complex.

* Notes to this chapter begin on p. 46.

Elementary teaching is a case in point. The role of the elementary teacher is defined in diverse and contradictory terms. As an "employee," the teacher is a salaried worker subject to the authority of the public body which employs her. Continual claims to "professional" status presume the existence of a unified occupational group with a system of collegial controls. The rhetoric of "teaching as an art," however, projects autonomy rather than control; to use the artist as prototype is to stress individuality rather than standardization through bureaucratic or collegial controls. Each definition implies alternative sources of control or, antithetically, the absence of external control.

The task of this chapter is to assess different depictions of the teacher's role and the consequences each possesses for control over elementary teachers. The approach is serial; organizational, professional, and individualistic aspects of the teacher's role are examined in turn. Sociologists have pointed to the flimsy base of empirical study underlying analysis of public schools; it is too early for definitive or dogmatic statements about educational organization.[2] The pressing need is for working models which generate hypotheses and originating questions.[3] The following pages make use of published research and recent inquiry by the author toward that end.

Legality and Actuality in the Control System of Public Schools

> The good administrator gets out of his subordinates' way and lets them get their work done.[4]

Employee status denotes subordination. It does not, however, specify the exact scope of control asserted over the subordinate; some employees experience minute, close supervision while others work under general and even distant control. Although the official rhetoric of school systems projects a high degree of hierarchical control over teachers, several important factors limit the extent to which such control is exercised. The focus of this section is on the structure of public schools, mechanisms of control within such systems, and the limits which are placed on the assertion of control over elementary teachers.

The Formal System of Control

The board of education is the official embodiment of the school system. Although state governments possess constitutional powers over public education, they have consistently delegated many powers to local school boards.[5] The body of law and tradition that has accumulated around American public schools therefore concentrates on the rights and obligations of school boards. Sometimes elected, sometimes appointed, boards hold the vast majority of specified powers in public schooling. Board members usually serve without compensation. Criteria for eligibility are similar to those used for other elective or appointive public positions; one rarely encounters special qualifications attached to the office. The authority granted them extends over all aspects of school affairs (unlike universities, for example, where faculties may be granted hegemony over curricular matters). Boards of education are empowered, in many communities, to tax citizens in support of the schools and most have considerable say in the allocation of local tax dollars. Boards may choose to delegate some of their powers to the superintendent and his subordinates, but such delegative acts do not dissolve the board's legal responsibility. State codes and system bylaws may itemize the superintendent's rights and duties but it is always clear that the board retains ultimate authority. Subordinates other than the superintendent possess no legally distinct areas of operation; they are clearly subordinate to the board and the superintendent.

The superintendent is the chief executive officer of the board and is charged with implementing board policies. He is not an independent executive with specific policy-making

powers, for the separation-of-powers doctrine does not prevail in public school systems. The superintendent is not
expected to represent substantive positions apart from the
board. He may recommend specific action to the board and his
exercise of administrative discretion may produce decisions
where the distinction between policy-making and administrative implementation of policy is moot. Yet the superintendent cannot refuse review of his activity by the board of
control. The superintendent is normally employed, on contract, for a stipulated period, and although some states provide
superintendents with a modified form of tenure, the usual
situation is one of tenuous rather than assured possession of
position. Several observers have based their work on the
assumption of the superintendent's vulnerability;[6] superintendents themselves, in meetings, conversations, and professional periodicals, lay repeated emphasis on the risks they
face "on the firing line."

In legal and formal terms the occupants of other school
offices are almost nonexistent. Central office personnel, where
they exist, are perceived as "extensions" of the superintendent—the rhetoric of titling (e.g., associate or assistant
superintendent) underscores that dependence. Principals,
apparently heads of visible and discrete units, direct sub-units
which possess no official policy-making powers or independent
fiscal resources.[7] Teachers, whether on term or continuing
contracts, are officially employees without powers of governance. Public schools, unlike major universities, have no
legally-based "senates" or similar arrangements for collective
participation by faculty members in the overall operation of
the organization.

The formal and legal allocation of authority in school
systems is monolithic, hierarchical, and concentrated; official
powers are focused at the apex of the structure. A system of
this kind implies that those in command set goals, oversee
their realization, and are accountable for outcomes. Accountability, our culture states, follows authority. It is this
accountability, as we shall see, that produces the vulnerability
experienced by both board members and superintendents of

schools. That vulnerability, in turn, acts to inhibit the full assertion of their legally-held powers.

Pluralism and Ambiguous Goals

Parsons argues that the primary function of governing boards is fiduciary; such boards act to legitimate the actions of officials who should not be judges in their own cases.[8] But members of school boards can rarely afford to act in a haughty or highly authoritative fashion—they are *not* members of an august court insulated from the hurly-burly of local interests. School affairs need not be enmeshed in party politics to become intensely partisan. Educational affairs need no such linkage to generate high emotion, bitter exchanges, and sometimes continuing feuds in rural and urban, large and small school districts.[9] Issues arise over athletics or desegregation or Christmas observances or the rate of placement in prestige colleges. Elected or appointed, school board members may experience direct hostility and retributive sanctions when their decisions alienate powerful groups.[10] The vulnerability of school board members is heightened by the great visibility of their decisions (state laws frequently require that meetings be open to the press and the public), the serious repercussions their fiscal decisions have for property owners, and the sensitive nature of their guardianship over children. Accountability is very real when things go awry or factions form.

Goal-setting can be an awkward affair for public school boards. It is easy enough to rule that some activities fall outside the purview of public schools. But the range of acceptable educational objectives is broad in American society; statements of educational objectives may include numerous outcomes, from health to citizenship, from vocational preparation to social poise.[11] Dahlke has shown that educational goals reflect deep cleavages in the life philosophies of different groups in our pluralistic society; arguments over educational goals may exacerbate differences which are normally ignored or muted in the interest of community harmony or national unity.[12] Boards frequently find it difficult to secure clarity in their mandate. Small wonder, then, that we frequently find them avoiding substantive matters. It requires more-than-ordinary idealism for impartial board members (whose rewards, after all, are limited) to fly in the face of politically volatile issues. Where motives are less pure (e.g., as where board membership is used to launch a political career or to gain special consideration in the awarding of contracts), such courageous action may be patently irrational.[13]

Pluralism of values creates difficulties for boards in assigning priorities among goals or in specifying particular goals; there is a tendency for boards to temper the divisive potential of such decisions by employing techniques of avoidance. A recent review of goal statements issued by boards of education documents the prevalence of vague, unordered, and even trivial policy announcements.[14] (In educational jargon, in fact, "board policies" usually refers to procedural agreements, e.g., the terms of board–superintendents relationships rather than substantive goals and major commitments for their realization.) When boards do issue substantive goal statements, such statements generally lack the directive power for principals and teachers that we associate with the phrase "goals of the organization." Such statements are normally so general that they do not help the staff choose between alternative courses of action in the choices they face. School systems do not possess the detailed specifications of policy we encounter, for example, in federal agencies.[15] Nor do we encounter the controls such as those built into many business organizations through complex systems of accounting, production control, and the like. Bidwell is justified when he asserts that school personnel work in a context marked by "structural looseness."[16]

The Limited Allocative Powers of School Management

The major function of managerial personnel, says Parsons, is to allocate resources within the organization.[17] As chief manager, the superintendent can play an important role in school system allocations. He may prepare the budget and may, by virtue of his continued and steady immersion in school affairs, wield heavy influence over board decisions. Perhaps his principal resource in asserting such influence is his control over personnel matters such as hiring, promotion, and transfer. Yet when we compare the superintendent to the chief executive in other organizational systems, the limitations on his allocative powers become apparent. Schools display certain characteristics which lessen the range and depth of administrative control.

The principle of *equality* is deeply rooted in the governance of American schools—a conception of equality as *sameness* pervades organizational life. In large city school systems, for example, allocations to individual schools of personnel and other resources are handled by "formulas" based on objective features such as number of pupils. There is widespread anxiety among school administrators lest some group of parents charge them with favoritism to any single segment of the populace.[18] Experimentation is reduced in curricular and other matters by this anxiety—what is done for some should be done for all. Impersonal mechanisms are employed by administrators seeking safe strategies; thus we have allocation of students to schools, in most systems, on the basis of chronological age. Current onslaughts on the use of impersonal mechanisms (e.g., the nongraded school) indicate some recognition of placement, but such reforms have yet to conquer the total territory. It is important to note that safety strategies, by relying on impersonal bases for allocation, reduce the decisional range of educational administrators. General rules for allocation, once announced, constrain administrators and administered alike. If allocative powers be central to managerial influence, then erosions in allocative power constitute erosions in total administrative power and control.

One of the most significant domains of equality definition lies in the way teachers are paid and in the range of promotions open to them. Money payment and promotion are not only rewards available to employees, they are, as well, potential sanctions available to those who govern organizations. Teachers are generally paid in terms of a salary schedule which prescribes specific salaries for persons of given experience and formal schooling; such schedules disregard grade or subject specialization and individual competence. Salaries are set automatically when the amount of compensation is beyond the power of administrators to determine. Promotion is also a relatively weak sanction as many teachers are not interested in leaving the classroom for administrative positions.[19] Most elementary schools, in fact, have no formal ranks between classroom teacher and principal; a flat organization of this type means fewer incentives in the form of promotional possibilities. The ultimate negative sanction, dismissal, is used almost exclusively with beginning teachers; tenure arrangements make it extremely difficult for school boards to discharge teachers on continuing contract. The pattern of monetary and role allocations in schools impose rigid limits on managerial power.

The rhythm of allocative decisions in schools is intermittent and infrequent in comparison with many other types of organizations. Major allocations occur annually: budget, personnel selection and placement, scheduling of students, and the like, take place before or at the beginning of the school year. Day-to-day administrative decisions serve largely to buttress strategies which are initiated and reviewed at relatively long intervals. Contrast such a rhythm with the immediate, continual need for decision in armies at war, large construction projects, or the treatment of accident victims! School administration offers few opportunities for dramatic and decisive action; events which call for such action may fall, in fact, into the category of "things that should have been prevented," such as student insurrection or teacher strikes. Once schedules are set and staff and students assigned, school is in motion and supposed "to keep." Unlike administrators in some settings, the school administrator acquires little of the glamour which comes from immersion in dramatic decisions and frequent emergencies.

Public school teaching possesses other characteristics which impede full realization of possibilities for close control that lie in the formal structure. The ecological patterning of students, for example, is one where students and staff are dispersed throughout separate buildings—the superintendent is usually isolated from daily school operations. Within buildings, students and teachers are distributed into separate rooms. Such self-contained classrooms are small universes of control with the teacher in command; administrators refer, ambivalently, to the "closed door" which the teacher can put between herself and administrative surveillance. Another impediment to close control lies in the relative indivisibility of the teacher's tasks. How does one subdivide a warm and empathic relationship established between teacher and class? How does an administrative superior assist a teacher maintain discipline—for administrators, no less than teachers, are concerned with maintaining control over students—without simultaneously undermining her authority? As teachers spend almost all their school time in the presence of their students, there are few occasions for superordinates to direct teachers without incurring the risk of embarrassing a "subordinate line officer."[20]

The relatively unrationalized nature of teaching technique also restricts initiations by administrative superiors. There are few settled matters in pedagogy. If greater agreement prevailed, superiors could, through mastery of that consensus, assert the right to prescribe for subordinates. Few elementary teachers can use specialized substantive knowledge to argue that their technical expertise exceeds the principal's. The largely intuitive nature of teaching does, however, permit the elementary teacher to communicate her conviction that intimate acquaintance with specific students is highly relevant. Who knows as well as she the particular characteristics and needs of her boys and girls? The teacher can "agree in principle" with her superordinates while feeling certain that the principle does not apply to her particular circumstances.

Resolving Dilemmas of Vulnerability and Control

School-system organization, as portrayed so far, presents some improbable characteristics. Few sociologists will be surprised to learn that the stated and actual are not identical—that disjunction is familiar since Roethlisberger's classic work on industrial organization.[21] What *is* unlikely is the juxtaposition of vulnerability at the apex of the structure with limited control over subordinates. School personnel can readily embarrass those charged with school governance. Why should any group of power-holders acquiesce in arrangements which increase their risks? The question draws our attention to a broader one: How do school officials, given the relative weakness of the "chain of command," attain the level and type of control they consider necessary? The pages which follow present a tentative answer to the question. The argument is that organizational control over teachers is accomplished through selection–socialization and subtle mechanisms which refine bureaucratic rule.

Those who acquire tenure status as elementary teachers have undergone extensive selection and socialization. Assuming that the teacher attended elementary and secondary schools in the usual pattern, she enters college with extraordinary familiarity with the work she will take on; all high school graduates have spent approximately 10,000 hours in close contact with teachers in the course of their schooling. Few occupations have entrants with more precise knowledge of the work activities of practitioners than does public school teaching.[22] Persons whose aspirations do not match the teacher's work round are not likely to enter the occupation willingly; those who do choose teaching do so on the basis of relatively accurate information about the nature of the work.[23] Teachers play a part in the development and encouragement of the ambition to teach and thereby introduce self-perpetuation into the recruitment process.[24]

Preparation for teaching does of necessity require coursework at college; but, more significantly, many teachers

attend colleges where most students have similar objectives
and where the student subculture is colored by that common
aspiration. Instruction in education courses is frequently given
by persons who have had experience in public school and who
bring public school standards to teaching and assessing
students. Colleagueship ties link supplying colleges and receiving school systems and reinforce the current conception
of teacher training as preparation for school work. The
common values and close relationships that unite teacher
training institutions, school employers, and state officials
responsible for certification lie behind Conant's depiction of
an educational "establishment."[25] A delivery system of this
type is unlikely to produce many persons with tastes and
attitudes unsuited to employment in the occupation. As school
systems have two or three years in which to assess new teachers,
further screening takes place, and further socialization occurs
as teachers learn what kinds of behavior are required to win
permanent status. The system of self-selection based on
familiarity, selection within training institutions and schools,
supplemented by the tenure testing point, produce sufficient
homogeneity to reduce strains which would otherwise be
placed on the control system of schools.

The authority structure of public schools meets the mini-
mal criteria of bureaucracy: there are rules surrounding conditions of employment, hierarchic offices filled through merit,
specific expectations that surround historical offices; but, as
Bidwell comments, these bureaucratic elements are found
only in "rudimentary form" in public schools.[26] Though
labor is divided, the divisions are comparatively few; though
careers exist for those who wish to spend a lifetime in schools,
many spend only a few years in such employment; though
some impersonality is present in relationships to "clients,"
warmth and attention to individuals are thought essential to
effective teaching. We can obtain a clearer picture of the
authority system by examining the series of relationships which
unify the ranks of school employees into a hierarchy, for it is
in these linkages and what transpires there that school systems
are particularly interesting.

It is clear that the hierarchic nature of school systems gives differential weight to decisions made at superior levels. Decisions made by school boards constrain the actions of the superintendent and others employed in the schools; similarly, the superintendent's decisions have serious consequences for his subordinates. But the effect of such successive constraints is not specified by the fact of hierarchy—we must know precisely *how* superordinate decisions act to affect the *scope* of the subordinate's decision-making range. A superordinate's decision may not only limit the remaining options for the subordinate but contain specifications as to priorities among those which remain; in such cases, higher level decisions effectively pre-empt the decision-making territory of the subordinate. Other decisions may constrain less by leaving the question of priorities open. This difference can be illustrated by referring to two board decisions affecting a superintendent. One may order him to assign all manipulable funds in a given order or priority; little remains for him to decide in such a case. Or the board might simply instruct him to cut 10 per cent off his total budget as he sees fit, thereby maximizing the options which remain open to him. A teacher may be given a detailed set of rules determining the exact circumstances under which students are to receive various punishments; such superordinate decisions constrain in detail. Another teacher may be informed that expulsion of students is not an acceptable way of enforcing discipline, yet be permitted to choose among alternative courses of action open to the subordinate. It appears that school systems, when contrasted to other organizational systems, feature a relatively high proportion of low-constraint decisions, particularly as far as teachers are concerned. Through use of such decisions, principals and other superordinates focus their control *on points of possible trouble* while avoiding the difficulties created by detailed specification and circumventing the resistance teachers might show to more direct commands. Note that where extensive use of low-constraint decisions is made goals may not be minutely specified from the top to the bottom of the organization. Succeeding layers of administration may narrow the range of goal selections possible at the teacher level, but persons at that level may be free to choose among the goals which remain. Under circumstances such as these, goals may be set at any level of the organization—set, that is, within the range of tolerated possibilities.

Conventional concepts of hierarchical control usually assume that superordinate–subordinate linkages are marked by uniformity on all matters, i.e., that all of a superordinate's wishes carry equal initiatory power over his subordinate's actions. Yet one encounters situations in school systems where this is not the case. Boards, for example, normally take budget review seriously and would be taken aback if the superintendent expressed reservations about their doing so. Yet one hears practitioners say that the wise superintendent will resign when his board questions major personnel recommendations. For boards to question the superintendent on these matters is viewed as evidence of the deterioration of their relationship. It appears that decision areas are subjected to differential definition, and that variable zoning exists in which, within the *same* dyad, initiatory power varies by topic. (One thinks of marriage, in which the husband has hegemony over some issues, the wife over others, and discussion or argument arises over the rest.)

Research is needed to clarify zoning within the school-system hierarchy. In the case of principal–teacher relationships, for example, we would expect that while matters of compliance with record-keeping would fall into the principal's zone of influence, in-class affairs (e.g., the specifics of a particular class) would fall within the teacher's territory.[27] Conflict would arise, then, in zones where hegemony is unclear. The author's observations of teachers and school administrators suggests that the chain of linkages is zoned so that executive dominance is clear over "administrative" matters but muted in "instructional" areas. The administrative line is marked, in other words, by "orders" on buildings and records and money; as one approaches instruction, the number and tone of administrative initiations change and the "suggestion" becomes more characteristic than the "order."

Variable zoning occurs as well in the rules and regulations which are issued in school systems. Some rules, for example, are "soft" where others are "hard." Regulations and practices surrounding the expenditure and recording of school funds are subject to the specific and mandatory conventions of modern accountancy and are literally enforced. The central office auditor is unlikely to heed a principal's claim of professional judgment when his actions conflict with regulations. One finds it difficult, on the other hand, to think of curriculum "guides" as "rules" at all—they lack the specificity and the literal enforcement associated with that term. Central office supervisors may feel that their visits act to "keep teachers within the spirit of the system's curriculum philosophy," but neither their rhetoric nor their behavior approaches that of the internal auditor. We can hypothesize that hard rules center on matters already codified in terms of the logics of cost and efficiency, i.e., matters subject to accounting practice or engineering modes of thought. Soft rules, on the other hand, are found where thorny issues of instructional policy are at stake—the exact aims of a particular class, the best way to present specific material, and general rules in regard to the conflict between distributive justice and the needs of an individual student. Indications are that that which is most central and unique to schools—instruction— is least controlled by specific and literally enforced rules and regulations.[28]

Through reliance on low-constraint decisions and variable zoning, school boards and top administrators reduce vulnerability that could stem from subordinates *without* rigorous specification in intangible and sensitive areas. Those at the apex exercise selective control on matters which, in their judgment, constitute critical points in meeting community expectations; in this respect, the structure is well-adapted to the exigencies of popular control. The decision to extend the areas controlled, however, rests with those in positions of authority; legally, they can make their decisions more constraining and broaden their zones of initiation. The protection granted teachers by the restrained exercise of authority is fragile; obstacles to greater administrative control mentioned earlier (diffuse goals, limited allocative powers, and the organization and technique of teaching) could, theoretically, be overcome and more centralized authority instituted in public schools.

The authority system described can, of course, result in a balance of administrative control and teacher autonomy. By leaving priorities open and critical zones relatively free, a school system may maximize the creative potential of a highly competent, well-motivated teaching staff. Depending upon the goals held by the teachers in question, the outcome may be effective performances in various directions (some teachers may stress some objectives, others different ones) or effective performance guided by similar objectives. Whatever the outcome in particular school systems, however, it is clear that the designation *employee* describes only part of the teacher's relationship to the school order.

The Partial Professionalization of Elementary Teaching

Public school circles are rife with talk of professionalism. Those familiar with the resistance administrators encounter from technical personnel in hospitals, universities, and business might surmise that the gap between the stated and the actual in school organization stems from the professionalization of teachers.[29] That interpretation, however, assumes that processes of professionalization among teachers are sufficiently institutionalized to constrain the actions of boards and administrators. How accurate is that assumption? What part do collegial ties among teachers play in "softening" hierarchical authority? In looking for answers to these questions, we shall examine several facets of professionalization among elementary teachers. Specifically, the examination includes a brief review of the history and current status of the occupational group, a comparison of the teacher's role with a model of professionalized work, and inquiry into teacher socialization and the technical subculture of the occupation.

A Brief History of Teacher Professionalization

Stinchcombe argues that conditions associated with an organization's founding have lasting effects on its subsequent development.[30] Ambiguities in the position of the elementary teacher today are rooted in the organizational history of schools; control by laymen, lack of clarity in colleague group boundaries, limited prestige and money income, and feminization of the occupation have taken place over a protracted period of time.

Bailyn writes that the contribution of the Colonial Era was to initiate the concept of school as a necessary instrument for socializing colonial children into a novel way of life.[31] Englishmen in Tudor times relied primarily on family and apprenticeship to conduct their young from infancy to adulthood. Migration to the New World meant rearing children in a setting where older forms of socialization, inappropriate to the new environment, lost their effectiveness and reliability. Education became a designed and conscious affair undertaken to replace the old. The advent of the school created financial problems, and the solution of these problems eventuated in local and public control. "Dependent for support upon annual and even less regular gifts," states Bailyn, "education at all levels during the early formative years came within the direct control, not of those responsible for instruction, but of those who had created and maintained the institutions."[32] Lower schools, unlike the colleges, failed to develop alternative sources of support; today elementary and secondary education are financed and controlled by the local citizenry. The persistence of such "layman control" has had significant consequences for the shape of the teaching occupation.[33]

Teaching was not regularized during the Colonial Period; no special arrangements existed to regulate entry, and the necessary credentials were limited to sufficient literacy to teach reading, writing, and elementary arithmetic.[34] Those who taught did so for limited periods of time, for most of them were on the way to something else—ministerial students preparing for a pulpit, indentured servants accumulating the price of their bond. Incomes and prestige were low. Teaching was ranked in terms of the age of the students, with those teaching the early grades receiving the lowest monetary and deference rewards. The men who taught (most teachers were male) were expected to show themselves proper and religious in conduct, and, as part of their regular duties, were expected to help out around the church by doing menial chores. Then, as today, these men needed extra income and often took on extra employment. Colonial Americans thought of teaching as a rather easy task—they did not think of it as taxing the full strength of a man.

State school systems as we know them today began to emerge between the Revolution and the Civil War. Those whose names are featured in histories of education (Mann, Bernard, Wiley) asserted the urgency of a free and public system of common schooling;[35] they managed to build the first such system in history. Yet few major changes occurred in the role of the teacher; during the Jacksonian years, public school teaching, like much else, was absorbed into the spoils system. As salaries were small and communities were loath to raise them, women entered the work and, in line with practices of the time, accepted incomes lower than those paid to men. Elementary teaching became work for girls with little formal schooling—most had finished elementary school and a year or two of grammar school. Normal schools (imported from Prussia) began before the Civil War, but it was several decades before a majority of teachers received the year-or-two's training they offered to elementary school graduates. The Civil War emptied the schools of men; veterans, finding numerous other opportunities in the expanding economy, rarely returned to the classroom.

The role of the elementary teacher took firmer shape in the years following the Civil War; by 1917, the principalship and the superintendency were institutionalized.[36] Elementary

schools expanded to cope with millions of children whose
parents had immigrated from Europe, and the demands for
teachers rose. "Tappan's Law," which stipulated that a
teacher should have completed the level immediately above
that which she aspired to teach, emerged as the guide to
school officials; elementary teachers came to be women with
high school education.

The superintendent emerged as the key school administrator around the turn of the century. Callahan documents
how superintendents were swept up in the enthusiasm for
"Scientific Management" which marked the first two decades
of this century.[37] This view of school management concep-
tualized the teacher much as industrial workers were seen by
their managers; the teacher was to execute, under minute
prescription and intimate supervision, the plans developed by
experts in the central office. The teacher associations which
had survived fused into the National Education Association
and its complex array of state and local affiliates. The domi-
nation of associational life by men in administrative positions
was flagrant, and in 1920 a reorganization, the result of a
teacher revolt, gave somewhat greater influence to classroom
teachers.[38] It is important to note, however, that the main
body of teachers who continued with the NEA did *not* insist
on separating out their role in professional development. The
formation of the American Federation of Teachers was in
opposition to administrators, but it failed to attract more than
a minority of teachers. The National Education Association
formed and sustained internal units which differentiated by
role, such as the Classroom Teacher's Department and the
American Association of School Administrators. But to this
day, those participating within the NEA complex have averred
the importance of a "unified profession" composed of
teachers, administrators, guidance personnel, and others who
perform "professional" functions in the school.

The years from 1918 to today have not, generally speaking,
seen many structural changes in the role of the elementary
school teacher. Tenure arrangements, begun just before
World War I, spread during the Twenties and Thirties; the

equalization of elementary and secondary salaries occurred in that period. Entry standards rose to require college attendance, and certification machinery was constructed; the National Education Association grew enormously (from 8,500 members in 1918 to almost one million today) and added numerous functions and functionaries to its central headquarters. Managerial ideologies shifted from "scientific management" to "democratic administration" to the analytic and social scientific orientation emerging at present.[39] The current ideology of administration appears somewhat uncertain and tentative; we are in a period marked by greater concern with means than with ends, with pedagogical efficiency within prevailing forms than with new conceptions of school purpose.[40]

The current situation reflects the centuries during which teachers were defined solely as employees. It is interesting that teachers have not challenged their formal subordination; unlike most who claim professional status, teachers have not contested the right of persons outside the occupation to govern their technical affairs. Although teacher associations have sought to influence legislation at all levels of government, they have generally accepted the structural order within which they work. The American Federation of Teachers, presumably the most aggressive of teacher organizations, has worked to define relations between teachers and superordinates as relations between employees and employers. Concentrating on "welfare" issues of money and working conditions, it has not launched any serious attacks on the right of citizen boards to control instructional affairs. Whatever the ideology of professionalism among teachers may be, it does not currently constitute a direct challenge to public, lay control over school affairs.

Elementary teaching has been "regularized" in the sense that pathways *into* the occupation have been institutionalized. It is not clear, however, what constitutes leaving the occupation. Are elementary principals members of the "profession?" Whereas most fields claiming professional status manifest great concern with the clarification of membership qualifications, the exact boundaries of colleague-group membership remain unclear within public school teaching. The definition put forth by the largest occupational association, the National Education Association, is extremely broad. NEA policy calls for a "unified profession" encompassing teachers, principals, superintendents, counselors, and—optimistically—college professors. Yet the same association, ironically, includes sub-groups which act in ways divergent from the policy of the group as a whole. The American Association of School Administrators recently revised its rules to make it more difficult for teachers and principals to gain entry. Although teacher unions stress solidarity among classroom teachers, they have not sought to capitalize on such solidarity as the basis for professionalization. If elementary teaching be a profession, it is a profession with ambiguous membership.

Professional status carries connotations of high prestige.[41] The prestige of elementary teachers, as distinguished from high school teachers, is not known, but the general standing of public school teachers can be inferred from the National Opinion Research Center's studies of occupational ranking. The survey conducted in 1947 accords "public school teacher" a rank of 35/90 and a position below such occupations as medicine, college teaching, the clergy, dentistry, law, and engineering, and above journalists, welfare workers, and the skilled trades of electrician, machinist, and carpenter.[42] No significant differences in overall rankings or the specific position of teaching occurred in the replication done in 1963.[43] It is useful, however, to examine the prestige of teaching in light of the sexual division of labor in our society. Although teaching ranks thirty-fifth on the NORC list in general, it is first among those occupations largely populated by women.[44] Within the range of occupations "open" to women (open in the sense that participation is clearly more than token), the prestige of teaching is very high. Teaching is socially desirable for American women, but for men it occupies a rank well below the topmost levels of work achievement.

Occupations can be arrayed in terms of the ratio between

those granted admission and those seeking entry. Some occupations regularly turn away large numbers of would-be members, while others, like teaching, fall into the category of fields of chronic "shortage." The percentage of college seniors choosing teaching has risen steadily of late, but expansion of teaching staffs, coupled with high turnover, has resulted in demand exceeding supply.[45] A situation of shortage undermines attempts to raise entry standards; the certification machinery already developed has been violated by thousands of teachers working with "temporary" certificates. The unfavorable competitive position of elementary teaching has prevented leaders from employing strategies of prestige enhancement based upon more rigorous or restricted entry. The social characteristics of teachers have added little to its overall standing, for as the National Education Association reports,

> teachers constitute, in social origin, a fairly representative cross section of the American people, except that the families of the managerial and professional groups appear to be over-represented by teachers and that unskilled and service workers appear to be under-represented.[46]

Although teaching salaries have risen steadily (particularly since 1947) they are marked by a "low ceiling" and are generally low in comparison with the average annual earnings of male college graduates.[47] Most men who teach in public schools find it necessary to supplement their salaries by additional employment.[48] The level of teaching salaries is not sufficiently high to maintain men and their families at a living standard associated with "professional" styles of life in our society.

Chapter Five ("Women and Bureaucracy in the Semi-Professions" by Simpson and Simpson) deals with issues of femininity and work in some depth. As far as elementary teaching is concerned, it is clearly congruent with feminine socialization, work styles, and familial roles. Compared to other realistic alternatives for women, teaching offers attractive prestige and money. The decentralized nature of school organization means local hiring in almost every community; teaching is thus accessible to women who are relatively immobile members of the work force.[49] The absence of interpersonal rivalry for monetary rewards fits the socialization experiences Caplow attributed to American women.[50] The work schedule of teachers facilitates the participation of women with school-age children—their work hours coincide with those during which their children are outside the home. The slow-changing technology of teaching permits teachers to be away for protracted periods (as during the early years of child-rearing) and to return without excessive loss of skill. An obvious but important correlative fact should also be mentioned: in our society, as in most, the care of small children is culturally defined as women's work.

It is easy to forget the recency of large-scale participation by women in the general labor market. To date the only occupations which have clearly achieved professional recognition have been male occupations. We have yet to see whether any occupation predominantly feminine in composition can or will achieve clear title to the honorific designation "profession."

Elementary Teaching and the Established Professions

Although sociologists have not achieved consensus on a single set of criteria for the identification of professions, there is general agreement that a few fields clearly belong within the category. Examples are medicine, law, and architecture. But such fields are fee-for-service professions where the practitioner renders service to an aggregate of clients. The problem is to find organizational characteristics peculiar to professions which can, with equal facility, be applied to salaried occupations. Direct and concrete applications of fee-for-service categories create confusion. (Who is the client of the elementary teacher: students? parents? taxpayers? the school system?) We can, however, locate certain issues which must be resolved in all occupations, and, noting the peculiar resolution employed in clearly established professions, test individual fields in terms of the proximity of their resolutions to professional ones. We use four such issues here:

1. How the individual relates to the market.
2. The nature of knowledge and skill possessed by members of the occupation.
3. The relation established to the polity.
4. The extent to which those performing similar activities influence the careers of members of the occupation.

The established practitioner in a well-established profession occupies a favored position in the market.[51] He can assert himself vis-à-vis a single client without serious economic risk, for the multiplicity of his clientele and their lack of organization reduces his economic dependence upon any single individual. This economic independence provides him with a basis for professional autonomy; he can choose to act in ways congruent with professional norms when the latter collide with the wishes of a client. He can withstand pressures which he considers contrary to his professional principles or interests.

Elementary teachers receive their income from "one big client." But is it not true that tenure arrangements serve to balance the exchange and give the teacher an autonomy similar to that enjoyed by the professional practitioner? There are differences between the functions served by multiple clienteles and tenure; tenure protects the individual in his position only within a given school district. It is difficult for elementary teachers to build a reputation which transcends their local area; teaching, even superb teaching, throws a short shadow. Since mechanisms for broadcasting one's competence are limited, the teacher cannot be entirely unconcerned with her employer's goodwill. Since employment elsewhere can be threatened by negative recommendations, the teacher is wise to avoid actions which would antagonize her "one big client."

The knowledge and skill possessed by those practicing established professions are recognized both as vital to individual and social welfare and as esoteric in nature. The layman

experiences here his vulnerable status—he knows he needs the
professional's service and lacks the professional's knowledge
and skill. The critical point is that of evaluation by relevant
publics; whatever the actual state of professional knowledge
in scientific terms, the relevant publics (clients, political
agencies, and the like) *believe* that knowledge to be both
essential and restricted to members of the professional group.
The possession of esoteric knowledge over a period of time
strengthens those within the profession vis-à-vis the public in
general terms. There are indications that protracted occupancy
of professional status permits an occupation to play an important role in defining the very nature of the service it will
provide. Thus, lawyers have influenced the meaning and substance of justice, and, in some respects, doctors have defined
the essential characteristics of health and illness.

"No one ever died of a split infinitive" is a quip which
throws the less-than-vital nature of teaching knowledge into
relief. Nor can elementary teachers point to an arcane body of
substantive or technical knowledge to assert professional status
vis-à-vis the school board or the public-at-large. That which
is taught in elementary school is presumed to be known by
almost all adults, and teachers have not been able to convince
many critics—and more importantly, legislatures—that
"methods courses" constitute a truly distinct and impressive
body of knowledge.[52] The subjects teachers themselves believe
useful in teaching (e.g., child psychology) are primarily the
property of others. Lacking the clear autonomy which leads
to the assurance that professional knowledge will provide the
basis of action, teachers have not developed codified and
systematic bodies of professional knowledge; lacking that
knowledge, their stance vis-à-vis laymen is, in turn, weakened.

The state can ill-afford to ignore well-established professions
and the claims of persons to their powers, for, since the
service is presumed to be vital, the charlatan can threaten the
welfare of citizens. Complex licensure arrangements develop
which are mainly delegated by political authorities to members
of the profession who implement them. Such delegation is
not, however, a formal abrogation of powers: there is the

implied threat to reclaim the government of affairs by political officials should the profession lose their confidence.

The situation in licensing elementary teachers is somewhat quixotic. A complex and elaborate procedure exists which, as Conant indicates, is by-passed by thousands of teachers.[53] Lieberman points out that educational licensing boards are *not* controlled by members of the teaching profession.[54] Further confusion is evident when we observe that some high-status schools, such as private preparatory schools, employ teachers without regard to such certification specifics where they can do so.

Those outside a well-established profession, acknowledging their ignorance of its special knowledge, are inclined to delegate much of its governance to members of the professions. It makes sense to conceptualize this process as one of exchange by means of which the profession can retain its self-governing perquisites as long as it retains the trust of political authorities. Professions possess and use complex formal machinery for the discipline of errant members who threaten that exchange. But what is less widely realized is that in important sectors of the professions, senior colleagues hold enormous and sustained power over the careers of those aspiring to full recognition.[55] Informal referral systems in medicine and partnership probation periods in law and architecture enable senior practitioners to undertake protracted testing of the technical competence and normative integrity of aspirants.

The ambiguity of colleague group boundaries makes it difficult for an observer to decide whether teachers are subjected to collegial scrutiny in their career progression. The tenure promotion, for example, is assessed by administrative superiors (the principal and superintendent normally recommend candidates to the board) but not by fellow teachers. It is a curious fact, unexplained by Sharma, that teachers in his national sample did not wish to participate in personnel decisions about other teachers.[56]

This review of four issues reveals as much dissimilarity as similarity to professional modes of resolution. We encounter serious ambiguities on each count: the role of the elementary teacher differs significantly from that found in situations where professional status is uncontested.

The Incomplete Subculture

The controls one finds in well-established professions are more than external mechanisms for rewarding the faithful and punishing the deviants. Members of a profession are supposed to internalize the standards of their profession—they talk of "professional conscience." But the inculcation of such standards requires an elaborate subculture buttressed by complex machinery for its transmission to neophytes.[57] Witness, for example, the protracted socialization we find in medicine with its pre-medical curriculum, its four years of specialized schooling, its complex internship and residency arrangements. Established professions take few chances with newcomers— the neophyte is subjected to years of scrutiny and indoctrination by professors and members of the profession.

Elementary teaching represents, at best, a faint replica of such inculcation of technical and moral practices. Although inquiry into teacher socialization is still very limited, it is possible to note some important ways in which teaching, as a subculture, differs from what is associated with a high degree of professionalization.

Entrants to most professions are, as materials for professional socialization, largely unformed. Few students entering law or medicine or architecture are intimately familiar with the working round of practitioners or feel qualified to make judgments about professional performances. Teaching, on the other hand, is well known to entrants, and they have already formed opinions about what constitutes an effective teaching performance. Teachers interviewed by the author were able to describe their outstanding public school teachers in considerable detail, and some volunteered the information that they currently employ techniques learned as young students.[58] Those seeking to socialize their students into a particular conception of teaching must overcome such pre-existing attitudes and values. It is noteworthy that the same teachers who found it easy to describe their former teachers had difficulty in describing colleagues of outstanding competence; their replies frequently contained the phrase "we never see each other at work." These data suggest that the flow of influence from generation to generation encounters less influence from colleagues than we associate with professional fields and may, in fact, account for the conservatism ascribed to school people by Waller and Durkheim.[59]

We have noted that the public school network, as a series of linked organizations, can eliminate those who, as students or beginning teachers, fail to show the appropriate characteristics and attitudes. To test for *general* acceptability, however, is not the same process as indoctrinating beginners with a set of clear, precise, and usable specifications for the performance of the occupation's tasks. The role of college preparation for teaching is not well understood at the present time, but it appears that its potency, in confronting students with extended prior exposure to teaching, is limited. Teachers themselves tend to discount the contribution of pre-service courses in influencing their current work habits and choices.[60] Some studies point to a shift in teacher attitudes as they move from professional training courses to actual classroom confrontation.[61] One study indicates that actual experience in teaching tends to "wash out" earlier differences associated with attendance at different types of undergraduate colleges.[62] There is no evidence that pre-service experiences provide those exposed to them with a significant body of directives for teaching or affect their work values in lasting fashion.

There is indication that work socialization occurs primarily during the beginner's actual confrontation with responsibility in performing occupational tasks.[63] Elementary teachers acquire their substantive knowledge through sixteen years of studentship, but what of the core interpersonal skills involved in their craft? Learning to control a class of thirty students, determining appropriate levels of vocabulary and effective sequences of presentation, realizing variations in individual potentials for learning—these are complex accomplishments requiring immersion in actual teaching. Elementary teachers usually undergo a period of practice teaching before assignment to a regular class and one study shows that the tutelage of the supervising teacher has an important influence.[64] But it is significant to observe that the first year of actual teaching experience—the point of full involvement in accountable teaching responsibility—is generally not accompanied by regular or intensive contact with senior colleagues. The beginning elementary teacher is, of course, "visited" by the principal and probably a central office supervisor, but the fraction of working time which is supervised is very small. (Twelve visits of two hours' duration each would be high and would consist of less than 3 per cent of the teacher's first year, estimated at thirty-eight weeks of thirty hours each.) Where obvious trouble arises with a beginning teacher, special attention will be paid; otherwise, she may be left almost entirely to her own resources in mastering her new role. Other teachers have little time available, for they too are caught in the time and space economy of elementary schools which permits them little time away from students. The system of supervising beginning teachers is compatible with the exercise of gross control and of centering on trouble points; it does *not* suggest a precise instrument of work socialization through which the organization or professional colleagues engage in on-the-spot assistance to the newcomer. Elementary teachers learn their core skills in isolation from other adults.

Occupational cultures, no less than other types, grow through protracted interaction and communication among members of the group. Teaching, as an activity involving contact with students, is carried on by individuals whose contacts with one another are essentially at the periphery of the central transactions. Such conditions are neither likely to produce a culture marked by rich, specific, and detailed technical terms and procedures nor calculated to develop norms which operationalize values. We can see this in the state of practical knowledge about teaching, for, in addition to the private nature of this activity, there are no regular mechanisms for overcoming its evanescent qualities. Teaching techniques are developed and used by thousands of individuals in restricted contact with one another; there are no general expectations that individual teachers should record their experiences in such a way that it becomes the general property of the professional group. No provisions are made in the daily schedule of the teacher for such activity. Yet we note that physicians since Galen (with important historical gaps) have identified and described syndromes and have tested and recorded alternative therapies and their effects. Law, through its elaborate, refined procedures for recording the deliberations and decisions of courts, represents the distillation of generations of practitioner effort. The successes and failures of architects are recorded in stone, wood, and steel. Experience in these professions has a cumulative quality; what teachers learn is largely lost. It is not possible for the professor of education to gain ready access to decades of "cases" for critical review and scientific testing; nor is it easy for the beginning teacher to get the feeling that she begins where predecessors left off.

The absence of a refined technical culture is evident in the talk of elementary school teachers. Analysis of long, somewhat "open" interviews with teachers reveals little by way of a special rhetoric to delineate the essence of their daily grappling with interpersonal and learning problems. The language one finds, as might be expected from the foregoing paragraph, is the language of persons of their general educational and class background.[65] Where trade jargon is used, it is frequently characterized by various meanings among different speakers (e.g., "growth" is advanced performance on achievement tests for one, the overcoming of shyness for another). Isolation and evanescence seem to have had the expected effects.

The general status of teaching, the teacher's role and the condition and transmission arrangements of its subculture point to truncated rather than fully realized professionalization. The ideology of professionalism among elementary teachers has yet to result in the structural characteristics or collegial assertiveness found in clearly established professions. It appears that considerable militancy and knowledge-building must occur if teachers are to acquire the work arrangements and technical apparatus associated with high-prestige professions.

In view of the truncated nature of professionalization among elementary teachers, it seems highly unlikely that collegial ties play a major part in reducing the potency of hierarchical authority. It may be, of course, that board members and administrators occasionally restrain their assertions of authority in deference to the attributed expertise of teachers. But professional ways of organizing work have yet to be institutionalized in the public schools. The absence of such institutionalization suggests skepticism rather than credulity on the count of teacher professionalization, and this skepticism should, in the writer's opinion, extend to ruling out *a priori* formulations which grant professional controls a major part in containing administrative authority. The autonomy possessed by elementary teachers is not the collectively shared right of recognized professionals.

Teacher Rewards and the Press for Autonomy

The organizational and professional constraints that act on elementary teachers are limited in scope and in specificity; individual teachers have latitude in what they do. Some measure of autonomy is structurally consistent with the widespread belief that teaching is, to some extent, a nonroutine "art" requiring judgment on the part of those practicing it. But there is no sociological magic which ensures the institutionalization of appropriate work arrangements; the development and perpetuation of a given set of social arrangements needs people who are able to initiate and sustain those arrangements. What part do teachers play in the creation and maintenance of patterns which give room for individual autonomy? What is there in the situation which gives them the opportunity to attain autonomy despite a hierarchical authority structure and a weak set of professional supports? The main argument of this section is that an answer can be found in the reward system of elementary school teaching.

We can classify work rewards into three groups. First are *extrinsic* rewards, defined as given quantities of money, prestige, and power, which are affixed to roles and "belong" to those who occupy the role. The second consist of *ancillary* rewards which are affixed to the role and may be perceived as benefits but which, since they are constant through time, become "part of the job" rather than "income" received for additional effort. Examples are security, the work calendar, and the physical environment. The third cluster is composed of the *intrinsic* rewards which persons derive from their work. Since intrinsic rewards are subjective, they vary to some extent from individual to individual. But occupations differ in the kinds of subjective rewards which are likely to prevail among occupational members. We can visualize occupations, therefore, as presenting unique combinations of probable intrinsic rewards. The sociologist can, through empirical inquiry, establish the existence of such patterns and, having done so, analyze and describe the components of those patterns.

This analysis postulates that an individual, having joined a given occupation, concentrates his reward-seeking energies at those points where effort makes the largest difference in his total rewards. Ancillary rewards, for example, are relatively unimportant once the person has become a teacher; he tends to take for granted such things as high security and a short work year and, which may be peculiar to teaching, realizes that ancillary rewards are largely similar for everyone within the occupation. Ancillary rewards may attract persons to a given field, but they have relatively little capacity to generate effort once they are in it.

The patterning of extrinsic rewards in teaching differs from the patterning of such rewards in most occupations. As we have seen, in-school effort has no effect on money rewards for classroom teachers, since money income is increased by course-taking and longevity. The package of formal prestige

Table 1–1. Types of Rewards for Dade County Elementary School Teachers

EXTRINSIC REWARDS	N	%
Salary	475	15.5
Respect from others	1159	37.8
Chance to use influence	1043	34.0
No satisfaction from these	387	12.6
TOTAL	3064	99.9

INTRINSIC REWARDS	N	%
Chance to study, read and plan for classes	105	3.4
Discipline and classroom management	32	1.0
Knowing that I have "reached" students and they have learned	2687	86.6
Chance to associate with children or young people	237	7.6
Chance to associate with other teachers	32	1.0
No satisfaction from these	8	.3
TOTAL	3101	99.9

ANCILLARY REWARDS	N	%
Security of income and position	700	22.9
Time (esp. summers) for travel, etc.	709	23.2
Freedom from competition, rivalry	159	5.2
Appropriateness for people like me	1054	34.4
No satisfaction from these	440	14.4
TOTAL	3062	100.1

ALL COMBINED	N	%
Extrinsic	340	11.0
Intrinsic	2400	77.8
Ancillary	343	11.1
TOTAL	3083	99.9

and power meted out to teachers is highly standardized—the absence of hierarchy among teachers neutralizes extrinsic rewards as an important incentive for individuals. Teachers may, of course, elect to change school systems or seek administrative office, but indications are that women teachers are relatively immobile and that interest in administration is low among women in elementary schools.[66] Thus extrinsic rewards are likely to affect the behavior of a minority of teachers; the majority will give them little thought on a *day-to-day* basis.

It seems that Veblen was too pessimistic in expecting the death of "the instinct of workmanship."[67] Recent studies have shown that pride in one's accomplishments and enjoyment of work processes, quite apart from external recognition, are still important to Americans at work.[68] Since effort *is* likely to make a difference in one's intrinsic satisfaction, we would expect that intrinsic rewards would be of great concern to elementary school teachers. Unlike ancillary and extrinsic rewards in teaching, intrinsic rewards vary with the effort one makes to obtain them.

This model was tested with data gathered from teachers in the Dade County school system.[69] Teachers were asked to select, serially, from among three sets of rewards the one, in each instance, which mattered most to them. After choosing one extrinsic, one ancillary and one intrinsic reward, they were asked to choose among the three total sets. The results are presented in Table 1–1.

It is clear that intrinsic rewards are dominant for this group and that for a very large proportion the most important intrinsic reward revolves around "transitive" aspects of the role. (The preferred item reads, "The times I know I have 'reached' a student or group of students and they have learned.") Transitive rewards arise when effective communication with students produces student responses which the teacher defines as "learning." The statement the teachers chose in such large numbers fuses product and process and credits the teacher with achievement of the former and effectiveness in the latter. There are, of course, important elements of indeterminacy in the statement; it does not specify the kind of learning, whether it is primarily by the group or by an individual, or how the teacher ascertained its occurrence. As we shall see, the predominance of transitive-intrinsic rewards has important consequences for the teacher's stance vis-à-vis controls emanating from the hierarchy and from peers.

One of the consequences of this patterning of rewards is that it renders teachers more sensitive to students and less sensitive to administrative or collegial reactions. Students have the capacity to grant or deny the responses which teachers consider their primary payment. Since the effects which administrators and colleagues have on such responses are indirect, they are secondary. Since the teacher's rewards depend primarily on what takes place in the classroom, she can be relatively independent of benefits controlled by administrators and peers.

Since her key rewards are largely independent of administrative action, the teacher's relationship to administrative superiors can move away from subordination towards exchange. A relationship of exchange implies that the teacher can assert as well as respond to claims. In the case of elementary teachers, her claims are buttressed by their legitimacy; "requests for assistance" can readily be justified in terms of her primary functions as a teacher. Teachers press their principals for help on difficult discipline cases and with "problem" parents. Teachers may show displeasure when supplies run out or when the principal "interrupts" them in their work.[70] The assertion of such claims is congruent with both teachers' core tasks and the enhancement of work rewards. Colleagues whose actions impede their effectiveness are open to criticism; teachers apparently feel free to complain about teachers whose classes disturb theirs. Social and psychological boundaries, in the form of norms and conventional practices, arise to augment the physical separation of teachers and classrooms.

Teachers face the problem of deciding when they have achieved the desired level of student response; in a sense, each teacher defines the outcomes she will consider gratifying and those she will consider unsatisfactory. This problem is compounded by the nature of teaching itself, for teaching has a particularly interminable quality. One can easily define teaching outcomes in such a way that it is never finished; one never teaches every student everything he could and should learn. The maximization of transitive rewards and the resolution of interminability press the teacher in the same direction—further "into" teaching. Thus are teachers carried away from other aspects of their role, such as involvement in general school affairs; the press toward core teaching activities exercises an organizationally "centrifugal" effect. Table 1–2 presents data which point to the teacher's disposition to spend marginal time on tasks directly connected with teaching. Dade County elementary teachers, when asked about the dispensation of ten extra hours, choose core teaching tasks over organizational matters in a ratio of nine to one.

The teacher's immersion in teaching tasks and her relative indifference to organizational affairs affects her relationship to the principal and colleagues. Caring less about school-wide than classroom affairs, the teacher is not reluctant to grant

Table 1–2. Use of Additional Time by Dade County
Elementary School Teachers

If you were to receive a gift of ten hours more a week, but with the provision that it be spent on work, which of the following would you choose to spend that time on first?

	N	%
Service on a school curriculum committee	98	3.1
Preparing lessons, reading and studying, and reviewing student work	1382	43.8
Enhancing the community's assessment of the school by working on exhibits, parent meetings, etc.	73	2.3
Teaching students either in groups or in individual conference	913	28.9
Improving school operations by work on scheduling, discipline, student government, etc.	76	2.4
Discussing student work and problems with their parents	148	4.7
Counseling individual students on problems they consider important	464	14.7
TOTAL	3154	99.9

the principal clear hegemony over those matters which do not
bear directly upon her teaching activities. The basis for zoning
decisions is laid; the principal's primary sphere is the school-
at-large, the teacher's is the classroom. The teacher may
participate (often voicing complaints) in committees which
deal with school-wide matters, but since these occupy the
fringes of her concern, such participation does little to
intensify relationships with colleagues. School affairs, which
might otherwise act to solidify colleagues jointly solving
common problems, are not sufficiently significant to add to the
import of collegial ties.

Intrinsic rewards can be assessed, by definition, only by
those experiencing them. Consequences flow from the
primacy of subjective rewards among teachers. Working alone,
the individual teacher selects behavior from the flux of classroom activity which *she* takes as evidence of learning. Cultural
and psychological differences among teachers may produce
dissimilar selections. A teacher oriented to achieving moral
objectives may take special pride in the deportment of her
students' march to assembly; the neighbor in an adjoining
classroom shows greater interest in her students' capacity to
plan and implement a special project. One teacher will assert
the importance of written tests in assessing student performance; another will argue that it is the quality of discussion
which really tells whether students are learning. Many
teachers apparently believe that the "good teacher" relies
primarily on her own observations and uses her own conception of desirable outcomes in monitoring her teaching behavior. Table 1–3 shows that Dade County teachers, by a
substantial majority, choose such self-directed monitoring over
reliance on the judgment of administrators, colleagues, or
students.

Individual teachers can make the most of transitive
rewards only if there is freedom for them to choose the criteria
and techniques to be used in assessing student performance.
Only then can individual teachers select the criteria and
techniques which, holding meaning for them, provide a sense
of genuine attainment of transitive outcomes. Thus teachers

Table I–3. Indications of Teaching Effectiveness Relied on by
Dade County Elementary School Teachers

How do good teachers, in your opinion, gauge the effectiveness of their teaching?
Which of the following is the good teacher most likely to rely on as indication?
Good teachers rely most on:

	N	%
The reactions of other teachers who are familiar with their work and their students	354	11.6
The opinions expressed by the students generally	161	5.3
Their general observations of students in light of the teacher's conception of what should be learned	1845	60.4
The assessments made by the principal	123	4.0
The assessments made by a special "supervisor" or similar person	18	.6
The results of objective examinations and various other tests	425	13.9
The reactions of students' parents	53	1.7
Other	77	2.5
TOTAL	3056	100.0

have a stake in warding off controls which reduce their options in the selection of working goals and assessment procedures. The resentment some teachers show toward the system-wide use of standardized tests is a case in point; such tests force the teacher to direct her efforts to the test itself and reduce her control over assessment. We would expect teachers to exert steady pressure on principals to keep supervision sufficiently loose to permit them to use a variety of assessment criteria and procedures.

There are few data available on what principals actually do in this matter of supervision. Data which are available, however, suggest that principals tend to accommodate to the teacher's wishes for looseness in classroom supervision. McDowell reported that Chicago principals expressed reservations over close supervision of tenure teachers.[71] Trask, in a detailed study of supervision in a Massachusetts city, delineated the caution exercised by principals in intervening in classroom affairs and their reluctance to initiate directly for any but beginning teachers.[72] Bridges shows that with increased experience principals' attitudes toward their role approach the expectations held by teachers, a finding which suggests that teachers tend to absorb the principal into their conception of his supervisory responsibilities.[73] The principal's reluctance to oppose teacher expectations is understandable in light of his interactive position. The principal's major relationships, day-in and day-out, are *within* the school; contact with administrative superordinates is intermittent and infrequent compared to the daily interactions he has with teachers. Principals normally rise from teacher ranks; the individual principal usually knows how teachers feel about "excessively close" supervision.

Although teachers do not want to be subject to highly specific supervision, they may turn to administrators or colleagues for advice in their work. Such voluntary advice-seeking is, of course, entirely consistent with the reward model used in the pages above. It is interesting to note, moreover, that teachers differ in their selection of sources of help. Table 1–4 shows that, although colleagues are cited most frequently, the principal and his assistant are mentioned by over a third of the teachers.

The rhetoric of supervision reveals how teachers view the issues in obtaining technical help from others. The question

Table I–4. Sources of Help for Dade County Elementary School Teachers

Teachers may receive assistance in curriculum and methods from a variety of sources. In your opinion, which of the following provides the most help to the classroom teacher?

	N	%
The Principal	446	14.3
Central Office Supervisors	67	2.1
District Directors	16	.5
Assistant Principal for Curriculum or Curriculum Assistant	895	28.6
The Department or grade chairman (or head)	306	9.8
Other teachers in the school	1297	41.5
Other	100	3.2
TOTAL	3127	100.0

used in Table 1–4 is based on analysis of intensive interviews with teachers; they refer continually to "help" or "assistance" or "advice" no matter whether the source is formally authoritative or not. In describing how the principal should act, teachers stress his obligation to be accessible and ready to help them when requested. Teachers stress that good colleagues are those who show a willingness to share their knowledge and effective practices with other teachers. In either case, teachers feel that initiation should come from the teacher who desires help and advice; neither the principal nor colleagues should offer unsolicited assistance. Teacher culture, apparently, permits the individual teacher to approach a peer *or* a superordinate. But most teachers apparently see the exchange of technical assistance as one which is theirs to control; ideas and suggestions may be solicited from various sources, but it is the teacher who tests them in the crucible of classroom experience. The norms maximize teacher freedom to seek assistance without granting authority to those who give it.

To sum up, then, the reward system within elementary teaching has important consequences for the teacher's relationships with superordinates and colleagues. The critical rewards—rewards we have termed "transitive"—flow from effective communication with students, not other adults. To maximize such rewards, teachers concentrate their energies on core teaching tasks and show little interest in organizational affairs which they "delegate" to the principal without question. Since their key rewards are relatively independent of administrative or collegial actions, teachers are emboldened to press their claims upon superordinates, and indications are that those claims are heeded. Informal understandings exist by which principals concentrate instructional supervision on beginning teachers, leaving more experienced teachers largely to their own devices. Teachers monitor their own work and seek to enlarge the zone of freedom which permits them to select goals and means of assessment which are congruent with their personal priorities. Advice is shared among teachers, and principals participate in offering such advice; it appears, however, that the teacher retains considerable independence as she shifts and sorts various ideas before applying them in ways *she* regards as effective.

Teacher Rewards and Teacher Autonomy

There is history behind the idea that a teacher's rewards are primarily intrinsic. We have noted the association of teaching with religious and moral concerns; the theme of low income and limited prestige is rooted in over three hundred years of American experience with teaching. It is not surprising, given the historical definition of teaching as poorly paid work, that those who chose the occupation place a relatively low emphasis upon economic values.

One may, in fact, attribute a special work ethic to teachers (including, probably, social workers and clergy), a "dedicatory ethic" which elevates service motives and denigrates material rewards as the proper motivation to work. Proper orientation lies in willing service to children and little thought to economic and other extrinsic benefits. Research is needed on the emergence of this ideology and its fate today as teachers, through unions and associations, seek higher incomes and better working conditions. Perhaps, like the professors described by Rudolph, teachers have come to see "dedication" as a form of subsidy to education they no longer wish to grant.[74]

There is irony in the position teachers take toward extrinsic rewards. While professing the unimportance of such rewards, teachers have consistently opposed attempts to introduce differentiation in money, prestige, and power within their ranks. Resistance to "merit pay" is widespread and fierce. Teachers show little enthusiasm for the differentiations that do exist in teaching (e.g., grade and department chairmanships) and no enthusiasm for additional ranks. They seem to share a kind of "uniformity pact" whereby agreement is secured among teachers that all should, insofar as extrinsic rewards are concerned, be treated largely alike. Pressed to explain these beliefs, teachers are likely to phrase their convictions in the language of solidarity among teachers;

differentiation, they argue, will lead to envy and hostility among teachers, preventing the cooperation which is necessary to effective education. One wonders at this: why does a group which expresses so little concern for extrinsic rewards perceive them as so dangerous to peer solidarity?

The answer may well lie in the fragile nature of the teacher's autonomy, an autonomy which, as noted in our discussion of school structure, possesses no legitimation in the official statement of authority distribution in American public schools. The introduction of greater differentiation in extrinsic rewards would, without doubt, strengthen the relative position of boards and administrators over teachers in a situation where teachers possess no formal power. Equality among teachers in extrinsic rewards neutralizes the exercise of administrative judgments and administrative sanctions. In focusing on intrinsic rewards, teachers simultaneously aver deep concern with their core functions while restraining the power of superordinates.

Although such assertions of concern with core functions strengthen teacher claims to "professional" standing, the resistance to differentiation within teaching ranks inhibits the emergence of senior colleagues in the field. This impedes the development of organizational arrangements found in established professions. Teachers face a true dilemma in this matter, for to create internal distinctions in a hierarchy where authority belongs solely to apex members would serve only to add to the number of administrative superordinates. Unless senior colleagues were given a measure of *formal* autonomy, the creation of such positions would add nothing to the overall independence of the teaching group.

Teachers protect the measure of personal autonomy they possess by a consistent refusal to accept changes in the uniformity of extrinsic rewards. Equality, it seems, is the foundation of their autonomy. As long as school systems feature a distribution of authority where those in authority hold all formal powers, it may be that insistence on equality is the main assurance that teachers possess sufficient autonomy to make the judgments they consider essential to effective teaching.

Suggestions for Research
on an Exploding Sector

Public education today presents the possibility of sharp and large-scale change in a social system which has been tradition-bound. Such a situation presents promising possibilities for sociological inquiry. We conclude this chapter by suggesting research in two main directions. The first is empirical study of the current balance of controls and autonomy among different school systems. The second is analysis, in process, of changes which are likely to alter the *overall* balance of control and autonomy in American schools.

This chapter has posited a control system containing several components. There is no reason to believe, however, that all school systems feature the same balance among hierarchical controls, collegial controls, and teacher autonomy. It should be possible to develop a typology based on the predominance of one or another of the elements, and it would be useful theoretically to learn what conditions produce different outcomes. The construction of such a typology would permit research into the effects which different systems of control have on students and their learning.

Hierarchical dominance probably varies with the size of the school system; the conventional wisdom of educational administration associates large size with numerous layers of authority and the development of rules and demands for teacher compliance. Subtle research may prove otherwise, however, for subordinates may use the formalization of procedures to increase control over their work.[75] Recent work by Anderson suggests that social class may be an important variable in affecting the nature of controls within schools; he reports that Baltimore junior high schools serving lower-class students make greater use of rules in governing teacher behavior.[76] It would be consistent with earlier analyses in this chapter if research indicated that communities with internal cleavages have more controls in their schools than communities without such cleavages. The press by apex officials to avoid trouble through adding controls presumably varies with the political sensitivity of their communities.

Not all teachers work alone. A new form of instructional organization, "team teaching" has developed and become increasingly widespread over the last decade.[77] Although such team arrangements vary in their specifics, some require persistent and close collaboration among teachers. Analysis of schools where team teaching has been in effect for some years might reveal incipient professionalization as collegial ties replace isolation and team leaders occupy leadership rank within the teaching force. Has collaboration and its needs led to a more precise and specific rhetoric of description and analysis of teaching practices? Do teachers, working together, begin to codify their experience in ways similar to the established professions?

Although "democratic administration" was the ideological vogue during the Thirties and Forties in schools of education, it is not easy to find systems in which teachers have a strong voice in the formation of school policy. Charters alludes to studies, however, which indicate that participation of teachers in school affairs influences their attitudes toward work.[78] Does the granting of de facto authority to teachers over curriculum intensify their concern with other than classroom matters? Does such concern lead to significant changes in their relationships with other teachers?

Teacher autonomy should be greater where board members and administrators feel relatively little vulnerability vis-à-vis their constituency. This hypothesis could be tested in homogeneous communities where parents support schools but hold moderate educational aspirations for their children. Some studies reveal that lower-middle-class parents, though reluctant to intervene in school matters, give their support to educational authorities.[79] High-prestige suburban school systems may be able to recruit teachers who accept the prevailing standards and conform without close supervision; research is needed into the extent of such conformity and its meaning for classroom behavior. The growth of collective bargaining and the specification of relationships involved in grievance procedures requires close examination; principals, for example, may be inhibited in supervising teachers lest alienation lead to "trouble with the union." Detailed contracts coming out of collective bargaining might result in complex work rules that act much like those associated with increased bureaucratization. The National Education Association, on the other hand, is searching to find new ways to give substance to its traditional ideology of professionalism.

Is Autonomy Obsolescent?

Public schools offer promising opportunities for sociologists who are interested in studying organizational change *in process*. An important shift has occurred in the public evaluation of education and the significance of schooling to our society. Public expenditures for education are rising rapidly. For the first time in the American experience the federal government is allocating significant resources for local school use. Conventional political parties stress the necessity for more educational resources; radical groups, left and right, attack current educational practices to draw attention to their dissatisfactions. Giant and aspiring business organizations (e.g., IBM, General Electric, Xerox, Raytheon) are undertaking large-scale capital investments in education in anticipation of an expanding educational "market." Universities compete for funds to establish centers for educational research; learned societies have appointed committees to work on curriculum in the elementary and secondary schools. Parents are increasingly concerned with gaining college admission for their children. Economists, who used to classify education as a consumer service and even a luxury, now treat schooling as a critical factor in the nation's productive capacity. It seems that education has moved from the periphery to the center of American social, political, and economic life.

Social scientists are participating in the new emphasis on educational change. Political scientists, for example, are questioning the separation of school affairs from other areas of local government.[80] Economists are beginning to apply models of input–output analysis to schools and are raising questions about the efficiency of current practices.[81] Psychologists, long interested in learning and education generally, have already stimulated such new techniques as programmed instruction and the use of computers in instruction. Private foundations, government agencies, and public school systems are trying to harness social science to increase the efficiency and effectiveness of public school instruction.

The new level of public and private interest, coupled with the use of social science, will probably lead to the "cracking" of tradition and less use of unquestioned practices in public schools. One result may be that the informal autonomy afforded the teacher today will be reduced as pressures mount for rationalization of the educational enterprise. It is easier to anticipate pressures toward greater centralization of authority or toward professionalization than it is to foresee the extension of individualistic autonomy. Yet the prediction of how given trends will affect either professionalization or centralization is extremely difficult; the ambiguity of single trends can be illustrated by reference to three: rising expectations of school performance, research and development activity, and emphasis on cognitive mastery.

Higher public expectations of school performance are likely to increase the political vulnerability of those who govern school systems. Confronted with such demands, board members and administrators will be prompted to increase the precision of controls they exercise over subordinates. The same increase in levels of public expectation, however, may lead to higher salaries for teachers, attract more candidates, and permit the occupation to raise entry standards and introduce more stringent occupational controls.

Sharp increases in public and private expenditures for research and development may have a similarly ambiguous result. New techniques (e.g., television) may require heavy capital expenditure and force their central location and economic use; in that instance, control over instruction may pass from individual teachers to the central administration.

New curricula and associated techniques may enhance possibilities for standardizing outcomes with diverse student populations and weaken the teacher's claim that her knowledge of students justifies decision-making autonomy. On the other hand, new knowledge about pedagogy may become the very esoteric knowledge whose absence has hampered teachers in their claims to professional standing. Training in education may become highly technical; the result may be a significant gap between those who have studied it and those who have not.

Current trends include a greater emphasis on cognitive mastery as an aim for teachers. As a high priority goal, cognitive mastery can be associated with defining educational outputs in measurable terms; defining goals in such terms permits the use of the technique of control which Blau considers the most effective—control by results.[82] Yet emphasis on cognitive mastery is also associated with specialization of teachers in particular disciplines (as, e.g., in colleges and universities). Possessing specialized knowledge of particular subjects and how to teach them, elementary teachers may gain autonomy through technical expertise not shared by generalist administrators.

The structural implications of current trends are not obvious. Elementary teaching may become more professionalized or, on the other hand, be subjected to closer hierarchical control. Perhaps the schools of the future will be marked by chronic tension between organizational and professional controls. Sociologists have an unusual opportunity to observe some basic social processes as they unfold in the elementary schools.

Notes

1. I wish to thank Mrs. Carol Kronus for her assistance in the preparation of this chapter. I am also indebted to Former Dean Francis Keppel, Harvard Graduate School of Education; Dean Roald Campbell, Department of Education, University of Chicago; Donald Mitchell and the New England School Development Council

for support which underlies the larger research from which this paper is drawn.

2. Orville G. Brim, Jr., *Society and the Field of Education* (New York: Russell Sage Foundation, 1958). Charles Bidwell, "The School as a Formal Organization," in *Handbook of Organizations,* ed. James G. March (Chicago: Rand McNally, 1965), pp. 972–1022. W. W. Charters, "The Social Background of Teaching," in *Handbook of Research on Teaching,* ed. N. L. Gage (Chicago: Rand McNally, 1963), pp. 715–813. Neal Gross, "Society of Education," in *Sociology Today,* ed. Robert K. Merton, Leonard Broom, Leonard S. Cottrell, Jr. (New York: Basic Books, 1959), pp. 128–52.

3. Robert K. Merton, "Notes on Problem-Finding in Sociology," in *Sociology Today,* pp. ix–xxxiv.

4. This saying is sometimes attributed to the late Paul Mort, an influential professor of educational administration who taught at Teachers' College, Columbia.

5. Roald F. Campbell, Luvern L. Cunningham, and Roderick F. McPhee, *The Organization and Control of American Schools* (Columbus, Ohio: Merrill Books, 1965), p. 160.

6. Raymond E. Callahan, *Education and the Cult of Efficiency* (Chicago: U. of Chicago, 1962); and N. Gross, W. S. Mason, and A. W. McEachern, *Explorations in Role Analysis: Studies of the School Superintendency Role In American Society* (New York: Wiley, 1958).

7. There is, of course, considerable variation in the actual decision-making power of principals. Generally speaking, elementary school principals appear to have less autonomy from central office control than their opposite numbers in high schools.

8. Talcott Parsons, "Some Ingredients of a General Theory of Formal Organization," in *Administrative Theory in Education,* ed. Andrew W. Halpin (Chicago: Midwest Administration Center, U. of Chicago, 1958), p. 48.

9. For example, see cases in Jack A. Culbertson, Paul B. Jacobson, and Theodore L. Reller, *Administrative Relationships* (Englewood Cliffs, N.J.: Prentice-Hall, 1960); also Cyril G. Sargent and Eugene L. Belisle, *Educational Administration: Cases and Concepts* (Boston: Houghton, 1955).

10. Recently the board president of a large Southern system suffered grave economic consequences as a result of a pro-integration stand. Opponents boycotted his business, a regional supply house, and forced him to change to another line of business. This and related incidents will be reported in a forthcoming book. Robert Crain, Morton Unger, and Gerald A. McWorter, *School Desegregation in New Orleans: A Comparative Study in Social Control*, NORC Report No. 110 (Chicago: National Opinion Research Center; May, 1966).

11. *The White House Conference on Education: A Report to the President* (Washington, D.C.: U.S. Govt. Printing Office; April, 1956), p. 8.

12. Otto H. Dahlke, *Values in Culture and Classroom: A Study in the Sociology of the School* (New York: Harper, 1958).

13. Donald J. McCarty, "Motives for Seeking School Board Membership," unpublished Ph.D. dissertation (Chicago: Department of Education, University of Chicago, 1959).

14. Donald C. Orlich and S. Samuel Shermis, "Educational Philosophy as Mythology: A Critical Analysis of School Philosophies," *Administrator's Notebook*, 14, No. 4 (December, 1965).

15. Herbert Kaufman, *The Forest Ranger: A Study in Administrative Behavior* (Baltimore: Johns Hopkins, 1960).

16. Bidwell, *op. cit.*, p. 976.

17. Parsons, *op. cit.*, p. 43.

18. This does not mean, of course, that all groups are always treated with equity; perhaps the "formulas" tend to be adjusted in some instances to the likelihood of complaint and the distribution of power. Patricia Cayo Sexton, *Education and Income* (New York: Viking, 1961).

19. In a survey of the teachers in a large school system, 53.9 per cent of the elementary teachers said that they would feel loss were they to leave the classroom. The community was Dade County Florida.

20. Willard Waller, *The Sociology of Teaching* (New York: Wiley, 1932), p. 455.

21. F. J. Roethlisberger and W. J. Dickson, with the collaboration of H. A. Wright, *Management and the Worker* (Cambridge, Mass.: Harvard U.P., 1946).

22. In a study of lawyers and their pre-practice image of their work, the author found that even the sons of lawyers expressed surprise at the difference between their romantic expectations and the realities of practice. See Dan C. Lortie, "The Striving Young Lawyer: A Study of Early Career Differentiation in the Chicago Bar," unpublished Ph.D. dissertation (Chicago: Department of Sociology, University of Chicago, 1958). The linking of "reality shock" to the public school teacher refers specifically to teachers who begin their careers in slum schools.

23. In interviews with 94 teachers in the Boston Metropolitan Area, the writer found that most respondents found it difficult to cite major ways in which their expectations of teaching differed from their experienced reality.

24. Over half of the teachers interviewed in the five school systems around Boston mentioned their teachers in discussing what persons had influenced their decision to become teachers.

25. James B. Conant, *The Education of American Teachers* (New York: McGraw-Hill, 1963).

26. Bidwell, *op. cit.,* p. 974.

27. One elementary teacher expresses her expectations about the principal as follows: "He should see that I have as near perfect an environment as I can have. I think that when he can he should take problems off my hands . . . things that don't deal specifically with things that concern our teaching. The administration of the school should run pretty smoothly." The theme here of separating the school generally from the classroom specifically is reiterated throughout interview materials with elementary teachers.

28. A recent test of this variable control was made by two students at the University of Chicago. Stephen Hazlitt and Bernard Watson found that the system of rules issued by the Gary, Indiana, school district matched the described pattern.

29. Howard M. Vollmer and D. L. Mills, *Professionalization* (Englewood Cliffs, N.J.: Prentice-Hall, 1966), esp. Section 8; and Amitai Etzioni, *Modern Organizations* (Englewood Cliffs, N.J.: Prentice-Hall, 1964), Chapter 8.

30. Arthur L. Stinchcombe, "Social Structure and Organizations," in *Handbook of Organizations,* p. 153.

31. Bernard Bailyn, *Education in the Forming of American Society* (Chapel Hill: U. of North Carolina, 1960), p. 21.

32. *Ibid.*, p. 44.

33. See Myron Lieberman, *Education as a Profession* (Englewood Cliffs, N.J.: Prentice-Hall, 1956).

34. R. Freeman Butts and Lawrence A. Cremin, *A History of Education in American Culture* (New York: Holt, 1953).

35. *Ibid.*, p. 256.

36. Paul Revere Pierce, *The Origin and Development of the Public School Principalship* (Chicago: U. of Chicago, 1935). T. L. Reller, *The Development of the City Superintendency of Schools in the United States* (Philadelphia: Author, 1935).

37. Callahan, *op. cit.*, chapters 2, 3.

38. L. Cremin, *The Transformation of the School: Progressivism in American Education,1876–1957* (New York: Knopf, 1961).

39. Raymond E. Callahan and H. Warren Button, "Historical Changes in the Role of the Man in the Organization: 1865–1950," in *National Society for the Study of Education Yearbook,* ed. Daniel Griffiths (Chicago: NSSE, 1964), pp. 73–92.

40. See paper by Dan C. Lortie in *Challenge and Change in American Education,* ed. Seymour Harris (Berkeley: McCutchan, 1965), pp. 149–56.

41. Howard S. Becker, "The Nature of a Profession," in *Education for the Professions,* National Society for the Study of Education Yearbook, ed. Nelson B. Henry (Chicago: NSSE, 1962), 61, pt. 2, 31 (whole section from pp. 27–46).

42. National Opinion Research Center, "Jobs and Occupations: a Popular Evaluation," in R. Bendix and S. M. Lipset (eds.), *Class, Status, and Power* (New York: Free Press, 1953), pp. 411–26.

43. Robert Hodge, Paul M. Siegel, and Peter Rossi, "Occupational Prestige in the United States, 1925–63," in *American Journal of Sociology,* 70, No. 3 (November, 1964), 286–302.

44. NORC, *op. cit.*

45. National Education Association, Research Division, "Teacher

Supply and Demand in Public Schools, 1965," *Research Report 1965–R10* (June, 1965).

46. National Education Association, Research Division, "The American Public School Teachers, 1960–61," in *Research Monograph 1963–M2*, p. 15.

47. Charles S. Benson, *The Economics of Public Education* (Boston: Houghton, 1961) pp. 403–4.

48. NEA, *Research Monograph 1963–M2*, p. 21.

49. Benson, *op. cit.*, p. 417.

50. Theodore Caplow, *The Sociology of Work* (Minneapolis: U. of Minnesota, 1954), p. 243.

51. Dan C. Lortie, *The Striving Young Lawyer*, p. 182.

52. The legislatures of California and New York have recently augmented the discipline-based study required of all elementary teachers.

53. Conant, *op. cit.*, Appendix G (pp. 242–46).

54. Lieberman, *op. cit.*, pp. 91–97.

55. Oswald Hall, "Stages of a Medical Career," in *American Journal of Sociology*, 53 (March, 1948), 327–36. Dan C. Lortie, "Laymen to Lawmen: Law School, Careers and Socialization," in *Harvard Educational Review* (Fall, 1959), 352–69.

56. Chiranji Lal. Sharma, "Practices in Decision-Making as Related to Satisfaction in Teaching," unpublished Ph.D. dissertation (Department of Education, University of Chicago, 1955).

57. Everett C. Hughes, *Men and their Work* (New York: Free Press, 1958), Chapter 9.

58. The interviews referred to were part of the Boston Area study.

59. Emile Durkheim, *Education and Sociology* (New York: Free Press, 1956); Waller, *op. cit.*, p. 108.

60. Teachers dismiss most of their courses as "too theoretical." It seems that they are referring less to an inappropriate level of generalization than to overly idealistic depictions of what it is possible to attain in classrooms.

61. J. W. Getzels and P. W. Jackson, "The Teacher's Personality & Characteristics," in *Handbook of Research on Teaching*, p. 574.

62. Egon G. Guba, Philip W. Jackson, and Charles E. Bidwell, "Occupational Choice and the Teaching Career," in *Educational Research Bulletin*, 38, No. 1 (January, 1959), 1–12.

63. Dan C. Lortie, "Laymen to Lawmen."

64. Laurence Iannoccone and H. Warren Button, *Functions of Student Teaching; Attitude Formation and Initiation on Elementary School Teaching*, Cooperative Research Project No. 1026 (St. Louis: Washington University, 1964).

65. Emil Haller, in the course of research on teacher socialization, sampled conversation from the author's tape-recorded interviews with elementary teachers and compared it with the Thorndike-Lorge Word List, a listing of the frequency with which English words are used. He found that 89.6 per cent of the words used in the interviews coincided with the 2,200 most commonly used words on the list. Words with prefixes and suffixes were not included; Haller estimated that such words would account for half the remaining words. Such heavy use of common vocabulary in discussion of their work does not support the beliefs that teachers possess and employ an extensive technical rhetoric. See Emil J. Haller, "Technical Socialization: Pupil Influences on Teachers' Speech" (unpublished Ph.D. dissertation, Department of Education, University of Chicago, 1966.)

66. In Dade County, less than 7 per cent of the elementary women teachers believed they would feel gain from leaving the classroom for administration.

67. Thorstein Veblen, *The Instinct of Workmanship* (New York: Macmillan, 1914).

68. F. Herzberg, B. Mausner, and Barbara Snyderman, *Motivation to Work* (New York: Wiley, 1959).

69. All teachers in the system participated in answering a self-administered questionnaire; there are no sampling problems as the questionnaire was administered during regular working hours.

70. Some of the empirical statements made in this section are based on analysis of open-ended interviews conducted in the Boston Metropolitan area. They are phrased so as to avoid the need for detailed quantitative description here. They will be fully described in a forthcoming monograph by the author.

71. Harold D. McDowell, "The Principal's Role in a Metropolitan School System: Its Functions and Variations," unpublished Ph.D. thesis (Department of Sociology, University of Chicago, 1954), pp. 150ff.

72. Anne E. Trask, "Supervision in the School: an Exploratory Study," unpublished Ph.D. thesis (Department of Education, Harvard University, 1962), pp. 8ff.

73. Edwin M. Bridges, "Teacher Participation in Decision-Making: Interaction of Personal and Situational Variables," unpublished Ph.D. thesis (Department of Education, University of Chicago, 1964), chapter 4.

74. Frederick Rudolph, "Who Paid the Bills?" *Harvard Educational Review,* 31, No. 2 (Spring, 1961), 144–57.

75. Gerald H. Moeller, "Bureaucracy and Teachers' Sense of Power," in *Administrator's Notebook,* 11, No. 3 (November, 1962), 1–4.

76. James O. Anderson, *Applicability of the Bureaucratic Model to the Organizational Structure of the School,* Cooperative Research Project S-043 (Washington, D.C.: U.S. Office of Education, 1964).

77. For example, see Judson T. Shaplin and Henry F. Olds, Jr. (eds.), *Team Teaching* (New York: Harper, 1964). A chapter by the author details a variety of possible research projects which could be undertaken on team teaching.

78. Charters, *op. cit.,* pp. 783–84.

79. R. J. Havighurst and Bernice L. Neugarten, *Society and Education* (Boston: Allyn, 1957), p. 121.

80. Robert H. Salisbury, "Big City Politics and the Schools," in *The NESDEC News,* 19, No. 2 (1965–66), 6–8.

81. See C. S. Benson *et al.,* "State and Local Fiscal Relationships in Public Education in California," *Report of the Senate Fact Finding Committee on Revenue and Taxation,* Sacramento, March, 1965.

82. Peter M. Blau and W. Richard Scott, *Formal Organizations* (San Francisco: Chandler, 1962), pp. 178–80.

CHAPTER TWO

Nurses ▲ Fred E. Katz

STATE UNIVERSITY OF NEW YORK AT BUFFALO

*T*HE MODERN NURSE IS CAUGHT IN THE throes of change. Medicine has increasingly made her into an administrative specialist, while her heritage is that of bedside care for the individual patient. From her leaders she is under pressure to become a professional, while the physician and she herself are apt to doubt her qualifications as a professional. She is a woman who finds herself in a work situation where the most prestigious positions routinely go to men. She ranks low in occupational prestige and financial rewards. All this has been described and documented again and again.[1]* The conflict inherent in the nurse's situation could doubtless be elaborated even further than the existing studies have already done, but more useful insight can be gained by taking a look at how the nurse fits into the movement to apply rational knowledge in modern

* Notes for this chapter begin on p. 77.

medicine. We shall look at how nurses fare in a context in which knowledge is systematically harnessed for solving problems but is also a weapon for giving or depriving people of distinctive social statuses. Although nursing is done in a variety of contexts—in schools, in factories, in the home— a look at nurses in hospitals will best serve to describe the nurse's professional situation while, at the same time, illuminating part of the organizational context that exists for the implementation of medical knowledge.

Knowledge Harnessing and Knowledge Guardianship

Ours is a society where knowledge counts. Those who know something and are able to put this knowledge to work influence us immensely. On a large scale, the development and organized deployment of knowledge is a major feature of our social existence. It is incorporated in the social order of our society in two distinctive ways: both formally recognized professions and complex social organizations are suited to harnessing existing knowledge and bringing it to bear on specific problems. Both are also involved in the process of creating new knowledge. The two modes are frequently combined as professionals increasingly work within large organizations. Yet the two have fundamental differences: professions are traditional guardians of bodies of knowledge; organizations, on the other hand, typically focus on the harnessing process itself, where efficiency and effectiveness are the main concerns. The organizational harnessing process includes not only a division of labor, by which specialists are enabled to concentrate on their own spheres of competence; it also includes distinctive "bargains" among its component categories specifying the form of personnel participation in the organization's primary mission and the rewards each category receives for its efforts. In time, these bargains tend to become frozen into relatively stable arrangements within the organization. Specifically, our argument is that in an age of high regard for science, hospitals harness both scientific and nonscientific resources for the care and treatment of patients. They do this chiefly by admitting the nonscientific, care-minded nurse into the hospital. In return for the right to practice nonscientific, nurturent care that has no clear place in the medical textbooks, the nurse accepts a low place in the hospital's status hierarchy. Part of the bargain is that the nurse not only helps the physician in his scientific tasks, but also helps overcome inadequacies in the scientific method of practicing medicine. She does this by helping to prevent knowledge concerning errors, ambiguities, and uncertainties from reaching the patients and their families. She virtually takes over where scientific methods are inadequate or non-existent, as in the care of incurable and senile patients in large mental hospitals.

There are probably few settings that display more direct application of vast areas of knowledge than the modern hospital. Here knowledge is routinely harnessed to alleviate the most intimate and severe personal crises. Here, too, exist both elaborate administrative arrangements that help co-ordinate medical activities and firmly established professionals who are the guardians of the knowledge that is being applied. As good health is increasingly regarded as a human right, hospital administrations and physicians are under pressure to adopt the latest results of the burgeoning new knowledge. At the same time, inertia affects both organizational and pro-fessional interests: the administration must make ends meet in the face of the increased cost of medical technology, while the physicians must display responsibility and caution in adopting new practices. Doubtless, less noble constraints (such as safeguarding habits and social image based on sheer comfort with things-as-they-are or protecting one's occupational career from the vicissitudes of competition with new pro-fessionals who offer new competencies) are also at work in many a hospital. Among physicians, however, competition is fairly well controlled, since the medical profession has a strongly enforced ethic of mutual respect. New specialists tend to be brought into the nest by being incorporated into existing consultation arrangements.

Hospitals are, in short, under pressure to implement existing knowledge but are, at the same time, involved in controlling knowledge. Physicians are chiefly responsible for deciding which items of knowledge are safe to use—safe for the patient and safe for their own reputations and the reputation of the hospital. Hospital administrators are responsible for deciding which items of knowledge are too expensive to use and which items fall within the hospital's financial capacity. These tasks may conflict with each other,[2] but underlying both is the shared sense of practicality of the applied scientist who sees the environment as something that can be manipulated and knowledge as the means of control.[3] For both physicians and hospital administrators knowledge is power, but power which must be applied cautiously and with predictability.

The question arises, then, how the nurse fits into the picture of the controlled application of knowledge in the hospital situation. How does she promote or hinder the harnessing and guardianship of knowledge? Two kinds of considerations suggest themselves: How does the nurse affect the flow and uses of knowledge? And, how does she influence the kind, i.e., the content, of knowledge that is used?

First, guardianship of knowledge implies that knowledge is not permitted to flow freely. Doctors do *not* always tell their patients the truth, and this is regarded as perfectly ethical professional behavior. Withholding of knowledge may, for example, be based on a particular, culturally produced bias against accepting the reality of impending death or permanent debility, or even pessimistic news of any sort. Reticence may also be based on a belief that, by pretending that the patient will improve—when the doctor does not actually believe this —the patient may, occasionally, actually improve. Here the idea is that the patient's own collaboration, based on optimistic faith, may be a factor that contributes to his improvement. In this situation the doctor's deception may be seen as an attempt to create a positive self-fulfilling prophecy: because the patient thinks he will get better he will harness emotional and physical resources that may actually help him to get better. The nurse's part in all this is to go along with the doctor, whatever the rationale and no matter how unfounded the optimism may be. She is usually expected to uphold the doctor's optimistic definition of the situation. Such optimism and deception is often more difficult for the nurse than it is for the doctor, because the nurse is in more frequent, immediate contact with the patient. She constantly sees his misery and hears his entreaties about his fate. However, this should not be taken to mean that the nurse is necessarily under severe stress as she withholds the hopeless truth from the dying patient. The well-socialized nurse—in contrast to the student nurse—is apt to feel quite at home when telling the terminal patient that he will get better and that he should, to be sure, ask his physician about his prognosis.[4] The blocking of pessimistic information, both from the patient and the nurse's own consciousness, may be a necessary prerequisite to the nurse's own effective functioning. In this regard, for example, some of the most cheerful and loving nursing can be seen in the care of severely defective patients in mental hospitals, patients whose mental and physical functioning is virtually nil and has been so from birth, for whom scientific medicine has nothing to offer, and whom doctors call vegetables.[5] Here any *rational* consideration could only lead to utterly hopeless prognosis. But the nurses do not permit this sort of knowledge to enter their own day-to-day awareness. In such a situation patients are completely dependent upon the nurse's nurturence, which is probably the fundamental ingredient of traditional nursing, far more so than the harnessing of rational knowledge.

Blocking the flow of knowledge can also serve to protect the existing status arrangements among hospital personnel. Studies have shown that nurses are apt to withhold knowledge about patients from aides and practical nurses. Thus, nurses may prevent attendants from seeing the patient's chart or attending the briefing sessions when work shifts change.[6] This doubtless has some justification, since most attendants have poor formal education and are not schooled in the ethics of constraint followed by medical people. The nurse controls the care of patients by controlling access to information about patients. But the situation can, on the other hand, be fairly ludicrous and self-defeating when attendants actually carry out considerable direct care of patients, and have in consequence much first-hand knowledge that they could contribute about the individual patient. One cannot escape the interpretation that in such a case some of the nurse's secretiveness is dictated by a desire to protect her own status from intrusion by underlings.

The nurse, however, is herself often denied knowledge in her dealings with physicians. The traditional picture has the nurse do the doctor's bidding with unquestioning, unknowledgeable-but-always-reliable dispatch. Although the nurse will occasionally learn a great deal about a patient from her direct dealings with him, her knowledge and her interpretations are regarded as less valid and less "educated" than those of the physician. The nurse, herself, has traditionally shared this view. The point here is not "who knows most?" but "who is the *rightful* knower?"—who is the guardian of knowledge? Both nurse and physician accept the physician as the ultimate guardian of knowledge about the patient's illness. Of course, the physician is quite apt to have knowledge about the patient that is not available to the nurse, which has doubtless helped to lower the nurse's status. In modern hospitals one finds nurses who are satisfied with the extent of knowledge provided by the patient's chart and the doctor's verbal instructions. But one also finds nurses who want more information than doctors ordinarily give them.[7] Physicians tend to be wary of a nurse's zeal for more knowledge on the ground that it changes the character of the nurse's contribution, that it causes her to bring different *kinds* of knowledge to bear than she should. To this point we will return.

The nurse is expected to react with moral passivity to her knowledge of happenings in the hospital. Doctors' mistakes are not to be discussed—not with doctors, nor with hospital administrators, and least of all with patients and outsiders in the community. While her own mistakes can be openly and drastically censured within the hospital, exposure of those by physicians is strongly tabooed, and the nurse herself helps enforce the taboo. The nurse acts as a buffer between the professional's and layman's world and between the hospital and its environment. In each case, the nurse blocks the flow of information so that it will not reach unfavorable ears.⌐ If she were a full-fledged professional peer of the physician she could, conceivably, take a more active moral stand against mistakes in medical treatment. But, as it stands, she is chiefly a sponge and a buffer. She is a silent partner to medical decisions for which she has little or no legal responsibility but in which she may recognize errors. She is expected, at all times, to protect the good name of the physician and the hospital, even if this means blocking or distorting information for public consumption. Thus, in a study of hospitals in the Midwest it was shown that when obstetricians failed to show up for the delivery of babies, the nurse would carry out the doctor's task. Not only did the nurse never claim the doctor's fee, she was usually careful not to let the patient know that she had performed the delivery. When a patient did discover it the nurse always protected the physician by finding ways of blaming the patient. She reported to the interviewing sociologist: "I stood behind the doctor the way I've been taught to do."[8]

Of course, the nurse also facilitates the flow of knowledge. The modern nurse increasingly formulates her job in clearly delineated tasks, tasks that can be written down on an assignment sheet and checked off when they are done. Such formulation promotes clarity and accountability and, therefore, accurate execution of the doctor's orders, the ingredients of rational deployment of knowledge. Hence, in the modern hospital the doctor's orders have an excellent chance of being translated into action; and, when there is a misinterpretation, there is a good chance of being able to trace the error, thanks to the "accounting system" that is built into this scheme. But there is a well-known price for this efficiency: the nurse must spend much of her time in administrative work. She must keep track of the accounting system. She must break down the doctor's orders into specific detailed task assignments and check the records to see that they are actually carried out. Habenstein and Christ suggest that the modern nursing station "resembles . . . the dispatcher's office of an urban taxicab company. The supervisory personnel—the head nurses—seldom find it necessary or desirable to leave the station.[9] One of these nurses stated: "My whole job is keeping records and . . . charting."[10] In another study a head nurse stated: "Seventy-five per cent of my time is spent kardexing orders. I feel like a robot . . . [I] get farther and farther away from patients every day."[11] The actual carrying out of the tasks increasingly (but not entirely) falls on the shoulders of relatively untrained subordinates of the nurse. As a result, the nurse is often frustrated in her attempt to express more than a very limited amount of her patient-centered interests. Instead, she has become a functionary, a crucial one to be sure, whose main contribution lies in the harnessing process. She translates the doctor's orders into discrete quanta of work, most of which she assigns to others, and collates the activities of aides and practical nurses. All this bears remarkable similarity to mass harnessing of knowledge in factories. The chief difference is that, since factories deal with inanimate products, even greater use can be made of machines. Much of the collation and translation can be done far more efficiently by computers than by humans. Not only are human collaters less efficient, they are also apt to get frustrated and bored with essentially mechanical activity. The solution for many nurses appears to be to leave nursing or to change jobs to see whether a different hospital may offer a better situation.[12]

In addition to the immediate tactical knowledge that the nurse brings to bear, she also represents the ideals that presumably prevail behind the ongoing activities. Her uniform, for example, and her demeanor provide a distinctive dramaturgy, to use Erving Goffman's term for the elaborate effort to create an impression.[13] Given Western cultural definitions, the white uniform represents selflessness and purity—moral as well as physical. The soft white shoes bring on the swift, quietly reassuring angel. Much of this symbolism is grotesquely outdated. Whiteness does not mean purity to a lot of people; angels are the helpers of a decreasing proportion of the world's population; and quiet is not reassuring to all people, although it probably comes closer to being a physiological universal than the purity of whiteness. Presumably these ideals permeate the hospital and are present in particular in the nurse. Realistically, however, the individual nurse has no say in the matter of uniform and rather little say in even the prescribed demeanor: engaging friendliness but not too close a personal involvement with patients. The hospital in which she works and the school from which she received her training, these organizations dictate most of the dramaturgy. They are the guardians of the venerable ideals. The individual nurse is their emissary and walking advertisement. She makes the message available to those who have the ability to perceive it.

Do nurses influence the *kind* of knowledge that is used in the hospital? Despite the effort of many nursing leaders for the professionalization of nursing, the physician is still the chief determiner of the kind of knowledge that is used in the medical setting. He has a recognized body of knowledge that he applies. He makes the assessment that determines the illness classification that is pinned upon the patient. The nurse, in contrast, does not make the major policy decisions about the treatment of patients, at least not legally; and she has no clearly formulated body of professional knowledge that is recognized and accepted by others.[14] Next to this picture, however, one must put the fact that the hour-by-hour, day-by-day ward life is still a world that is actually ruled by the nurse. She is *there*; and when she is not physically present her supervisory hand is still tangibly at work—far more tangibly than that of the physician. In situations calling for extensive custodial care—in long-term illness and especially in treatment for the senile aged and patients with drawn-out mental illness—the nurse tends to be the *de facto* chief of service. It would be quibbling over semantics to say that in these situations the nurse is merely carrying out doctors' orders. In state mental hospitals with three thousand patients it is not unusual to find only half a dozen physicians, only half of whom (usually residents, who are learning) are likely to be trained in psychiatry.[15] Given this sort of ratio and, in addition, the physical dispersion of patients over several acres of hospital grounds, the nurse and attendants are the actual medical team. It is under these limiting circumstances that we may consider what sort of knowledge the nurse brings to bear.

Under pressure from their leaders to establish nursing as a full-fledged profession, nurses are trying to create a distinctive body of knowledge by doing research. In nursing journals one can find reports on standard physiological topics (as, e.g., "Clearance Rates of 131 Iodine in Mechanically Injured and Normal Muscle Tissue"[16]) which one might also find in journals written by and catering to physicians. But physiological research by nurses is comparatively rare. One is far more likely to find an article such as "Characteristics of Graduate Students in Four Clinical Nursing Specialities."[17] Knowledge from the behavioral sciences—psychology, sociology, and anthropology—has found considerable acceptance by nurses, especially faculties of university schools of nursing. Recent nursing graduates are under pressure to implement it. But it is not clear to what extent nurses are actually able to put the insights into effect. Older nurses and physicians have been less receptive to the behavioral sciences. In custodial hospitals where nurses have been given fairly free reign they have occasionally met with dramatic successes when they have implemented knowledge from behavioral sciences.[18]

The relevant behavioral science knowledge has not been clearly formulated in precise, objective language—neither by nurses nor by the behavioral scientists themselves. What the nurse has adopted ranges from the "manipulative" possibilities gleaned from the Human Relationists[19] to increasingly sophisticated realization that such things as the patient's social class, ethnic membership, and education are apt to influence his disease symptoms and his response to the hospital and its staff's efforts to treat him.[20] In this perspective the intention is to recognize that not only drugs and surgery constitute medical treatment but that the "environment of the hospital is an instrumentality."[21]

On the other hand, when deploring the lack of formalization of the behavioral sciences, one must recognize that the physiological sciences that form the content of medical treatment are also not very tightly organized. To be sure they contain numerous formulations proven to a level of validity that transcends most behavioral science formulations. But the total expanse is made up of enormously disjunctive bits of knowledge about particular diseases, particular organic units, and particular *sub*systems of the human body. The large amount of memory work that goes into medical education illustrates the lack of theoretical integration of the physiological sciences; it also means that computers will be able to share an increasing part of the burden of making medical diagnoses and running surveillance on the course of treatment. After all, where memory work is concerned, including the quick and reliable harnessing of isolated iota of information, computers enjoy great superiority over ordinary humans. Yet this points to dehumanization in the wake of modern medicine. The proverbially impersonal reports by physicians—"a broken leg just arrived in ward four . . . and take a look at the pleurisy in room twenty . . . ."—have too much truth to them to be amusing. In this scene, many a nursing leader believes that the behavioral sciences can help put the pieces together again, and can help the medical staff to see that the patient is a significant entity rather than a series of disjointed disease processes—and that the nurse is best equipped to bring this transformation about.[22] Whether or not the behavioral sciences can actually do this has not been proven.

The nurse has been the traditional bastion of humanized medical care. Her "knowledge" has been assumed to be the knowledge of the heart. To be sure, traditionally the whole of medicine was less scientifically focused than it is today; doctors, too, were probably more humanistically inclined before this century. But it was the nurse who was seen as the nurturent provider of Tender Loving Care (TLC). In the modern world science has enjoyed great successes but has also raised issues that it has not been able to solve. One of the fundamental unsolved issues is the problem of humanizing scientific knowledge. How does one utilize scientific knowledge without destroying human rhythms? How does one develop knowledge that is specifically concerned with preserving humane considerations? This requires a look at the social roles of both physician and nurse.

In the medical context physicians are the harnessers of science, which means that they harness scientific knowledge from a variety of sources—from physiology and anatomy, biochemistry, and so forth—and translate it into specific programmatic action for the individual patient. It also means that they must adopt a distinctive posture toward the patient. They must have a degree of rational detachment from the patient: they must isolate and concentrate on the specific features of his illness—to the exclusion of a total immersion in the patient's life. If at all possible, they must try to apply universal canons of science rather than trying to devise utterly unique solutions to each and every patient.[23] Additionally, since they work in applied rather than pure science, they must be willing to use the available scientific knowledge in highly eclectic ways.[24] These priorities are geared, ideally, to implementing available scientific knowledge. But they obviously mean that the physician cannot concern himself with a great many features of the patient's life, even though those features may be relevant to his illness and course of treatment. If a doctor is to be successful in exploiting and focusing the available scientific knowledge, he cannot, for example, afford much emotional involvement with the patient. Yet each patient *is* different from every other patient; each patient *does* have emotional loose ends that enter into his reaction to illness and the therapeutic measures that are being used on him. Here the nurse's lack of full-scale induction into the scientific outlook can be a boon. The nurse traditionally allows herself considerable emotional openness to the patient. A nurse with twenty-eight years of experience put it this way: "It's listening to the patients, smiling at each of them, and talking with them about their families, their jobs, etcetera, that's important—and satisfying—to me."[25] This approach can permit the patient to express, and thereby face, many of his own personal problems as they relate to his illness and affect his willingness to accept the medical regime around him.[26] Stated differently, the nurse has a posture toward the patient that is less universalizing than that of the physician: she emphasizes the uniqueness of each patient and the need for emotional contact between patient and those around him. This posture can allow the patient to have a measure of autonomy that can be highly useful for him and the hospital. He can, then, be more than a person with a unique history and "background." He can, to some extent, *be himself* while in the medical context. Thus, a person who is encouraged to feel free to talk rather openly about his family, his work, and his stay in the hospital is by this means still participating in his own real, natural circumstances. He is, at the same time, *actively participating* in working out an adaptation to the fact that he is now physically removed from his family and work; he is *actively* working out an adaptation to being in the hospital, even if the "adaptation" includes little more than expressing anger at the medical staff.[27] In short, the nurse's administering TLC can create autonomy for the patient which the patient can use to participate actively in adapting to his life in the hospital and the facts of his illness. As noted, such "adaptation" may not be friendly to the hospital; but at least it may dissipate hidden fears and facilitate realistic solutions to real problems. If the behavioral studies of hospitals have any message it is that blocked emotions and fears of patients—or, for that matter, those of staff members—are apt to be translated into tensions *in other sectors of life in the hospital*.[28] The patient's active participation in working out an adaptation is apt to be fruitful not only for his own peace of mind, but also for the peace and orderly pursuit of goals in the hospital.

There are various obstacles to the nurse's adopting such a role. Under the pressures of staff shortage and the demands of administering the technical side of scientific medicine (giving injections, collecting specimen, etc.) she simply has little time to spend with individual patients. The nurse is also under pressure from her leaders: she is encouraged to increase her "professional" participation in medicine, even if this means increasing her administrative work and diminishing her personal concern with the patients. By such professionalism she will presumably improve her social status. TLC, it must be remembered, tends to be paid for in the non-negotiable currency of temporary pleasant feelings, not in social recognition that takes the form of a respectable wage. Nurses' professionalism has mixed reception from physicians. Nursing leaders tend to look at this as physicians' efforts to block the progress of nurses as a profession. This motivation may in part be present, but it is also likely that the wise physician recognizes that his emphasis on scientific techniques in medicine leaves many of the patient's needs unmet. The physician relies on the nurse to cater to these needs, and the traditional nurse concerned with TLC may have done this rather better than her modern professional counterpart.

Among nurses there is no absolute uniformity about the sort of knowledge that is favored. A guideline may be taken from the study by Habenstein and Christ,[29] who found that nurses differed very decidedly in their beliefs about the usefulness of formal knowledge as against rather unformalized TLC.[30] Thus, one nurse stated:

> TLC is important, but you can go too far with it, and before you know it you have your hands full of chronic complainers.

while another said:

> I feel best when I am with the patient.[31]

The authors suggest a typology according to which nursing includes the Professionalizer, the Traditionalizer, and the Utilizer.

> [The] focus of the professionalizer is not specifically upon the patient to be healed but upon the special things that must be done and the special modes of operations that must be evolved if the problem of healing is to be more adequately

and intelligently met. Her case rests with *knowledge,* and knowledge in this case represents the application of rational faculties of experience . . . .[32]

Here science represents doing things *to* the patient. There is no recognition that, if given the right sort of autonomy, the patient might do things of his own volition that will also contribute to his recovery or, at least, facilitate the work of those who are doing things to him. The authors describe the traditionalizing nurse as one who, along with her *dedication,* takes a highly uncritical stance with regard to knowledge and existing practices in the hospital: she is a guardian, not a harnesser; she mainly guards the traditions of the hospital and the physicians. Such a nurse is not likely to try to suggest innovations based on her own experiences in the hospital. The Utilizing nurse, finally, has a strong commitment neither to professional knowledge nor to traditions of the hospital and medicine. She "asks only to be judged in terms of the efficacy and diligence of her task performance as they [her duties] are accomplished, one by one."[33] She is the prototype of the nurse as a piece-rate worker, a low-level, nonprofessional, organizational employee who simply does her job. She "utilizes" the medical context for her own outside interests. Developing and using a distinctive body of knowledge has little intrinsic appeal for her.

Habenstein and Christ also note that the three types of nurse differ in their choice of hospital services. Professionalizers, for instance, do not like obstetrics since there is little *medical* drama involved—" . . . after all, the mothers are not *ill.* . . ."[34] A traditionalizer says, on the other hand, " . . . obstetrics is such a happy place. These mothers are so happy and the babies are so helpless. . . ."[35] To the professionalizer disease is the challenge, a challenge for harnessing scientific knowledge and making a distinctive "medical" contribution to the course of events. To the traditionalizer, the patient is the challenge, but challenging also are the reputation of the hospital and the medical profession. The traditionalizer is probably closer to being a guardian of humane concerns than are the professionalizer and utilizer. Her passivity and lack of intellectual focus, however, do not always augur well for zealous protection of the patient's humanity. A clear guardianship of the patient's autonomy might provide her with a suitable focus for her efforts.

The Uses of Knowledge and Skills and the Nurse's Own Status

The Caste System

So far most of the focus has been on harnessing and guarding knowledge for the sake of reaching medical objectives, implying that contributions by various sorts of medical personnel are collated and applied to solving medical problems. But in the collation process not all contributions are treated as being equally important: the contributions by physicians are rated as more critical than those of nurses and aides. This evaluation is formalized in hospitals in a rather rigid social stratification system that places physicians at the top in caste-like superordination above nurses. The important point to note is that the semi-professionals, such as nurses and laboratory and X-ray technicians, are not located on a continuum with doctors: there is no hierarchical pattern with a gradual approach to and fusion with the highest status, that of physician. Instead, the caste-like system puts an unscalable wall between the physician and the semi-professionals in the hospital. Among modern nurses there are movements to increase their own professional independence and thereby to improve their status on the medical team. Before considering these movements it will be well to consider the existing system more fully.

The nurse at work discusses few of her activities with the patient she is tending: as she takes the patient's temperature and weighs him she is apt to remain silent; if the patient asks how much he weighs, he will be told to ask his physician. The nurse may explain her silence as her way of preventing anxiety for the patient;[36] in fact, it may increase his worry. But it is her way of not trespassing into the domain of the physician, of "knowing her place"—just as she would not presume, ordinarily, to sit at the doctors' table in the hospital dining room. Further, physicians generally hold the nurse in low esteem:[37] they are willing to see nurses receive income infinitely smaller than their own, and frequently treat the nurse as a nonperson[38] who can be ignored and reprimanded with impunity. To be sure, physicians often acknowledge individual competence and are fond of individual nurses. But this is still in the character of a caste system, just as southern whites in the United States traditionally held specific Negroes in fond regard and treated them kindly, even lovingly.

In economic and in democratic-humanitarian terms, the nurses' low status must seem harsh indeed. But in the medical system there is a positive side to the nurses' low status. As noted earlier, the prestige of modern medicine rests on science: it is the scientific (and technological) advance in the treatment of illness that has received the great public acclaim. The nurturent care of patients, as given by families and nurses, has not had any comparable recognition; indeed, it occupies a rather residual place in "scientific" medicine. Physicians are the promoters and guardians of scientific medicine. Nurses assist them in many specific ways, but they do so as distinct underlings who follow instruction. The caste-like separation of nurses from physicians suggests that nurses are really not part of the scientific fraternity that exists in hospitals. Nurses are largely disfranchised from equal participation in this prestigious sector of medicine. How, then, do hospitals get the loyalty and cooperation of nurses if they do not give nurses full-fledged membership in the scientific fraternity? The answer seems to be that in partial payment for such denial, nurses are permitted to enact functions that have no clear place in modern medicine: namely, the nurturent care functions. It is as though the nurse receives the right to engage in her traditional tasks as a bonus for accepting second-class citizenship in the dominant medical system. The system benefits from this arrangement, since nurturent care of some sort is doubtless essential for most patients. For the nurse it provides continuity with the traditions of her occupation, and it fulfills the expectation of most young nursing trainees of giving *bedside* care to patients. It provides such continuity despite a situation in which the nurse must spend a large portion of her time being quasi-scientist and ward administrator rather than dispenser of personal care to patients.

It must be noted that there are cracks in the caste system. The young nurse is less likely than her predecessors to jump when the doctor enters. She is apt to say, as one university-trained staff nurse put it: "I was educated to serve the patient . . . I have different responsibilities than the doctor has . . . ."[39] Yet the perspective that the nurse has responsibilities different from those of doctors can also lead nurses to be well satisfied with being doctors' nonequals. It involves recognition that doctors give the orders for the patient's medical treatment, and supervisory and head nurses "act as overseers"[40] to see that the staff nurse carries them out, but that in her immediate care of patients the nurse enjoys considerable autonomy. As one staff nurse put it: ". . . really it's the nurse who controls herself . . . ,"[41] and a head nurse said: "I control my own work . . . just myself. . . ."[42] These nurses claimed to have "a good cooperative relationship with doctors . . . [and that they] wouldn't want to be on an equal basis with doctors. . . ."[43] In terms of organizational control over the nurse, this suggests a blend of quite specific controls over some activities—those involved in carrying out doctors' orders for medical treatment—and considerable freedom in bedside care, where the nurse may assert her own initiative.

Toward Professionalization

Few professionals talk as much about being professionals as those whose professional stature is in doubt. Nursing leaders, especially those teaching in university schools of nursing, talk a great deal about being professionals. Their objective is to give nursing full-fledged professional status.

Sociologically, the development of a profession involves more than developing a distinct body of knowledge. It involves realization, as Emile Durkheim would have put it, that professionals are part of a moral community;[44] that they have social links not only to their clients and colleagues in their profession, but also to other groups with whose activities their skills must dovetail; and that the legitimacy of their professional contribution must be acknowledged by these other groups. In short, the legitimacy of professional guardianship of a body of knowledge depends not only on *having* a distinct body of knowledge, but on acceptance of the guardianship by those beyond as well as those within the ranks. In the case of the nurse, the outside acceptance would have to come from physicians and hospital administrators and would probably require drastic rearrangement of social roles in the hospital. As yet neither the development of a clear-cut body of professional nursing knowledge nor the acceptance of nurses as full-fledged guardians of the existing knowledge has proceeded very far. It will be instructive to examine the ongoing struggle.

Among nursing leaders one can hear statements to the effect that modern, college-trained nurses, having "been nurtured and allowed to develop their intellectual potential, find a pitifully scarce market for their capabilities in the very institutions that are in desperate need of their talents,"[45] and that nurses suffer disillusionment upon beginning their work in hospitals.[46] The leaders believe that nurses are not sufficiently aggressive in spelling out the distinctive nursing care requirements but are too subservient to the demands from other professionals. One nurse states:

> Over and over again I have heard nurses telling their patients that they don't have time to do thus and so for them. Is this because the nurses are busy caring for other patients? In most cases no. It's because they are doing work that members of other service professions (administrator, doctors, and therapists, for example) have loaded upon them.

> It doesn't occur to these nurses that it is their responsibility
> to spell out just what nursing care is needed and to estimate
> the *time* that will be needed to give this care. Instead, they
> do all kinds of work that has been assigned to them, then
> give their patients whatever nursing care they can in the
> amount of time that is left.[47]

But another side of this picture is that practicing nurses often
seem to be quite satisfied with the amount of professional
responsibility they actually have.[48] This is especially so among
nurses who have diploma rather than collegiate nursing
training.[49] Rank-and-file nurses generally appear to have less
commitment to *professionalism* than their leaders.[50] This is not
merely a matter of belief: it is apparently translated into action,
namely into high rates of departure at the time of marriage and
high rates of part-time nursing when economic and family
circumstances permit.[51]

There have been various suggestions about re-focusing the
nurse's role so that her professional contribution will be more
fully recognized: she should become the manager of patient
care (as against the physician's focus on patient therapy);[52]
she should delegate many of her present managerial duties to
the hospital's administration, so that she can get back to the
bedside of the patient.[53] Neither of these seems to offer the
nurse clear-cut professional autonomy. If she is manager of
patient care, she still must assist the physician in giving
therapy; and her "care" would probably come under the
physician's surveillance as well. Her return to the bedside
might offer better prospects if she could persuade physicians
that her skills are of professional caliber comparable to his
own. Some nurses are indeed trying to do this, but the road is
rocky. Here is an insightful assessment of the present "eroded"
state of nursing as seen from the perspective of a physician:

> A physician develops a very specific and responsible
> relationship with his patients . . . around his direct clinical
> practice with patients. Nurses have by-passed this direct
> relationship and are organized in bureaucratic hierarchy.
> Unlike physicians, nurses attempt to resolve the shortage
> of nurses by trying to give nursing care through others.

This move to a managerial practice of nursing resulted in a proliferation of nursing personnel with different kinds of training, much of it mediocre.

A physician for the most part attends to all the medical needs of his patients . . . [on the other hand] one nurse may be responsible for all treatments, . . . and another for all the nursing information on the patient. . . . In addition to fracturing clinical nursing practice by the [above] method of organizing nursing care . . . nurses are responsible to three major departments . . . when this major distraction is compounded by nursing staff with widely different types of training, spread over three shifts with rotating days off, . . . the exact transmission of messages [to and from the physician] is likely to occur only by chance. When nurses adopted the managerial means of practice, they did much to disrupt the communication with their clinical colleagues . . .[54]

There is considerable antagonism between physicians who want dependable, servile nurses and nurses who want professional dignity and autonomy.[55] Physicians obviously have the upper hand.

In the past twenty years nurses have been very receptive to the work of behavioral scientists, especially sociologists, psychologists, and anthropologists. Nurses have enthusiastically incorporated behavioral science into their teaching curriculum and have engaged in or supported a considerable amount of research on occupational studies of nurses[56] and situational studies of nursing care.[57] There can be little doubt that this interest in behavioral science is part of the effort to gain professional respectability. The actual dealings between nurses and the behavioral scientists have had successes, but also difficulties. In the early period nurses were probably over-eager to accept the behavioral scientists into their midst, and probably exaggerated the gifts they might receive. Some disenchantment has set in—with nurses realizing that their guests cannot tell them what their goals and professional focus ought to be, that their guests are occasionally unmannerly enough to treat them as suitable subjects for research, even when the nurses do not want to be and when the objectives of the research have little practical relevance to nursing problems. Some nurses have begun to believe that they must eventually renounce this "patronage" by outsiders.[58] The behavioral scientists, too, occasionally chafed under nursing regimes that seemed to lack traditions of open intellectual inquiry.

Much of the behavioral research deliberately focused on nurses' professionalization, yet no real formulas on how nursing is to become a profession have emerged, although, as E. C. Hughes has pointed out, "there has been much fruitless argument whether or not nursing is a profession."[59] To be sure, much of the content of the modern nursing curriculum supplements physiology and anatomy with behavioral science items. This has doubtless added a measure of socio-cultural sophistication to innocent, undifferentiated TLC. But nurses have not thereby achieved a distinct body of knowledge that has been accepted by their medical colleagues. In addition, the behavioral knowledge about her professionalism has done little to alter the nurse's subservience to the hospital physician. Behavioral scientists have not really proven that they are capable of aiding the ladies in their professional distress.

Some behavioral scientists have stated that nursing cannot become a profession—that nurses are deluding themselves by their professional efforts, that they simply lack the professional guardianship over a body of knowledge.[60] Many, perhaps a majority, of the physicians would probably agree. It is not clear how much of this situation is an inherent fact of life about nursing and how much, if any, the end-product of a vicious cycle. If the latter, it may be that nurses have not developed a viable body of sophisticated knowledge because they have been kept in caste-like subservience to doctors, and their lack of success has then been used to justify keeping them in their low status.

Two things seem to be needed if nursing is to develop into a profession: (1) its corpus of knowledge, e.g., behavioral knowledge relevant to the care of patients, must be greatly refined and organized, with nurses themselves taking a leading part in this process; (2) nurses' caste-like status separation from physicians must give way to the colleagueship that now prevails among the various medical specialties. It may be asked whether the nurses' *assistance* of the doctor in therapeutic measures (e.g., in the operating room) does not inevitably make her into the physician's assistant rather than his colleague. It would seem that these medical assistance functions could be carried out more profitably by those who are training to be physicians, namely medical students and interns. The nurse's participation in this area is anachronistic; such assistance might better be part of the apprenticeship of those who will later assume the full responsibility. This would free the nurse to concentrate on the tasks of patient care, where she can lay claim to some degree of genuine expertise. Once hospitals are free of the caste system—a system that is inevitably expensive and that takes its toll in disrupted and distorted flow of knowledge—they can truly harness the contributions of groups that are now kept ritualistically separate. But the destruction of the caste system will take more imaginative effort than has been put forward thus far.

Hospital nurses who were recently interviewed pointed out that the heart of being a professional nurse is a commitment to personal care of patients, not a commitment to abstract systems of knowledge.[61] From this point of view, the traditional hospital arrangement that makes the nurse subservient to physicians but autonomous in regard to nurturent care is a viable system. The new professional aspirations, however, with their focus on the nurse as a scientific colleague of the physician, hold the promise of making personalized care of patients increasingly sophisticated. But hospitals will have to develop adequate arrangements for translating the new sophistication of nurses into workable organizational patterns.

Notes

1. For recent surveys, see Fred Davis (ed.), *The Nursing Profession* (New York: Wiley, 1966); Ronald G. Corwin and Morris J. Taves, "Nursing and Other Health Professions," in Howard E. Freeman, Sol Levine and Leo G. Reeder (eds.), *Handbook of Medical Sociology* (Englewood Cliffs, N.J.: Prentice-Hall, 1963); Fred Davis and Virginia L. Olesen, "Nursing," in Howard M. Vollmer and Donald L. Mills (eds.), *Professionalization* (Englewood Cliffs, N.J.: Prentice-Hall, 1966).

2. There is a sociological literature that emphasizes how different functions of professionals and administrators lead to tensions. Much of this literature was generated by an insightful paper by Alvin Gouldner. See his "Cosmopolitans and Locals: Toward an Analysis of Latent Social Roles–I," in *Administrative Science Quarterly*, II (December, 1957), 281–306.

3. For a fuller discussion of the perspective of the applied scientist, see Fred E. Katz, "The Third Culture," in *Studies in Sociology*, ed. Milton Albrecht (Buffalo: State U. of New York, 1967), 133–47.

4. Fred E. Katz, unpublished study of nurses in a 500-bed hospital in a northeastern city, 1967.

5. Based on personal observations and interviews in several state hospitals.

6. Robert A. Habenstein and Edwin A. Christ, *Professionalizer, Traditionalizer, and Utilizer* (Columbia, Mo.: U. of Missouri, 1955), p. 29.

7. Katz, unpublished study of nurses.

8. Hebenstein and Christ, *op. cit.*, p. 99.

9. *Ibid*, p. 29.   10. *Ibid*.

11. Katz, unpublished study of nurses.

12. The turnover rate of nurses in hospitals is very high and so is the proportion of nurses who do not practice nursing. See E. C.

Hughes, H. M. Hughes and I. Deutscher, *Twenty Thousand Nurses Tell Their Story* (Philadelphia: Lippincott, 1958), Chapters II and III.

13. Erving Goffman, *The Presentation of Self in Everyday Life* (New York: Doubleday Anchor, 1959); Victor Thompson, *Modern Organizations* (New York: Knopf, 1961).

14. See William Goode, "Librarianship," in Vollmer and Mills, *op. cit.*, pp. 34–43.

15. Garland L. Lewis, Marguerite J. Holmes and Fred E. Katz, *An Approach to Education of Psychiatric Nursing Personnel* (New York: National League for Nursing, 1961).

16. Joan E. Mulligan and Gail E. Casse, in *Nursing Research,* 14, No. 2 (Spring, 1965), 126–31.

17. Doris I. Miller, in *Nursing Research,* 14, No. 2 (Spring, 1965), 106–11.

18. See, for example, Lewis, Holmes, and Katz, *op. cit.,* Chapter VI.

19. Charles Perrow, "Hospitals: Technology, Structure, and Goals," in *Handbook of Organizations,* ed. James G. March (Chicago: Rand McNally, 1965), pp. 910–71.

20. For examples of sophisticated application of social sciences to nursing, see: Francis C. MacGregor, *Social Science in Nursing* (New York: Russell Sage Foundation, 1960); and Esther Lucille Brown, *New Dimensions of Patient Care* (New York: Russell Sage Foundation, 1964), Parts 1–3.

21. Brown, *op. cit.,* Part 3, p. 7.

22. *Ibid.*

23. This is an application of Talcott Parsons' pattern variables. See Talcott Parsons, Robert F. Bales and Edward A. Shils, *Working Papers in the Theory of Action* (New York: The Free Press, 1953), Chapter 3.

24. Katz, "The Third Culture," pp. 134–38.

25. Katz, unpublished study of nurses.

26. *Can* permit is said advisedly. Wholly unsophisticated emotional interplay on the part of the nurse can also be psychologically destructive to the patient: it can be smothering rather than nurturing.

27. This point of view contrasts with Parsons' emphasis on the patient's exemption from his ordinary, work-a-day duties, his general passivity, and the discontinuities between his home and the hospital. See Talcott Parsons, *The Social System* (New York: The Free Press, 1950), pp. 440ff.

The extent to which patients are encouraged to be passive in modern hospitals is, of course, an empirical question. The suggestion for greater participation by patients is a sociological rationale for practices that actually do exist in many hospitals.

28. The first, and classic, study of this was Alfred H. Stanton and Morris S. Schwartz, *The Mental Hospital* (New York: Basic Books, 1954).

29. Habenstein and Christ, *op. cit.*

30. *Ibid.*, pp. 39ff.   31. *Ibid.*, p. 40.   32. *Ibid.*, p. 41.

33. *Ibid.*, p. 42.   34. *Ibid.*, p. 27.   35. *Ibid.*

36. Rose L. Coser, *Life in the Ward* (East Lansing: Michigan State U., 1962), e.g., Chapter V.

37. Hughes, Hughes, and Deutscher, *op. cit.*, 194ff.; and MacGregor, *op. cit.*, p. 266.

38. Coser (*op cit.*, Chapter II) gives vivid illustrations of the nurse being treated as a nonperson by physicians. For instance, physicians stand, bunched up, in a hallway. A nurse trying to go through has to stand aside and wait mutely. She dare not ask the doctors to move, and the doctors pay no attention to her discomfort.

39. Katz, unpublished study of nurses.

40. *Ibid.*   41. *Ibid.*   42. *Ibid.*   43. *Ibid.*

44. G. Simpson (trans.), *The Division of Labor in Society* (New York: The Free Press, 1960).

45. Lauraine A. Thomas, "Is Nursing Service Administration prepared for the Professional Nurse?" in *The Journal of Nursing Education,* 4, No. 1 (January, 1965), 6. This author blames nurses' own administrative regimes for the present state of affairs.

46. Corwin and Taves, *op. cit.,* p. 198.

47. Gertrude Bertrand Ujhely, "Servant? No! Service Professional? Yes!" *RN,* 27, No. 1 (January, 1964), 56–60.

48. See, for example, Leonard Reissman and John Rohrer (eds.), *Changing Dilemmas in The Nursing Profession* (New York: Putnam's, 1957), Chapter IV. Being satisfied with their existing responsibilities should not be taken to mean that they are satisfied with their wages.

49. Ronald Corwin, "The Professional Employee: A Study of Conflicting Nursing Roles," *American Journal of Sociology,* LXVI, No. 6 (May, 1961), 604–15.

50. It is also interesting to compare American nurses with nurses in other countries. For instance, Glaser's studies of nursing in several European countries suggest that these nurses do not try to promote the nurse's professionalism to the extent that American nurses attempt to. See William A. Glaser, "Nursing Leadership and Policy," in Fred Davis, *The Nursing Profession,* pp. 1–59.

51. *Ibid.*

52. Hans O. Mauksch, "The Organizational Context of Nursing Practice," in *ibid.,* pp. 109–37.

53. Luther P. Christman, "Nurse-Physician Communications in the Hospital," in *International Nursing Review,* 13, No. 4 (July-August, 1966), 49–57.

54. *Ibid.,* p. 54.

55. For a review of both sides see MacGregor, *op. cit.*

56. For example, see Hughes, Hughes, and Deutscher, *op. cit.*

57. For example, see Reissman and Rohrer, *op. cit.*

58. See, for example, M. D. Ellison, D. Diers, and R. C. Leonard,

"The Uses of Behavioral Sciences in Nursing: Further Comment," in *Nursing Research,* 14, No. 1 (Winter, 1965), 71–72.

59. Hughes, Hughes, and Deutscher, *op. cit.,* p. 4.

60. Goode, *op. cit.,* p. 36.

61. Katz, unpublished study of nurses.

CHAPTER THREE

Professional Employees in a Bureaucratic Structure: Social Work ▲ W. Richard Scott

DEPARTMENT OF SOCIOLOGY
STANFORD UNIVERSITY

*T*HE TERM PROFESSIONAL HAS MANY connotations. There is little agreement as to which dimensions it encompasses, and few of the several dimensions usually identified are very precisely defined. To the extent that the term has any common meaning, however, it refers to a person who by virtue of long training is qualified to perform specialized activities autonomously—relatively free from external supervision or regulation. The word *bureaucrat* has many connotations. Again, there is little agreement as to which dimensions are encompassed, and few of those usually mentioned are precisely defined. But to the extent that *bureaucrat* has any common meaning, it refers to a person performing specialized but more routine activities under the supervision of officials organized in a hierarchical fashion. Obviously, then, two very different arrangements for organizing work are implied by these two terms, and should a person trained to function as a *professional* find himself in the role of *bureaucrat*, there is at least the possibility of conflict.

The study reported here focuses on the problem raised when professional workers operate within a bureaucratic structure—the conflicts and tensions generated and the reconciliations and accommodations attempted. The precise nature of the problems and attempted solutions will vary with the characteristics of the particular professional groups and employment settings examined, but the problems are expected to be present in some form in all circumstances where professionals are employed by bureaucratic organizations. It is the intent of this paper to illuminate these generic problems by examining in some detail their manifestations and repercussions within a specific organization, a social work agency.

Social workers, viewed as an occupational category, exhibit an extraordinary amount of diversity. They range from the proverbial little old lady in tennis shoes, armed with good intentions and a high school diploma, ministering to the needs, as she interprets them, of her caseload, to the young man with a Ph.D. degree from a graduate school of social welfare engaged in a program of evaluative research on the merits of a new casework technique. Matching the variety of training undergone and tasks performed by workers is the diversity of settings in which they operate, some few functioning as solo practitioners, most typically as family counselors, others working for specialized private agencies, and the majority serving as employees in a variety of public settings—schools, hospitals, correction facilities, and public assistance agencies. To attempt to describe and, more particularly, to generalize in any meaningful way about the characteristics of social workers or the settings within which they function is, hence, a formidable and hazardous enterprise which will not be undertaken here. Instead, the present essay will concern itself exclusively with a particular group of social workers all of whom were employees of a single county welfare department. No claim is or can be made that this group of workers or this agency is in any sense "typical" or "representative" of other workers and agencies,[1]* and caution should be exercised in attempting to extrapolate the results of this study to other organizations.

The Agency and Its Program

Because all data to be reported were gathered within a single public assistance agency, which will be referred to as "County Agency," it is appropriate at the beginning to describe briefly the nature of the public assistance program in the United States, as well as to detail some of the more salient characteristics of the particular organization investigated. Such background information is intended not only to provide orientation to the reader, but also to specify some of the conditions under which the findings reported in subsequent pages were observed to obtain.

The Public Assistance Program

The present system of public welfare organizations is a fairly recent arrival on the American scene. The inability of local administrative units to provide relatively long term assistance to the indigent, the incapacitated, and the dependent became painfully clear during the great depression of the Thirties and resulted in the federal government stepping into the breach with the passage of the Social Security Act of 1935 to encourage the establishment of state programs of public welfare to be administered at the state and/or local level. The incentive for the adoption of the federal plan by the individual states was the provision of grants-in-aid to states meeting the general requirements outlined by the Act—these grants to be supplemental to and a certain percentage of state and local funds expended for the program. The act provided for federal participation in the assistance of certain categories of recipients: the aged, dependent children living with responsible

* Notes to this chapter begin on p. 134.

relatives, the blind, and, by a 1950 amendment, the permanently and totally disabled. In addition, although no federal funds were made available for general assistance, provisions were made for the support of various other child welfare services. Legislation in 1939 brought all employees of public welfare agencies under civil service codes. All states came to participate in the program.

The original Social Security Act, together with its several amendments, established certain general policies which were intended to secure the equitable, impartial, efficient, and responsible administration of the program.[2] Within these policies the individual states were allowed to establish more specific regulations to govern eligibility criteria for the various programs. Considerable variation remains among state programs with regard to these criteria, there being differences in state requirements with respect to age, citizenship, residency, need, property and income limitations, maximum payments, recoveries, liens, and specification of the extent to which relatives are held responsible for support.[3]

It is important to realize the extent to which the policies and programs of the public welfare agency are determined by laymen rather than by professionals within the field of social work. The broad framework for the public welfare program was established by Congress and is under its control; state legislatures specify and further determine the contents of the program; finally, even at the local level, a lay board participates in the setting of policies which govern agency operations. That many of the lay-determined laws and policies within which public welfare departments operate constitute a source of strain and tension for the professionals who man the agencies would seem to go without saying. Organizational adaptations and worker reactions to these provisions will be analyzed subsequently.

County Agency: Formal Structure and Staff Characteristics

Because public welfare programs are shaped in considerable measure by state laws, a few comments are in order on the

character of these regulations in the state where County
Agency is located. In general, this state legislature was con-
servative in its stance toward welfare legislation relative to
other states. Although high on per capita income, the state
was low on welfare expenditure. Further, many of its legislative
provisions pertaining to such matters as citizenship requirements, maximum payments, responsibility of relatives, and
property liens were among the most stringent in the nation.

By contrast, County Agency was regarded as having one
of the most, if not the most, progressive welfare programs in
the state. Budgetary standards used to calculate client needs
were the most generous in the state, and much emphasis was
placed on the accumulation of various special funds to assist
clients which would not be subject to the various federal or
state restrictions. The agency conducted in-service training
programs for all members, including refresher courses for the
older employees, and employed a variety of techniques to
encourage and assist staff members to take graduate training
in social work. County Agency's progressivism was no doubt
in part due to its urban location in a largely agricultural state
but was also attributable to the efforts of its two former
directors and its current director, all of whom were regarded
as hard-driving individuals, strongly committed to the ideology
of the social work profession.

County Agency, with a main and a branch office, served a
city of approximately 100,000 and its surrounding county. It
employed 170 persons at the time of the study, but the research
focused on the professional casework staff of ninety-two workers
and twelve supervisors. Caseworkers were organized into units
consisting typically of seven workers and a supervisor; seven
of the units handled public assistance caseloads (the categorical
programs), four worked with child welfare clients (placing
children for adoption, placing and supervising children in
foster homes and in institutions), and one smaller unit was
engaged in "special services" (family counseling, research).
In the main office, units handling each of these programs were
organized into divisions (Public Assistance, Child Welfare,
Special Services) each under a division head. The three units

in the branch office were all under a single division head, who also served as assistant director of the agency.[4]

Requirements for employment in the several divisions were uniform throughout the agency, and all caseworkers were paid on the same wage scale, special increments being given to workers with graduate training or previous social work experience. Minimum requirement for employment was a college degree and the passage of an exam administered by the state personnel bureau; nevertheless, twenty-five of the older employees had no college degree although seven of these did possess some sort of diploma, e.g., R.N. diploma or Bible school certificate. Thirty-nine caseworkers had taken some graduate training in social work, although only fourteen of these had completed more than fifteen hours and only two of the fourteen had an advanced degree. All of the twelve supervisors had taken some graduate training in social work, four of them less than fifteen hours and the rest thirty hours or more. Two of the twelve supervisors held advanced social work degrees, as did all of the division heads, the director, and the assistant director. While it might appear that the level of training acquired by the County Agency staff was somewhat low, it compared favorably with that reported for a national sample of social workers as of 1950.[5] This survey indicated that only about 60 per cent of all the casework employees of state, county, and local welfare departments had a college degree, as compared to 73 per cent of the County Agency employees; and only 27 per cent of the national survey respondents had taken some graduate training in social work, as compared to 42 per cent of the County Agency workers.

Other staff characteristics may be briefly summarized. Of the ninety-two caseworkers in County Agency, fifty-four were white (59 per cent) and thirty-eight Negro, while among supervisors, ten were white and two were Negro. One of the three division heads was Negro. Women predominated among the caseworkers, sixty-six (72 per cent) being employed. This was also the case at the supervisory level, with ten of the twelve supervisors female. The predominance of females over males is also characteristic of social workers in

the nation as a whole: 70 per cent of the social workers sur-
veyed by the Department of Labor were female. The average
age for County Agency workers was approximately forty
years, as compared to thirty-seven years for the national
sample. The average age for supervisors in County Agency
was fifty-three years, and for the national sample, forty-four
years. The average length of service for workers in County
Agency was 5.8 years, compared to 5.5 for the national sample.
Twenty-eight per cent of the caseworkers in County Agency
came from lower-class origins, as measured by father's occupation (unskilled and semi-skilled work); 30 per cent from
the lower-middle-class (fathers employed as skilled manual
or white-collar workers); and 42 per cent from the upper-
middle- or upper-classes (fathers with managerial or professional
occupations). No data were reported for the national sample
with respect to either class of origin or race. But on all other
variables the County Agency staff appeared to be fairly comparable to the U.S. sample of social workers, with the exception that the agency staff was on the average slightly better
educated in terms of both college and specialized social work
training.

Data Collection

All data were collected by the author over a ten-month period
in 1959. Several months were spent in informal interviewing
and observation, primarily within the Public Assistance and
Child Welfare Divisions. The researcher was permitted to
attend all administrative meetings, including the monthly
welfare board meeting, and to sit in on orientation sessions
for new workers, in-service training sessions, professional staff
meetings, and worker–supervisor conferences. Considerable
time was spent observing the daily work routines in the two
largest agency divisions.[6] Systematic data were also gathered.
Lengthy questionnaires were completed by ninety of the
ninety-two caseworkers and eleven of the twelve supervisors,
and all of the higher administrative personnel were interviewed

formally. Agency records were utilized to obtain measures of worker "productivity" and the yearly service ratings of all workers were made available to the researcher.

Professional Orientation of Staff

In many respects, the professional person employed by a bureaucratic organization is the modern marginal man, his feet uncertainly planted in two different and partially conflicting institutional environments. It is not necessary to describe here the characteristics of these two organizational forms, as they have been discussed at length in the literature of organizations, but some of the major areas of conflict may be briefly noted. Generally, professional workers —having been exposed to independent training centers where professional norms and standards are inculcated and having been bolstered by the social support received from like-minded colleagues—are likely to be critical of the organization's goals and performance standards, particularly in cases where these are not set by members of their own profession. In addition, professionals desire and expect a large degree of autonomy from organizational control: they wish to exercise maximum discretion in carrying out their professional activities, free from hierarchical interference or confining procedural regulations. Finally, professionals are less likely to be responsive to organizationally controlled sanctions: they care more for the good opinions of colleagues than for high evaluations from administrative superiors, and they prefer movement from one organization to another with better facilities or a more congenial professional atmosphere to mobility through the administrative hierarchy within a particular organization.[7]

Numerous empirical studies have shown some or all of these generalizations to hold for such professional groups as physicians,[8] college professors,[9] and scientists.[10] To what extent can they be said to be applicable to groups such as social

workers, whose claim to full-fledged professional status is,
perhaps, less secure? To approach this question, it is first
necessary to distinguish among social workers in terms of
their orientation to the professional community. No professional group is homogeneous in this respect, but it is
particularly important when dealing with the less secure
professions to characterize their members by this variable
because of the large differences among them in amount of
training and in other kinds of contacts with their profession.

Caseworker Orientation

Two dimensions of professional orientation were tapped in the
County Agency study: (1) exposure to professional training
centers, as indicated by the worker having taken some graduate
training in social work, and (2) sensitivity to professional
reference groups external to the agency, as indicated by the
worker's response to a questionnaire item dealing with the
location of sources of intellectual and professional stimulation.[11]
It was expected that workers with graduate training would be
more likely to choose professional reference groups external
to the agency. There being only a slight tendency in this
direction (39 per cent of the thirty-six workers with some
graduate training selected external reference groups, as compared to 22 per cent of the fifty workers lacking graduate
training), it was decided to continue the analysis with four
instead of two orientation types. These types were defined in
the following manner:

a. *Professionals*—workers with graduate training and
sensitivity to external professional groups ($N = 14$)
b. *Reference Group Only*—workers lacking graduate training but sensitive to external professional groups
($N = 11$)
c. *Training Only*—workers with graduate training but
sensitive to reference groups within the agency
($N = 22$)
d. *Bureaucrats*—workers lacking graduate training and

sensitive to reference groups within the agency
($N = 39$)
The classification received some external validation from data indicating that *Professionals* were most and *Bureaucrats* least likely to hold attitudes and engage in activities commonly associated with a professional orientation, while the two mixed types were intermediate in these tendencies.[12]

CASEWORKER ATTITUDES TOWARD THE AGENCY

The orientation types were employed to investigate the extent to which assertions posited for other types of professionals employed by organizations also held for social workers. The data presented in Table 3–1 indicate that professional orientation among the group of social workers examined results in the predicted consequences: criticism of agency standards and of procedural regulations, desire for more autonomy, and low loyalty to the employing agency were positively associated

Table 3–1. Caseworker Orientation and Attitudes Toward Agency

	TYPE OF ORIENTATION			
Attitudes	Professional	Reference Group Only	Training Only	Bureaucratic
Standards				
Agency is far from professional	43%	9%	10%	5%
Discrepancy between social work theory and agency practice is large	31%	24%	18%	8%
Procedural Regulations				
Laws limit casework	77%	82%	73%	32%
Procedures interfere with helping clients	50%	36%	36%	21%
Autonomy				
Like to be "Independent" worker	58%	50%	46%	27%
Loyalty				
Would leave present job for one in private agency	31%	27%	18%	8%
N (=100%)	12	11	20	36

with degree of professional orientation. Thus, *Professionals* were more likely than the mixed types (*Reference Group Only* and *Training Only*) who in turn were more likely than the *Bureaucrats* to agree "strongly" with the statement that County Agency has "a considerable distance to go before it can claim to be offering a fully adequate, professional welfare program," and that there was a "large" discrepancy between "professional standards and social work theory on the one hand and the actual work performed by this agency on the other." Professionally oriented workers were also more likely to agree with the following statements critical of the agency's procedural regulations: "Some federal and state laws and some county policies limit my performance of casework services"; and "Some procedures required by the agency actually interfere with my helping the client."[13] Professionally oriented workers were more likely to wish to function as "independent" workers, a status reserved for caseworkers who were considered by their supervisors capable of operating relatively independent of supervision.[14] Finally, professionally oriented workers were more likely to state that they would consider leaving their present position in County Agency to join a "fairly large private family service agency," at an equivalent or even a lower salary, if such an agency were established in their community.[15]

CASEWORKER EXPECTATIONS OF SUPERVISION

The preceding discussion suggests that a professional orientation among social workers has much the same effect on attitudes toward the employing organization as does a professional orientation among other kinds of professional groups, even though it may be the case that relative to these groups, a smaller proportion of social workers is oriented to their professional community.[16] However, when attitudes toward supervision are considered, there appear to be important differences between social work and most other professions. Social workers, unlike members of these other professions, expect to enter an organization where their work will be subject to routine hierarchical supervision. In general, the social work profession appears to justify the existence of supervisors as necessary to provide in-service training for those workers with little or no graduate training, of whom there are many in social work, and to furnish "internship" experiences for trained workers. (One social worker has pointed out acidly that such "internships" tend to be continued indefinitely in many agencies.[17]) While the value of routine supervision for caseworkers has recently become a subject for debate within the profession,[18] caseworkers in County Agency were not disposed to express strong opposition to the practice. When caseworkers were asked:

> Social work is one of the few professions that provides for the persistent routine supervision of both the new and the experienced worker. Do you think, all things considered, that this is a good arrangement?

exactly half (44) stated that it was "a good arrangement," and the other half admitted that it had both "advantages and disadvantages," but none felt that it was "not a good arrangement."

Professionally oriented caseworkers in County Agency were slightly more likely than their less professionally oriented counterparts to express ambivalence about the value of routine supervision.[19] Further, caseworker orientation was found to be associated with differences in the type of supervision preferred. The more professionally oriented caseworkers were more likely than those less professionally oriented to believe that supervisors should hold a master's degree in social work.[20] To determine further the extent to which caseworkers' orientation to the profession affected the kinds of expectations held for supervisors, workers in County Agency were invited to choose from among several alternatives those qualities they desired in a supervisor. The alternatives provided were:

> a. a supervisor well-versed in social and psychological theory
> or
> b. a supervisor with several years of on-the-job experience

a. *a supervisor who will require the worker to make most of the decisions*

or

b. *a supervisor who will make most of the decisions himself*

a. *a supervisor who will stick very closely to procedure*

or

b. *a supervisor who is quite flexible with regard to procedure*

a. *a supervisor who checks quite closely on your work*

or

b. *a supervisor who lets you work pretty much on your own*

a. *a supervisor who is skilled in teaching casework techniques*

or

b. *a supervisor who is skilled in agency policy and is a good administrator.*

Professionally oriented caseworkers were more likely than others to prefer a supervisor well-versed in theory and skilled in teaching casework techniques who would willingly delegate responsibility for decision-making to the caseworker and flexibly interpret agency policy. Thus, 40 per cent of the ten *Professionals*, 27 per cent of the (eleven) *Reference Group* workers, 30 per cent of the (twenty) *Training* workers, and 14 per cent of the (thirty-six) *Bureaucrats* confronted by the above alternatives selected responses *a, a, b, b, a*. The desire expressed by professionally oriented caseworkers to be allowed to make their own decisions and to work in an autonomous fashion rather than under close supervision is one seemingly shared by all types of professionals, and is certainly consistent with the generally accepted view of what a professional person is. Their preference for a supervisor well-versed in social and psychological theory suggests that these professionals, like others, wished their superiors to know the theoretical fundamentals of their discipline—knowledge not readily obtainable from on-the-job experience. Finally, the desire among professionally oriented workers for a supervisor skilled in teaching casework methods again underlines their interest in supervisory competence—in this case competence in a skill deemed all-important by the social work profession—and at the same time hints at the more general model that social work uses to define, and defend, supervision. Supervision for the social work profession is typically viewed more as an educational than as an administrative function. As Wilensky and Lebeaux note:

> In an extensive literature devoted to developing effective supervisory technique, and in courses in supervision in schools of social work, leadership is more often conceived in terms of education than of command, as a channel for obtaining collaboration among workers on difficult problems than as a method of case review by higher authority.[21]

In sum, the expectations held by professionally oriented workers for supervisory behavior emphasized their interest in autonomy of functioning and their desire for professionally competent assistance—expectations which, if fulfilled, would go a long way toward reconciling the potential conflict inherent in an arrangement prescribing routine supervision for professional employees.

SOURCES OF PROFESSIONAL STIMULATION

Attention to a variable like professional orientation tends to emphasize the extent to which workers in a common situation react differentially to it, and, in the present case, has perhaps led to an over-exaggeration of the extent to which worker attitudes were formulated independently of agency influence. To counteract this impression, the location of worker reference groups should again be examined. When workers were asked to select three sources of intellectual or professional stimulation, 29 per cent of them selected at least two groups or individuals outside the agency. By subtraction, we have 71 per cent of the workers selecting predominantly agency sources. A similar result is obtained if worker choices of the single most important source of stimulation are examined. Using this criterion, 50 per cent of the workers selected their own immediate supervisor; 11 per cent, the director of the agency, and 10 per cent, one of the division heads. In short, for almost three-fourths of the workers in County Agency, by their own report, much of whatever professional stimulation they received was filtered through the agency's administrative apparatus.

This last phrase, "filtered through the agency's administrative apparatus," may appear to be too strong a description, suggesting as it does that professional values were somehow diluted by contact with the agency's hierarchy. However, this is exactly what is being suggested. For evidence, Table 3–1 (p. 91) may again be examined. Here are reported caseworker evaluations of County Agency in the light of professional values. Consulting columns 2 and 4, *Reference Group Only* workers differed from *Bureaucrats* only in their report of whether they sought professional stimulation from persons outside or within the agency. There is little question from the data that *Bureaucrats*, those whose professional stimulation came primarily from agency officials, were considerably less likely than those whose professional ideas came from external sources to be critical of the agency's program. And even among those workers who had had some exposure to social work schools (columns 1 and 3), caseworkers relying primarily on agency officials for professional stimulation (*Training Only*) were likewise less critical of the agency program than were workers oriented to external sources (*Professionals*).

Why was it that reference to agency officials was associated with acceptance of the agency's program and, by implication, with the adoption of a less stringent set of professional standards?[22] Clearly, it is not because these administrative officials were not themselves social workers. All County Agency officials, as has been noted, had some graduate training in social work and many held advanced degrees. Rather, it seems reasonable to argue that accepting a position in the agency's hierarchy entailed some commitment on the part of the individual to the organization and a willingness to accept and work within the agency's policy framework. As committed professionals, some of the agency officials were working to change and improve various aspects of the agency program; but as representatives of the agency, they were also expected to attempt to reconcile and adjust some of their professional values to fit within the limitations of the existing program. They could not hope effectively to administer a program of which they were consistently critical.

It appears, then, that in attempting to understand the relation between bureaucratic and professional principles and the manner in which potential conflicts are managed, the analysis cannot remain at the level of the worker but must move up the hierarchy to examine the posture of administrators, in particular, that of the supervisory officials.

Supervisor's Orientation

It seems plausible to believe that the conflicts between bureaucratic and professional principles in a welfare agency will be most severe at the position of the supervisor. Supervisors are likely to have higher commitment to the profession than are workers—in County Agency at least they had on the average much more graduate training—and yet the organizational position they occupy is one requiring them to adhere to and enforce agency policies. Such conflicts may in fact have been present, but there is little evidence from interviews with 11 of the 12 County Agency supervisors to indicate that they were particularly severe. Supervisors were found to be less critical of the agency's program and policies than the professionally oriented workers and less critical of the agency's procedures than workers irrespective of the latter's orientation type. In contrast to worker attitudes (see Table 3–1), only one of the eleven supervisors felt that the agency had a considerable distance to go before it offered a fully adequate professional welfare program, and only two felt that the discrepancy between social work theory and agency practice was large. Four supervisors did agree that some laws interfered with the performing of casework services but, interestingly enough, none believed that the procedures required by the agency interfered with attempts to assist the client. Given these attitudes on the part of supervisors, it is perhaps more understandable why caseworkers selecting their supervisor as their primary source of professional stimulation (as 50 per cent of them did) were less critical of the agency program than workers oriented to professional sources external to the agency.

While the attitudes of supervisors toward the agency were not greatly affected by the supervisor's orientation to the profession, their *style* of supervision was related to this variable. In order to ascertain the orientation of supervisors, the same type of indicator previously employed for workers was adopted: namely, exposure to professional training centers. However, since all supervisors had taken some graduate training, number of hours of graduate work was used as the criterion measure, with the median employed as the point of division.[23] Given the small number of cases, it was deemed impractical to utilize more than two orientation types. The seven supervisors having eighteen hours of graduate work or less were assigned to the low-exposure category; the four having more than eighteen hours, to the high. With respect to the location of reference groups, supervisors were less likely than workers to select outside-agency sources of professional stimulation, only two of the eleven supervisors listing more than one outside-agency source. However, if just the location of the source of professional stimulation designated by supervisors as *the* most important is examined, all four of the high-exposure supervisors chose an outside-agency source as compared to two of the seven low-exposure group.

STYLE OF SUPERVISION

This single indicator—amount of training exposure—did appear to discriminate among supervisors with respect to style of supervision. To ascertain supervisory style, caseworker reports of their supervisor's techniques were employed rather than depending on supervisors to provide valid self-descriptions. Caseworkers were asked to express agreement or disagreement with a series of statements describing the characteristics and behavior of their present agency supervisor. As is clear from Table 3–2, subordinates of the more profes-

Table 3–2. Supervisor's Orientation and Style of Supervision

Worker descriptions of Supervisor's style	SUPERVISOR'S ORIENTATION	
	More Professional	Less Professional
Professional statements		
My supervisor:		
tries to teach and help me when I make a mistake	82%	63%
has a good background in social work theory	89%	45%
is a good teacher of casework methods and techniques	64%	45%
Bureaucratic statements		
My supervisor:		
sticks very closely to rules and procedures	43%	63%
is pretty strict with workers	14%	31%
checks my work very closely	36%	53%
is quite expert on the laws and policies pertaining to the agency	64%	69%
sometimes forces his decisions on me	14%	27%
N (= 100%)	28	49

sionally oriented supervisors were more likely to attribute to them such qualities as having a good background in social work theory and as being both better able and more willing to assume the role of teacher than their less professionally oriented counterparts. Also, while supervisors were not perceived to differ appreciably in their knowledge of agency laws and policies, professionally oriented supervisors were seen as less likely to adhere closely to agency rules and policies and to be generally more permissive and nonautocratic in their relations with workers. Professionally oriented supervisors were also more likely to be described by their subordinates as self-confident and willing to back workers in conflicts with clients; they were less likely to be described as impatient or as reluctant to make decisions which were theirs to make than the less professionally oriented supervisors.[24] In summary, the data suggest that supervisors did differ somewhat in the manner in which they carried out their supervisory role, those supervisors with more graduate training adhering more closely to the professional model of the supervisor—

that of a permissive educator who allows caseworkers a large measure of autonomy.

It is also important to note that caseworkers in County Agency apparently preferred the style of supervision offered by the more professionally oriented superiors. As will be recalled, when caseworkers were asked about the value of routine supervision, half stated that it was "a good arrangement" and the other half felt that it had "both advantages and disadvantages." Worker attitudes toward supervision, however, were found to vary considerably depending on what type of supervisor the caseworker was presently serving under: workers under the more professionally oriented supervisors were more likely than those under less professional supervisors to see advantages in the practice of routine supervision. Thus, 77 per cent of the (twenty-two) caseworkers serving under the more professionally oriented supervisors but only 45 per cent of the (forty-two) caseworkers under the less professional supervisors felt that routine supervision was "a good arrangement." And, as might be expected, worker evaluations of supervisors were also found to vary with worker orientation. For example, caseworkers with some professional training under both types of supervisors were more likely than caseworkers lacking training to have reservations about the value of routine supervision.[25] Specifically, 46 per cent of the (thirteen) trained caseworkers, as compared to 34 per cent of the (fifteen) untrained workers, under the more professional supervisors felt that there were "both advantages and disadvantages" associated with routine supervision; and 75 per cent of the (sixteen) trained caseworkers, as compared to 47 per cent of the (thirty) untrained workers, under the less professional supervisors expressed similar reservations. In general, caseworkers, regardless of orientation, were more favorably disposed to the more professional than to the less professional supervisors, but for either type of supervisor, professionally oriented workers were more likely to be critical of the professional qualifications of their supervisor than the nonprofessionally oriented workers.[26]

Turning from the effect of supervisor's orientation on caseworker attitudes to its effect on caseworker performance, there was some indication that workers under the more professional supervisors were slightly more "productive," as measured by agency standards. Performance statistics for professional workers are always difficult to interpret and may be completely misleading. There is no single indicator or set of indicators for accurately assessing quality of performance for a social worker. Nevertheless, one measure faithfully recorded for each worker in County Agency on a monthly basis was the number of visits made to clients. Although the number of workers for whom this information was available is small,[27] it appears that workers under professionally oriented supervisors were slightly more likely to visit clients frequently than workers under less professionally oriented supervisors. Thus, 80 per cent of the (five) trained workers and 67 per cent of the (six) untrained workers under the professionally oriented supervisors had a high or medium number of client visits, as compared to 56 per cent of the (thirteen) trained workers and 57 per cent of the (thirty) untrained workers under the less professional supervisors. These data are far from overwhelming, but they contain at least the suggestion that professionally oriented supervisors were the more effective group in motivating workers to perform well as measured by agency criteria.

The performance ratings of workers by supervisors provide yet another indication of the differences in supervisory approach between the two groups of supervisors. Each worker employed received a formal evaluation from his supervisor at the end of his first six months of employment and thereafter on an annual basis.[28] Workers serving under professionally oriented supervisors were considerably more likely to receive a high performance rating than were workers serving under less professional supervisors. Thus, 45 per cent of the (eleven) trained workers and 54 per cent of the (thirteen) untrained workers under professionally oriented supervisors received a high rating; but only 13 per cent of the (fifteen) trained workers and 15 per cent of the (twenty-six) untrained workers under the less professional supervisors received high performance ratings. Note that workers who had taken some graduate training in social work did not receive higher performance ratings from either type of supervisor. It is perhaps the case that workers under professionally oriented supervisors because of selection or training were, in fact, superior to those under the less professionally oriented supervisors and that the higher performance ratings they received were simply indicative of this fact. It was true that their performance as measured by client visits was somewhat superior, but it did not appear that differences in performance were great enough to account for differences in ratings received. A more plausible explanation for the distribution of ratings was that professionally oriented supervisors tended to adopt a reward-centered approach with workers and were more likely to look on ratings as a means for motivating and encouraging their subordinates. While definitive evidence on this point is lacking, the interpretation is at least consistent with other differences of supervisory style previously described.

THERAPEUTIC SUPERVISION

Any discussion of supervisory style as observed in County Agency would be incomplete without some consideration of a general approach adopted by some of the supervisors which will be referred to here as "therapeutic supervision." No systematic data were gathered on these techniques, the following analysis resting primarily on informal observations within the agency—in particular, observations of numerous supervisor–caseworker conferences; hence, these comments should be regarded as speculative. Therapeutic supervision involved the use by supervisors of psychiatric concepts and techniques in dealing with workers. Psychiatric theory has had a pronounced impact on theory and practice in social work, and although many observers have noted that its influence has been on the wane in recent years, there was much evidence to suggest its continuing appeal to some members of the supervisory staff in County Agency.

Therapeutic supervision is based on the implicit premise that instances of caseworker nonconformity are due to ignorance or to unconscious forces over which the worker had little or no control, rather than to knowing and willful actions.[29] Given this view of the causes, it follows that any attempt to control or correct the worker will necessarily entail his "re-education," in its broadest possible sense, rather than punishment. It should be obvious that therapeutic supervision is an essentially professional rather than a bureaucratic control technique, a point which will be amplified after some examples of its use in County Agency have been presented and discussed.

To illustrate this therapeutic approach, the failure of caseworkers to include a summary report of their interactions with clients in the case record was interpreted by some supervisory officials as due to a psychological block preventing the reporting of feelings, their own and the clients'. Workers had other explanations for this shortcoming, as is illustrated by the following interchange recorded during a meeting between a supervisor and his casework staff:

> SUPERVISOR. The records indicate the difficulty of recording interaction with the client. Now this is just between you and me. We're not asking for process recording. We're asking for a report of the feelings of the client, her reactions to what you tell her. Some of you are leaving yourselves out of the narrative. That's where we find out if the client has any motivations— by how she responds to the worker's comments. Why is this so hard to do?
> CASEWORKER. I can tell you if it won't be taken cynically. We have to get our cases to [the welfare] board on time.
> [The supervisor ignored this comment and changed the subject.]

This caseworker believed that worker nonconformity in this area was caused by the time pressures incurred by agency deadlines rather than by unconscious resistance to including oneself in the narrative.

Another illustration: worker resistance to the use of psychiatric concepts in understanding client behavior was

interpreted by some supervisors as resulting from the workers'
realization that these concepts were applicable to their own
behavior and were, hence, "striking too close to home." In
yet another case, a worker's criticism of agency deadlines and
the pressures of work was interpreted as being due to a
displacement of his feelings against his supervisor for giving
him a low rating.

Setting aside the question of whether these explanations
were accurate in whole or part, it should be noted that as a
general form this type of explanation tends to shift attention
away from the situation out of which the behavior arose and
to focus on the subjective condition of the actor involved.
The assumption is made that the worker's complaints or
nonconforming acts have a nonrational basis; hence, the
content of his complaint is ignored.[30] In short, this approach,
by focusing on the psychological state of individual actors,
tends to direct attention away from possible deficiencies in
organizational arrangements.[31]

Another facet of the therapeutic orientation to supervision
is best illustrated by events observed in connection with the
weekly conferences between supervisors and caseworkers. In
these meetings, supervisors would aid caseworkers in solving
the technical problems involved in determining client eligibility for assistance, help workers to understand the behavior
of their clients, make suggestions for dealing more effectively
with them, and on occasion would attempt to show workers
what impact their own feelings and needs were having on
their relationship with the clients. There were, of course,
legitimate grounds for sometimes subjecting the worker's
behavior and feelings to critical scrutiny. Caseworkers were
often involved in counseling relationships with clients and
in acting for the client in various capacities. As a protection
to the client it was important that the worker refrain from
projecting his own needs and values into the relationship. It
is precisely for these reasons that the profession advocates
routine supervision for caseworkers. As one supervisor in
County Agency explained to his workers, "All we have to
offer is our relationship, and so there has to be continuous

re-evaluation and self-examination of ourselves and our needs.''
And supervision was viewed as one means to this end, as the
supervisor went on to point out: ''When we deal with the
lives of human beings, we must keep subjectivity out, and
this sort of working together [the caseworker–supervisor
conference] is one way of doing this.'' The necessity for
agencies such as the one under study to rely on the services of
workers with little or no professional preparation served to
make even more compelling the close scrutiny of worker
feelings and actions in the interest of protecting clients.

Some notion of both the benefits as well as the possible
problems of therapeutic supervision may be obtained by
reproducing here a short portion of one caseworker–supervisor
conference. By way of background, the worker had made
numerous attempts over the past few months to establish a
relationship with an unwed mother having several children
and, because she felt she was having little or no success,
requested that the case be transferred to the ''intensive
unit''—a group of workers in the same division carrying a
small caseload comprising the most difficult clients.

> CASEWORKER. I have tried to reach this woman, but she wards
> off attempts to help her. [Gives more details]
> SUPERVISOR. Then the client feels that if she is on welfare, she
> can be immoral if she keeps from getting pregnant.
> C. I don't think she really believes this.
> S. We just had a lecture on mechanisms of defense. What could
> this be? What about rejection plus projection? She feels that
> others get by with things that she can't because she is on
> welfare.
> C. But she is very sweet.
> S. Then her hostility is being repressed.
> C. The client would prefer that I just came to determine eligibility
> [for financial assistance].
> S. Because the client is resistant, we no longer can work with her?
> C. But I have tried.
> S. You have only tried a direct approach.

C. I have tried a number of times.

S. We'll just have to do better. We have to go back, even when it's frustrating and discouraging.

C. We have to go back, but with what approach?

S. There are not too many ways to approach a human being.

C. Then just keep trying?

S. The client has already distinguished you from the other workers by your persistence.

C. But she doesn't want a relationship.

S. But she can be helped to see that a professional relationship makes fewer demands on her than other relations.

C. I explained that to her. Maybe she could relate better to a male worker.

S. You aren't exhausted yet. Keep going after her with warmth and human interest.

C. Then I don't get to transfer it, I take it?

S. Human beings all have a need for warmth and human interest.
[C. continues to explain why it is impossible for her to handle case.]

S. What is this, an example of a hopeless case or of a hopeless caseworker?

C. I still think we should transfer it to a male worker in the intensive unit.

S. Why are you resisting this case? What is the purpose of casework?

C. To help the client.

S. Help her to do what?

C. Reach her own goals.

S. All right. ·

C. But I have the conviction that I can't reach her.

S. This is your block. It's your own feelings.

C. I have concrete evidence that I'm not helping her.

S. Casework must be imaginative and optimistic.

C. But when your approach doesn't even result in your being able to get anywhere . . .

S. You have concluded that this client can't be reached. You're not getting any emotional gratification from her. She is not reaching goals at the pace you would like her to.

C. *What I am trying to say—there is a girl in the home entering her teens. Casework is needed on this woman. A relation needs to be established.*

S. *You're just like some other workers. You get scared out when you see a teenager coming along.*

C. *That's not true.*

S. *Yes, comes the adolescent and you want out.*

C. *No, I get scared out when I see a client I can't handle.*

S. *I don't think it is necessary for this case to go to the intensive unit. You have worse cases than this.*

C. *Yes, but I have a relationship with them.*

S. *You object to a client rejecting your help?*

C. *I believe that a caseworker with more skill could help her.*

S. *But how are you going to develop these skills? You know we have no M.A. workers.*

C. *What about intensive?*

S. *They are intensive only on a time basis. You've had graduate courses.*

C. *Yes, one!*

S. *I don't deny that problems could be found to make this case acceptable to intensive. But I have a responsibility to you to help you to learn.*

C. *But I think I have tried, and failed, and this is reality.*

S. *I think it's a rationalization.*

C. *Let's go to another case.*

Note that in this interaction, the supervisor's wishes prevailed over those of the caseworker: the case was not transferred. Note, too, that the supervisor would not accept the caseworker's interpretation of the situation. The caseworker attempted to focus on the lack of progress made by the client and her own difficulties in establishing a relationship. The supervisor directed attention primarily to the worker herself—to her "hopeless" attitude, to her need for emotional gratification, to her resistance to the case, to her fears, and to her rationalizations. No attempt will be made here to evaluate the outcome of this episode. Whether the case should or should not have been transferred is not at issue. Rather, the interaction is intended to illustrate the use by a supervisor of a therapeutic approach as he interprets both the client's and the worker's behavior in psychiatric terms.

There are certain important advantages associated with this approach for all concerned, including the client, the supervisor, the caseworker, and the agency. As noted, the client gains some protection from having the motives and goals of his caseworker periodically examined and questioned. The supervisor is able to exercise considerable surveillance and control over worker actions, but in a manner which is consistent with his own professional self-image. The therapeutic supervisor does not issue directives to caseworkers nor does he threaten them with punitive action for noncompliance. He attempts to refrain from using the sanctioning power attached to his office as supervisor and relies instead on his superior knowledge and casework skills to guide and control the caseworker. In the language of Etzioni, the therapeutically oriented supervisor controls his subordinates through the use of normative rather than remunerative or coercive sanctions.[32] In this way, the supervisor emphasizes his role as educator rather than administrative superior and confirms his self-image of professional rather than bureaucrat. The caseworker, for his part, is also likely to perceive the benefits associated with this approach. If he sees himself as a professional person, this supervisory orientation reinforces that image, granting him freedom from overt direction and access to professional consultation which assists him with his case problems and his own professional development. Finally, the Agency itself was probably a beneficiary of this supervisory technique, which by masking the power differences present in the administrative structure protected the professional self-images of both supervisors and subordinates and thus contributed to job satisfaction and morale of the professional staff.

Recognizing the existence of these quite considerable benefits, however, one should not overlook the dangers associated with the practice of therapeutic supervision. The routine use of methods by which a caseworker's motives are scrutinized and questioned raises problems because such tactics are subject to abuse: from worth as a method of helping the worker to attain insight, such procedures can degenerate into devices for the manipulation of the worker. The danger inherent in the possibility that at any moment the worker can be reduced from a participant in the discussion to its subject may act to curb the working out of honest differences of opinion between worker and supervisor. The worker who disagrees with his superior may be met with the response that he is "unable to accept supervision," or that he is exhibiting "resistance," or "immaturity." At worst, the supervisor becomes omnipotent: a worker is not even entitled to his own opinion in an honest disagreement with his supervisor because the latter can devalue his arguments by questioning his motives. That such tactics were not completely unknown in County Agency was indicated by the frequent reference among caseworkers to the supervisory practice of "caseworking the workers."

Psychiatric techniques can be employed with complete safety only in a professional relationship—one in which the "client" is assured that his best interests will dominate all others in guiding the practitioner's actions. Clearly, however, the caseworker cannot assume that his own interests will always govern the course of interactions with his supervisor. Many other legitimate interests are involved: those of the agency, the clients of the agency, and the public, to name only the most obvious. Further, the worker is not free—as is the client in a professional relationship—to reject his supervisor's directives when he feels that they are contrary to his own best interests. He is, after all, an employee, a subordinate in a hierarchical structure.

Informal observations of worker–supervisor conferences indicated that professionally oriented supervisors were more likely to utilize the therapeutic approach in their supervision of caseworkers. There is some evidence that caseworkers also perceived this difference between the two types of supervisors. Thus, 37 per cent of the (twenty-seven) workers under professional supervisors as compared to 2 per cent of the (forty-five) workers under the less professional supervisors described their supervisor as tending to "over-emphasize" the psychiatric viewpoint. Whether these caseworkers had in mind the kind of abuses just described as potentially associated with the practice of therapeutic supervision is a matter for conjecture. The data are not specific enough to support such a conclusion. In any event, caseworkers apparently did not regard the overly psychiatric views of the professionally oriented supervisors as too great a deficiency. In general, as already noted, they preferred the flexible, therapeutically oriented, teaching supervisor—whatever the defects of this approach—to the rule-following, close-supervising, bureaucratic administrator. The psychiatric approach allowed caseworkers to maintain their conception of themselves as professionals in a manner not possible under the more direct control attempts associated with the bureaucratic approach.

Agency Policy and Its Interpretation

The views of laymen and professionals seldom coincide on all issues affecting the conduct of professional activities. The better established professions have been able to negotiate arrangements with the lay society whereby they are granted a large measure of autonomy in the performance of their professional services, in return for which they agree to exercise self-restraint and colleague surveillance.[33] The social work profession, on the other hand, has been less successful in securing such arrangements. As has been noted, to a very large extent social workers in public agencies operate within a legal and procedural framework not of their own making. This fact has not escaped the attention of professional social workers, one of whom has written:

> Much of social work administration and social-policy determination, as well as elaboration of procedures, is done

by laymen. These laymen may function on high administrative levels or may exert their influence as members of
agency boards.

And this same observer goes on to express her reservations
concerning these arrangements:

> What may be laid down as desirable program goals and
> procedures may be at variance with professional values and
> professional conceptions regarding the nature of the needs
> of human beings. Professional staff members may not
> always be able to make their conceptions strongly explicit
> or to influence policy and administration. The practitioner
> then must work within a framework which in part may
> be incompatible with professional values, ethics, and
> standards.[34]

An example of one of the federal provisions that many
social workers feel to be inimical to the establishment of a
therapeutic relationship between worker and client is the
1952 amendment to the Social Security Act requiring the
states promptly to notify criminal prosecuting authorities of
the desertion of a father before aid can be granted to a mother
and her children. Wilensky and Lebeaux comment on the
problems this provision causes for the social worker:

> Strict legal enforcement of parental duty to support young
> children is, of course, strongly upheld in the American
> value system. But at the same time social caseworkers
> know from several decades of sad experience that legal
> compulsion is rarely successful in obtaining compliance
> from these fathers. The dilemma for family service here is
> that law and public opinion require action which is techni-
> cally and professionally unwise.[35]

Another federal requirement to which many social workers
are opposed is contained in a 1951 amendment that permits
states to make a matter of public record the names of recipients
and the amounts of their assistance payments if certain safe-
guards are in effect. Social workers opposing this provision

argue that such listings violate the privacy of clients, an important value for the service professions, and can be used to harass or ridicule recipients.

Caseworkers in County Agency were found to be overwhelmingly opposed to certain of the state requirements. For example, 84 per cent of the workers felt that residence requirements governing client elegibility for assistance were too strict and believed that they should either be removed or reduced; and 99 per cent of the workers felt that budgetary ceilings set by the state to govern the amount of assistance should be either removed entirely or raised. More generally, 88 per cent of the workers expressed agreement with the statement that "the professional progress of this agency and others like it in this state is held back by the conservatism of the [state's] public and legislature."

A large proportion of the casework staff was also found to disagree with certain of the requirements imposed by the local agency administration. It is impossible to separate in these data those policies imposed on a reluctant administration by the lay board from those policies established by agency officials, who were themselves social workers, in the interest of organizational efficiency or because of administrative necessity. Lay values and the perspectives of administratives often coincide in that both groups tend to be concerned with organizational efficiency. The administrators of bureaucratic organizations attempt to routinize and regulate work in order to assure adherence to minimum legal standards, to obtain equity and continuity of service to clients, and to achieve efficiency of operation and administration. The professional casework staff is usually less than sympathetic to such arguments, questioning the wisdom of many of the legal requirements, protesting procedural regulations and policies which interfere with their discretionary response to the differing problems of individual clients, and willingly sacrificing administrative efficiency in the cause of increased worker autonomy and client service. Thus, in County Agency, 59 per cent of the caseworkers believed that the laws under which the agency was expected to operate unduly limited their attempts to provide casework services to clients; 72 per cent believed their caseloads to be too large to permit adequate service to clients; and 85 per cent felt that they were required to spend too much of their time in filling out the various forms required by agency procedures.

In short, agency policies—some imposed by the lay representatives of the taxpaying public and others originating out of administrative concerns—were not always viewed by social workers as compatible with professional values. In a number of very important respects, the system of rules— federal, state, and local—governing operations was perceived by a majority of County Agency caseworkers to hinder professional progress and to interfere with their attempts to assist clients. Agency officials were not unaware of the problems faced by those workers struggling to retain their professional identity. The director was very active in lobbying for and even in helping to draft more progressive welfare legislation at the state level, and most administrative staff meetings (involving the director, the assistant director, and the division heads) were filled with critical discussions of federal, state, and even local policies. Nevertheless, these same officials were responsible for administering the existing program. It was their task to help caseworkers accept and work within the existing agency framework. To do so they attempted to interpret the role of the caseworker in a way which would be acceptable to the professional caseworkers and, at the same time, consistent with agency policy. These attempts may be illustrated by examining the interpretations given by agency officials to two central functions performed by workers: establishing client eligibility and caseload management.

The Interpretation of Caseworker Functions

Hughes has noted that one way in which professionals dispose of unpleasant tasks is to define them as sub-professional and assign them to less favored occupational groups. Thus:

Some functions are down-graded: bed-making and house-
keeping for nurses; the dusting, handling, chasing, cata-
loguing, date-stamping of books for librarians; "means
test" interviewing for social workers. The people who do
them are also down-graded or else a new category of
non-professional people is introduced into the system to
perform these *infra dignitatem* tasks.[36]

As Hughes suggests, some social workers have proposed that
clerks be hired to establish the eligibility of clients for
assistance (do " 'means test' interviewing").[37] In County
Agency, however, regular caseworkers were not only
expected to establish client eligibility—they were repeatedly
told that performing this task was one of their most important
professional functions. Establishing and periodically reviewing
the client's eligibility for assistance was not to be regarded
merely as a routine clerical task but as an opportunity to work
intimately with the client in solving his problems. In addition
to gathering data to substantiate the client's claim to financial
assistance, these interviews were to be used by the caseworker
to gain insights into the client's basic social and psychological
problems. In other words, eligibility determination was
defined by agency officials as a professional operation rather
than as merely a clerical one. Workers had a difficult time
perceiving it as such because the elaborate specification by
rules controlling the eligibility investigation and budget-setting
process left them little discretion in carrying out these
functions. Also, workers attempting to approach the determination of the client's financial needs in the spirit of a
conscientious professional were continually frustrated by the
fact that legally established ceilings arbitrarily restricted the
size of grants to clients, often at a level far below the amount
budgeted as necessary to the maintenance of a "reasonable
subsistence compatible with decency and health." In spite
of these limitations, agency superiors continued to insist on
the essentially professional character of these activities. More
generally, it appears that when for some reason a professional
group is unable to slough off a task in the manner indicated by

Hughes, there may be attempts to redefine it in such a way as to invest it with professional dignity and importance.

A second area of worker functioning requiring interpretation by agency officials related to the quantity of work to be performed. Social workers traditionally distinguish between "casework"—the providing of professional services to clients —on the one hand, and "caseload management"—organizing one's work so as to meet agency deadlines and make visits to clients on schedule—on the other. County Agency superiors attempted to convince workers that caseload management was an important part of their professional responsibilities, that quality and quantity of work were of equal importance.[38] Of course, there is nothing inherently nonprofessional in expecting workers to provide casework services to all and not just to some of their clients[39] unless—and this is an important condition—caseloads are so large that to cover all of them virtually guarantees substandard service from a professional standpoint to individual clients. In County Agency nearly three quarters of the workers felt that caseloads were too large to allow the performance of adequate casework services.[40] If worker perceptions of the situation were in fact accurate, the stress laid by superiors on quantity of work performed could have had the effect of lowering quality, that is, reducing the amount of attention devoted to the performance of casework services. The important point, however, is that such a consequence could be defended by superiors by defining caseload management as a professional function equal in importance to casework.

These interpretations of two important areas of caseworker functioning were fairly consistently reinforced by the supervisory staff of County Agency. However, there did appear to be some important differences among them in the manner in which they interpreted other aspects of agency policy.

The Interpretation of Agency Policy

First-line supervisors were expected to enforce the laws,

statutes, and regulations which together comprise agency
policy, and from all appearances, did so. There were some
variations apparent in their attempts to interpret and defend
agency policy: three somewhat different approaches were
distinguishable. Informal observation of a number of caseworker–supervisor conferences indicated that the less professionally oriented supervisors were more likely to attempt
to disassociate themselves from certain agency policies. In the
manner of some industrial foremen, they would express
solidarity with the workers by placing the onus for unpopular
policies on "top management." Thus, on one occasion, one
of these supervisors told a worker who resisted a policy: "It's
all clear-cut in this manual if you just follow it. I have my own
feelings about this and I know that you do too, but I heard
long ago, 'Follow policy!' " In a somewhat similar vein, these
supervisors would remind workers that some restrictions on
worker autonomy were always present in an organized
program. This type of explanation is illustrated by the following interchange between a worker and her supervisor:

> C. Do we still have to write up these long transfer summaries?
> S. Yes.
> C. I don't think it's necessary.
> S. Someday you can establish an agency and you can set it up
> just like you want it—but there will be a board and they will
> give you a certain budget and pass certain rules.
> C. Limitations, huh?
> S. Yes, limitations.

These interpretations were clearly *bureaucratic* in character.
In the first illustration, the content of the policy was not
defended by the supervisor. He, on the contrary, led the
worker to believe that he was in disagreement with it.
Nevertheless, the worker was reminded that it was the policy
of the agency and that she, as a good bureaucrat, was expected
to conform to it regardless of her personal beliefs or feelings.
In the second illustration, the supervisor did attempt to provide
a rationale for the policy, but it was a bureaucratic explanation, not a professional one. The worker was reminded of the

administrative framework within which all welfare programs
are conducted and the limitations inherent in such frameworks.

A second type of approach taken by supervisors differed
only slightly from the bureaucratic and is, perhaps, an
approach peculiar to social work. This approach is interesting
because it identifies an essentially bureaucratic trait—the
ability to accept authority—as a professional characteristic.
Supervisors, both the more and the less professionally oriented,
held that the truly professional social worker should be able to
exercise enough self-discipline to function effectively in an
agency setting. Disciplined conformity to authority was
regarded as a sign of maturity. As one supervisor explained to
a recalcitrant worker, "Maturity is involved in working with
existing authority and in accepting it." Another phrase often
used to justify working within agency policy was that to do so
was to "accept the reality factors in the situation." To resist
agency policy was considered unrealistic and a waste of
energies which could be devoted to constructive work.

This approach advocating *disciplined professional* behavior
on the part of caseworkers was not unique to County Agency.
A number of discussions in the social work literature are
consistent with this perspective. One series of articles suggests
that appropriate self-discipline on the part of the professional
is acquired only gradually. Accordingly, dissatisfaction and
even rebellion may be expected and condoned in the early
stages of the worker–agency relation because they represent
merely the "growing pains" of the novice. For example, in
discussing criteria by which the progress of first-year graduate
students in social work is to be evaluated, the writer explains:

> We should expect that he can identify sufficiently with the
> agency to work for it. This does not mean that he accepts
> all its policies without question—indeed, if this were so, it
> would be a sign of some trouble.[41]

By the beginning of his second year, the student is expected to
have made progress in learning to work within the agency

framework although he is still permitted to retain his independence of judgment. Thus:

> He should show ability to assimilate agency policy and procedure as they are interpreted to him within the community structure and legal framework of the agency. He should also learn the means by which agency policy is changed. He should retain freedom in raising questions about agency policy and evaluating it for himself.[42]

However, by the end of his second year, the student is expected to have overcome most if not all of his conflicts or doubts:

> He should be ready to fit into an agency setting (for which he has prepared professionally) with a minimum of difficulty in his relationships to staff, policy, procedures, and work routines and to assume his place as a professional caseworker and as a representative of his agency in the community. . . . His identification with the agency should be strong and he should support the client's use of it.[43]

Both the bureaucratic and the disciplined professional approach encouraged caseworkers to work within the limitations of the policies governing the agency. Both undoubtedly contributed to the efficiency and effectiveness with which the agency's program was carried out, and the latter did so in a way allowing workers to retain their self-conception as professional social workers. One cost borne by these approaches was that they may have worked to undermine any interest caseworkers might have in attempting to change and improve the existing program. Another cost was that caseworkers were probably encouraged simply to apply existing policies rather than go to the extra effort required to justify deviations. Deviations from federal and state requirements could not, of course, be sanctioned, but policies set by the local board and administration could be departed from at the discretion of local authorities. Given an atmosphere in which policy acceptance was stressed, however, workers were sometimes not sufficiently motivated to make a case for deviation, as one professionally oriented supervisor explained:

> Agency policy is flexible enough. Deviations from it are permitted if they can be justified and validated. The worker can list his reasons, discuss them with his supervisor and then send them to the director for his approval. The problem is that workers often refuse to take the initiative required to do this. In one case, I suggested to the worker that the department could pay for pre-natal care of a client if the worker would explain why it was essential. But the worker didn't want to: he preferred to adhere to the general policy that the agency does not furnish such care. Just a lack of initiative, a refusal to take the responsibility necessary. In another case, after I repeatedly urged the worker to try it, the director did approve monthly insurance payments of $8.00 started by a man when he was in the army although the policy maximum is $1.50.

Such are the possible costs in service to clients of establishing routine procedures for handling client needs and fostering an atmosphere in which workers are rewarded for the unquestioning application of them to individual cases.

In addition to advocating disciplined professional behavior on the part of workers, most of the professionally oriented supervisors also attempted to provide a professional rationale for certain of the agency's policies. This approach, the third and last to be discussed, may be viewed as one of *professional reconciliation*, in that supervisors using this technique would attempt to show caseworkers that agency policies which on their surface might appear to be contrary to professional norms were in fact consistent with them. The interpretive skills of supervisory officials were particularly taxed by those policies regarded by many social workers as being detrimental to client welfare and punitive in character. One example of such a policy was the requirement which stipulated that a client having an illegitimate child, in order to continue to be eligible for assistance, was to file paternity charges against the alleged father unless the child was being placed for adoption. Another was the federal provision described earlier which

required that cases involving the desertion of a father were to
be reported to the prosecutor before being accepted for
assistance. The professional reconciliation approach to such
policies was to de-emphasize the punitive character of the
action and emphasize its protective nature. The worker's
attention was focused on the party most likely to benefit from
the action rather than on the party whose interests might be
injured. In the case of the paternity policy, for example, the
interests of the child—"the innocent victim"—would be
emphasized rather than those of the parents. Thus, in discussing with a new group of workers the requirement that
paternity charges be filed against fathers, one supervisor
explained:

> We try to stress the importance of this for the child. It is
> not a matter of accusing anybody; rather it allows the child
> to be identified. The child needs to have its rights established
> —this is important for social security, natural inheritance,
> and so on. Our central focus is always this: to help the
> child.

Similar interpretations were used to justify the policy on
desertion of father, the supervisor emphasizing the protective
features of the law from the point of view of the mother and
her children.

The professional reconciliation approach was perhaps even
more difficult to employ in interpreting those policies where
it was not clear that there was any beneficiary of the action
required other than the taxpaying public, whose interests
were accorded little legitimacy by professional workers. For
example, the state in which County Agency was located had
a rather severe "responsible relative" law which provided
that children who had been supported through their minority
and who were receiving more than a specified income[44] were
responsible for the care of their parents and could be legally
prosecuted for failure to furnish financial assistance of a
stipulated amount. Many parents and children objected
violently to this requirement. Parents often chose to forgo
assistance rather than to press charges against their children.

In many of these cases, then, the interests of both parties—parents and children—appeared to suffer from enforcement of the law. In discussing such cases with workers, supervisors utilizing the professional reconciliation approach were observed to direct attention away from the individual parties involved to emphasize the total family as the unit to be served. One supervisor discussed the responsible relative policy with workers in the following terms:

> The matter of responsible relatives is very important. This is discussed in the manual in chapter three. In this state we do stress this. Other states don't pursue relative responsibility to the extent we do. The caseworker should try to build family relationships—he should contact relatives not only for financial support, but for other kinds of support as well. He should attempt to pull these families together. This is a casework service—to reinforce these relationships.

Thus, by shifting the focus of the worker from the individual parties (the parents *or* the children) to a larger unit (the family) and by interpreting this aspect of eligibility determination as a casework service, it was possible for supervisors to reconcile this legal requirement with professional social work values. The philosophy of this approach is nicely summarized in a hoary aphorism voiced often by one of the division heads: "If they give you lemons, make lemonade!"

The professional reconciliation approach, unlike the advocacy of disciplined professional behavior, was more closely akin to traditional professional practice. Supervisors using this approach did not appeal to the virtues of self-discipline and conformity for its own sake but faced up to the content of the particular policy and attempted to defend it as being fundamentally consistent with social work values and the best interests of clients. Because the emphasis was on reconciliation, however, this supervisory approach probably incurred some of the same costs associated with the bureaucratic and disciplined professional techniques: namely, the discouragement of caseworker attempts to reform the program and the encouragement of worker conformity to rules, even in those circumstances where conformity could be detrimental to client welfare.

Supervisors in County Agency, regardless of their professional orientation, defended the policies of the agency. A variety of defensive tactics were employed, but all had the same end result: support for agency policies. It may not be seen as particularly surprising that agency superiors rose to the defense of agency policies: they were, after all, members of the agency hierarchy and responsible for the administration of its program. But if their behavior is contrasted with that of other professional groups occupying similar kinds of administrative positions—for example, the director (and his assistants) of a group of clinic physicians studied by Goss[45]—then it is clear that all professionals do not inevitably become champions of the policies of the organizations by which they are employed. More precisely, while the physicians-in-charge studied by Goss took great pains to carefully delineate professional from bureaucratic considerations and were always watchful to see that the interests of clinic administrators did not encroach upon the making of professional decisions concerning patient care, professional superiors in County Agency appeared often to blunt the distinction between bureaucratic and professional concerns, holding conformity to agency rules to be a professional virtue and seeking to provide professional justifications for many of the agency's policies. Of course, physicians in a hospital clinic are in a very different position with respect to amount of social power than are social workers in a public agency, and it may be to the credit of the professional staff of County Agency that they were able to introduce some non-bureaucratic considerations into the operations of the agency.

There is some indication, however, that social workers are becoming restive with their present lot. Objections to current working arrangements are more and more frequently found in the professional social work literature. This discussion may be fittingly concluded with a single, admittedly extreme, statement of the posture of this more militant group.

Organizational Man and Woman have been determining the future of social work for a long time, so long that the

Organization is now supreme. Those who enunciate *its* function, *its* policies and procedures occupy places so high in the hierarchy that they get only a dim view of the people the organization was originally set up to serve. . . . For one often sees practitioners reenacting The Charge of the Light Brigade—"Theirs not to make reply, theirs not to reason why, theirs but to do and die"—only, of course, they do not die; they either leave the profession or linger on until they thoroughly learn the ritual of "acceptance of agency," "acceptance of supervision," "acceptance of limitations," "acceptance," "acceptance," "acceptance!" It may be true that a patient who has lost an arm or a leg and fights through to an acceptance of his limitations may find a sense of freedom within limitations, but only the devotees of the folklore of confusion will turn this fact into an excuse for their own apathy in the face of agency policies and community conditions inimical to human welfare.[46]

Caseworkers and Clients

The agency as a means, a mechanism—the *agency*—for carrying out welfare policy becomes an end in itself. Between the altruist with his desire to help and the client with his need lies the machine, with its own "needs."[47]

The central characteristics of the professional–client relationship have been outlined by Parsons and include the following elements: (1) the professional is a specialist and is expected to limit the scope of his interaction with clients to matters related to his speciality; (2) the professional is expected to relate to the client in an affectively neutral manner; and (3) the professional is to put the client's needs uppermost in the encounter.[48] The client's needs, not his wishes, are to govern the relationship, and it is the task of the professional to determine what these needs are and how they may best be served. The client is regarded as a layman who cannot adequately evaluate the services he receives, let alone determine which services he requires. However, in the ideal case, the client is free to withdraw from the relationship whenever he feels that his interests are being inadequately served.

A Diffuse Relationship

Relationships between social workers and clients in County Agency conformed only in part to this ideal characterization. Workers were not really specialists but were expected to deal with a large number of problem areas presented by clients. At various times, caseworkers found themselves assisting clients in such varied and complex areas as substandard housing, insufficient clothing, special diets, insurance, arranging for medical care, child-rearing, delinquency, marital adjustment, employment, mental illness, unwed motherhood, and so on. One worker, seeing a sign on the bulletin board in the Public Assistance Division notifying workers where used sewing machines could be obtained by clients, laughed and commented: "No area is too small for the ADC worker." Thus, one of the characteristics of the caseworker–client relationship was that in practice it was quite diffuse.

The lack of specialization was a source of both satisfaction and concern to most workers. On the one hand, there was continual variety in the problems presented by individual clients, and most workers viewed with favor this absence of routine. On the other hand, there was a gnawing feeling of inadequacy expressed by many workers as they were confronted daily by such varying and complex problems. In response to a questionnaire item, over half of the workers (59 per cent) in County Agency stated that they were sometimes or frequently faced with problems which they were not qualified to resolve. And almost all workers stated that they would strongly or probably favor the Agency's hiring more specialists with whom they could consult on their case problems.[49]

But the diffuse relationship between worker and client had a more important implication: it meant that unlike most other professional–client relationships, the area in which the worker exercised authority by virtue of his professional competence was not clearly demarcated. The area of skills defined included the client's financial, social, and personal problems—a sizable arena. In fact, few human problems were automatically excluded from the social worker's care. With so broad a definition of professional responsibility and competence, the client had no basis for determining categorically which demands of the worker were based on special knowledge and expertise and which lacked this foundation. Perhaps because of this uncertainty, many clients appeared to reject most, if not all, of the claims of agency workers to professional competence.[50] Given this situation, in order to obtain the necessary compliance from clients, workers were often forced to fall back onto the bureaucratic authority they possessed as representatives of an agency that dispensed services desired by clients.

Emotional Detachment and Client Interests

Caseworkers, as professionals, were expected to relate to the client in a detached, emotionally neutral manner. The control of emotional affect in relationship with clients is meant to encourage impartial service and to insure that the practitioner's judgments are guided by reason rather than emotion. It is also instrumental in preventing over-involvement with clients, giving the worker some emotional insulation from their problems. However, for professionals in a bureaucratic setting, detachment takes on special significance in the worker–client relationship.

ELEMENTS OF A "GOOD" RELATIONSHIP

The elements of a professional relationship were a matter of frequent discussions in County Agency. In-service training sessions and supervisor–worker conferences furnished occasions for the consideration of criteria for a "good" worker–

client relation. During these discussions, the point was made invariably that a good relationship was *not* one in which the worker merely "stayed on good terms with the client" or where the worker "got the client to like him." Rather, a good relationship was held to exist when the client felt free to express hostility toward the worker and when the worker could make demands on the client and still retain his trust and confidence. Thus, in one of the supervisors' bi-monthly meetings the topic was discussed in the following terms:

S1. They [the workers] want to get the client on their good side.
S2. Or get on the good side of the client.
S3. It's very misunderstood. Workers think they have a good relationship if it's a positive one. If the client has negative feelings this is threatening to the workers, and they are afraid that the clients won't like them.
S4. One of my workers told me she had a good relationship with her clients because there had been no complaints.
[All laugh.]

Agency superiors believed that client hostilities toward caseworkers should not be repressed but brought out into the open, where they could be examined and discussed; and, they argued, their mere expression could have therapeutic benefits.

Some hostility directed at practitioners by clients would seem to be normal. As previously discussed, professionals are not expected to always follow the wishes of their clients but are to serve the best interests of clients as they interpreted them. This helps to explain why workers in the welfare agency were not expected always to enjoy the good favor of their clients. But this explanation assumes that client interests were, in fact, the overriding ones in determining the actions of workers, and this was probably not always the case. Just as the supervisor–caseworker relationship was not and could not be a purely professional one, neither was the caseworker–client relation. The client's interests did not always take precedence, because the worker was under considerable pressure to follow supervisory directives, and all his decisions were expected to conform to federal, state, county, and agency regulations. In a very real sense, the client's interests were defined in large part by the agency. It is true that clients were "free" to refuse to follow the directives of their case-worker, but to do so was to forfeit their claim to assistance.[51] And, unlike the more traditional professional–client relationship, the client did not have the option of turning to another professional: the agency possessed a monopoly in the dispensing of public welfare funds and services.

Given these circumstances, it is even more clear why workers could not be permitted to simply "get along well" with the client: the customer was not always right—the worker had to learn to give priority to the demands of the agency. And the very nature of the agency program meant that client hostility would sometimes be evoked. Clients were expected by the agency to do things that they would not ordinarily do voluntarily—e.g., to provide highly personal information to the worker; prosecute their relatives for failure to support them; agree to an agency lien on their property; and file paternity charges against their lovers. Supervisors attempted to prepare workers for these unpleasant situations by insisting that even a good performance by workers would sometimes elicit client hostility.

THE MANAGEMENT OF CLIENT HOSTILITY

As a protection to the worker's ego, it was essential that workers be taught to interpret client hostility in nonpersonal terms. It was also essential from the agency's standpoint that client resistance not deter the worker from enforcing agency policy. For instance, in one worker–supervisor conference, a worker reported to her supervisor that her client had refused to allow the agency to take wardship of her child, had become quite abusive, and had threatened to take her child and move to another city outside the county. The supervisor responded:

> We know what this is, don't we? She is projecting blame on to others. We recognize this for what it is—a big defense. We anticipated some kind of reaction, didn't we? This is what to us? A threat! Is this going to take us off our course?

Using psychiatric interpretations of the client's remarks, the supervisor attempted to defend the worker by disarming the client. Note the similarity of these techniques to those described earlier in the discussion of the therapeutic approach to the supervision of caseworkers. The same techniques were employed with the same results: differences in power—this time between the client and worker—were obscured, content was disregarded, and emotion was depersonalized. Such generalized terms and phrases as "helping the client to work through his problems," "interpreting agency policy" to the client, helping the client learn to "cooperate with the agency," assisting the client to "accept reality factors"—these and others like them helped to justify actions aimed at forcing the client to conform to the worker's plans and to the agency's program.

SOURCES OF WORKER SATISFACTIONS

Just as the worker was taught to ignore the client's hostility and anger, he was warned to disregard the client's praise and gratitude. Two episodes illustrate this attempt to control the sources of worker satisfactions. The first was recounted by a supervisor to a group of new workers during their orientation period:

> Just the other day one of our workers rushed around to get a sewing machine for a client—then came back disgusted and said that after all her effort the client didn't even thank her. I asked her who she picked the machine up for—herself or the client? These are deprived people; it's not easy for them to thank anybody for anything. We can't get our satisfactions from the client but from the job. We must get our satisfactions from bringing resources to the client, or we will be very frustrated in our work.

The second incident occurred in the conference discussed earlier between the worker and supervisor who were planning to institute wardship proceedings:

> C. *The problem for the mother is that taking the child away*

> *from her will mean that she can't get any more money [from ADC].*
>
> S. *The problem is that in that area of the city the people don't want any motivation to change. In your own security rests your ability to motivate. Don't come out with explanations. You are there to tell her what must be done. What are your satisfactions? Sometimes you get very few from the client herself. Your satisfactions must come from seeing your duty and role as a social worker and performing it.*

The worker then proceeded to talk of the difficulties she had experienced in working with clients in this area of the city. The supervisor sympathized:

> It's frustrating, it's disheartening. There are few satisfactions from clients. But we forget that a negative situation can also be the result of good casework.[52]

These supervisory comments point up two major reasons why supervisors were anxious to de-emphasize client reactions as sources of worker satisfaction. The first indicates that client gratitude was capricious and might not be forthcoming in any given case; hence, it could not serve as a dependable source of gratification for workers. The second comment amplifies a point made earlier: if the caseworker was to perform his job as a representative of the agency, it was often necessary for him to act in ways eliciting client anger rather than approval. By discounting the client as a source of job satisfaction, agency officials hoped to make the worker less sensitive to the client's responses in any given situation. In this way the work of the agency could be carried on and the caseworker could find satisfaction in the knowledge that he had "seen his duty and role as a social worker and performed it."

The Caseworker–Client Relationship

Up to this point, only anecdotal evidence has been presented on the nature of the caseworker–client relationship. That caseworkers were aware of the limitations imposed by the agency on their role as caseworker is indicated by some more systematic data obtained from the questionnaire distributed to all workers. Workers were asked to respond to the following question: How do you think *most* clients view the caseworker? Nine different responses were offered, and the worker was invited to check as many as he thought applicable. Responses most often selected and the percentage of workers choosing them were:

As a friend	34%
As a professional helper	43%
As a means to financial assistance and little else	48%
As a confidant with whom problems can be shared	55%
As an investigator	77%

Whether one takes the view that the above question elicited accurate reports from the workers on the clients' perceptions or that workers merely projected onto their clients their own role definitions—in either case the data are instructive. About 40 per cent of the workers felt that clients perceived some professional qualifications in the caseworker. One-third of the workers felt that clients viewed the relationship as a more personal one, a deviation from the professional norm in the direction of over-involvement. Half felt that most clients viewed the worker in an instrumental fashion—as a means to financial assistance rather than as a helping person in his own right, but at the same time half did emphasize their role as confidant to the client. Most important, three-fourths of all workers felt that most clients viewed caseworkers as "investigators." This term has essentially bureaucratic connotations: workers were viewed (or viewed themselves) as checking up on clients to see that they continued to be eligible for assistance and were conforming to agency regulations, as rule-followers concerned with the enforcement of agency policy.

Conclusion

Professional social workers on the one hand, and lay officials and some social work administrators on the other, appear to have differing conceptions of the public welfare agency and the groups it is designed to serve. There is little question that for the professional social worker, the client is held to be the prime beneficiary of the agency services —the *raison d'être* for the agency and its program. Laymen and often administrators, by contrast, seem often to be more concerned with protecting the interests of the public at large, and more particularly, the taxpayer. The determination of who is to be the prime beneficiary of an organization's services is a critical decision, as one typology of organizations is designed to show.[53]

Powerful laymen would like to define the public welfare agency as a "commonweal" organization, the employees working with clients, to be sure, but in such a way as to protect and serve the interests of the larger community of decent, self-respecting, self-reliant citizens. A bureaucratic model is the appropriate one, given these objectives, because routinized procedures must be instituted to insure that no one will receive financial assistance who does not meet all the legal requirements, and the eligibility of recipients must be continually checked to guarantee that the client is not "chiseling" the taxpayer. Some casework services may be permitted on the chance that some recipients may be "rehabilitated"— that is, made to be self-reliant again. No great amount of training is required for the lower-staff participants, for they need make few decisions, most of their performance being regulated by detailed rules and regulations. A supervisory staff is required to insure that workers adhere to rules, to assist workers in handling those problems not fully covered by the rules, and to see to it that they put in a full day's work.

Professional social workers prefer to view the social work agency as a "service" organization established to meet the complex and varying needs of a client population. The client is viewed as a person in trouble who must be helped to find his way in a puzzling world. If he is in financial need, he should be given assistance, but, more often than not, financial difficulties are just a symptom of much more basic problems. Clients' needs and their responses to attempts to assist them are infinitely variable, so that assistance must be offered on a case-by-case basis. No body of rules can be complex or subtle enough correctly to regulate contacts with clients, although there are some general principles and techniques, to be obtained from prolonged professional study, that can provide some guidance to caseworkers. The individual caseworker must be granted sufficient autonomy to allow him to exercise his discretion in the application of these principles to particular cases. Training is also required to enable the caseworker to gain sufficient emotional maturity to establish a relationship with the client within which his needs, and not the social worker's, are defined and served. Routine supervision of the caseworker is a valuable professional asset so long as the supervisor assists the worker in her professional development —both intellectual and emotional—and respects the case-worker's right to act as an autonomous professional.

Obviously, these idealized views of the function of the agency and the role of the social worker are incompatible and spell problems for the agency that combines participants subscribing to both. Although the models presented are almost caricatures, it is clear that County Agency at the time of the study reported here, corresponded more closely to the lay-controlled bureaucratic than to the professional model. As a result, while bureaucratically oriented workers were relatively satisfied with the agency's program, professionally oriented workers were often quite critical, regarding many agency standards as subprofessional and objecting to many of the procedural regulations as interfering with client service.

Caseworkers could freely complain about agency policies and even, on occasion, defy them, but such options were hardly open to supervisors. Supervisors did critically discuss some aspects of agency functioning in supervisory staff meetings, and such discussions sometimes resulted in policy changes, but many regulations were outside their control, having been set by legislative bodies and the lay board. Regardless of their own feelings, supervisors were expected to enforce all current agency policies. These circumstances created problems for all supervisors, although professionally oriented supervisors were placed in a particularly difficult position. It was their task to help workers to accommodate to the agency's program—to reconcile bureaucratic requirements with professional principles. Both bureaucratic and professionally oriented supervisors exercised considerable control over worker performance, but the latter, by adopting a therapeutic–educator style, did so in a manner more acceptable to their caseworker subordinates. And both types of supervisors enforced agency policy, but while the bureaucratically oriented supervisors were sometimes content to enforce policies simply on the grounds that they were policies, professionally oriented supervisors were concerned to provide workers with a professional rationale for following a given directive. There appeared to be little doubt about the short-run effectiveness of the control techniques utilized by professionally oriented supervisors. However, in some cases, service to clients appeared to suffer and in others, caseworker initiative for bringing about improvements in the existing program may have been retarded.

In spite of the efforts of higher administrators and professionally oriented supervisors, caseworkers had difficulties in ascribing to themselves a professional self-image in their interactions with clients. The diffuseness with which their role vis-à-vis clients was defined, and the restrictions put upon their performance by agency regulations, among other factors, caused workers to view themselves primarily as "investigators" in the eyes of clients. Superiors in County Agency attempted to interpret the type of work in which caseworkers were engaged as "professional" in nature. They sought to strengthen the worker's self conception by discounting the views of clients and enjoining workers to look to the agency for their professional role definitions and satisfactions. From all appearances, the supervisory staff in County Agency was an

important force in shaping worker conceptions of the role of
the professional social worker.

Notes

1. It is appropriate to note, however, that the great majority of
social workers employed in this country are affiliated with public
agencies, of which county agencies are a predominate subtype. See
U.S. Department of Labor, Bureau of Labor Statistics, *Social
Workers in 1950* (New York: American Association of Social
Workers, 1952).

2. For a compilation of these provisions, see U.S. Congress, House,
Laws Relating to Social Security and Unemployment Compensation, com-
piled by Gilman G. Udell (Washington, D.C.: U.S. Govt. Printing
Office, 1958).

3. See U.S. Department of Health, Education, and Welfare, Social
Security Administration, *Characteristics of State Public Assistance Plans
under the Social Security Act,* Public Assistance Report No. 27
(Washington, D.C.: U.S. Govt. Printing Office, 1956).

4. For a more complete description of the formal structure of
County Agency, see Peter M. Blau and W. Richard Scott, *Formal
Organizations* (San Francisco: Chandler, 1962), pp. 254–57.

5. U.S. Department of Labor, *op. cit.* All statistics describing the
characteristics of social workers in the U.S. reported in this section
are based on the survey reported in this publication.

6. The benefits as well as some of the problems associated with an
extended period of informal observation have been discussed elsewhere by the author. See W. Richard Scott, "Field Work in a
Formal Organization: Some Dilemmas in the Role of Observer," in
Human Organization, 22 (Summer, 1963), 162–68.

7. These areas of potential conflict are discussed at greater length in Amitai Etzioni, *Modern Organizations* (Englewood Cliffs, N.J.: Prentice-Hall, 1964), pp. 75–93; in William Kornhauser, *Scientists in Industry: Conflict and Accommodation* (Berkeley: U. of California, 1962); and in W. Richard Scott's "Professionals in Bureaucracies—Areas of Conflict," in *Professionalization: Readings in Occupational Change*, ed. Howard M. Vollmer and Donald L. Mills (Englewood Cliffs, N.J.: Prentice-Hall, 1966), pp. 265–75.

8. See, for example, Mary E. W. Goss, "Influence and Authority among Physicians in an Out-Patient Clinic," in *American Sociological Review*, 26 (February, 1961), 39–50.

9. See Alvin W. Gouldner, "Cosmopolitans and Locals," in *Administrative Science Quarterly*, 2 (December, 1957; February, 1958), 281–306, 444–80.

10. See, for example, Kornhauser, *op. cit.*

11. Workers were asked to select and order in terms of importance three sources of professional stimulation selected from the following list: (1) colleagues in the agency; (2) my supervisor; (3) my division head; (4) the director of the agency; (5) professional persons outside the agency; (6) professional books and journals; and (7) other, to be specified. The first four sources were considered to be inside-agency sources; the next two, sources external to the agency. Responses to (7) were classified as internal or external depending on the nature of the source listed. Workers checking two or more external-agency sources among their three choices were considered to be sensitive to professional reference groups external to the agency.

12. *Professionals* were more likely than the mixed groups and the mixed groups were more likely than the *Bureaucrats* to have attended two or more social work conferences in the past year, to be active in two or more local welfare groups, to believe that agency supervisors should have an M.S.W. degree, and to think assistance to clients should be increased. The data are reported in full in Blau and Scott, *op. cit.*, pp. 67–68.

13. A behavioral indication of the professionally oriented workers' disdain for procedural regulations was provided by the finding that they were more likely to have a high number of "delinquent cases" —cases not visited according to the agency's schedule—than the

bureaucratically oriented workers. Forty per cent of the (five) *Professionals*, 33 per cent of the (six) *Reference Group* workers, 8 per cent of the (twelve) *Training* workers and none of the (twenty-nine) *Bureaucrats* had a high number of delinquencies, according to the agency's performance records. These data were available for a relatively small subset of the workers but do represent average numbers of delinquencies over a 12-month period.

14. At the time of the study only two or three agency workers, all of high seniority, occupied this status. It should be noted here that the professional commitment typology was found to be unrelated to worker seniority.

15. The argument is not that professionally oriented workers desire to leave an organization simply for the sake of leaving, but that they are more likely to desert one organization for another if they consider it to offer a setting more conducive to professional practice, such as might be the case with a "large private family service agency."

16. To make one very crude comparison, Gouldner used a roughly comparable indicator of location of reference groups in his study of professors at "Co-op" College (See Gouldner, *op. cit.*, pp. 290–95.) By his measure, 41 per cent of the 125 professors were oriented to reference groups external to the college. In the County Agency study, by contrast, only 29 per cent of the social workers were oriented to professional sources external to the agency.

17. See Lucille N. Austin, "Supervision in Social Work," in *Social Work Year Book, 1960*, ed. Russell H. Kurtz (New York: National Association of Social Workers, 1960), p. 580.

18. The social work profession has begun to exhibit a good deal of ambivalence on this subject, some members arguing that routine supervision is not only unnecessary, but inimical to the whole idea of what a professional is, with others rushing to the defense of the system, noting its usefulness both administratively and professionally. Representative views are contained in the following articles: Charlotte Babcock, "Social Work as Work," in *Social Casework*, 34 (December, 1953) 415–22; Lydia Rapaport, "In Defense of Social Work: An Examination of Stress in the Profession," in *Social Service Review*, 34 (March, 1960), 62–74; Frances Scherz, "A Concept of Supervision Based on Definitions of Job Responsibility," in *Social Casework*, 39 (October, 1958), 435–43; Esther Schour, "Helping

Social Workers to Handle Work Stress," in *Social Casework, 34* (December, 1953), 423–28; and Florence Sytz, "The Folklore of Social Work," in Cora Kasius (ed.), *New Directions in Social Work* (New York: Harpers, 1954), pp. 238–51.

19. Some data relevant to this point are reported subsequently in the section on Supervisor's Orientation.

20. When workers were asked, "In general, do you feel that supervisory positions in this agency should be filled only by workers with a master's degree in social work, or by any good worker with sufficient experience?" 86 per cent of the (thirteen) *Professionals,* 50 per cent of the (ten) *Reference Group Only,* 45 per cent of the (twenty) *Training Only,* and 34 per cent of the (thirty-seven) *Bureaucrats* preferred supervisors equipped with an M.S.W.

21. Harold L. Wilensky and Charles N. Lebeaux, *Industrial Society and Social Welfare* (New York: Russell Sage Foundation, 1958), p. 237.

22. Of course, cross-sectional data of this type do not themselves support any particular causal interpretation, although it seems more reasonable to believe that choice of reference groups had more weight in determining attitudes toward the agency than vice versa. In any case, the interpretation offered here would be consistent with either this view or one which posited mutual dependence between location of reference group and attitudes toward the agency.

23. Use of the median as the division point was not quite as arbitrary as is sometimes the case, because all supervisors assigned by this procedure to the high-exposure group had taken the equivalent of at least a full year of graduate work (thirty hours or more), while those assigned to the low-exposure group had taken only a half year's work (eighteen hours) or less, there existing a large gap in the distribution at the point of division.

24. The data in support of these latter statements are reported in W. Richard Scott, "Reactions to Supervision in a Heteronomous Professional Organization," in *Administrative Science Quarterly, 10* (June, 1965), 65–81.

25. For the purposes of this analysis, in order to have sufficient cases, it was necessary to utilize two, rather than four, worker orientation types. Worker training rather than location of reference groups was selected as the single indicator of worker orientation, making comparable the type of indicator used for workers and supervisors.

26. Additional data in support of this summary statement appear in Scott, "Reactions to Supervision . . . ," pp. 77–81.

27. Only workers employed for a full twelve months were included in this analysis. Results were based on the average monthly performance of each worker over this period and were separately treated for each type of caseload.

28. Five qualitative evaluation categories were used by the Agency: unacceptable, fair, competent, commendable, and distinguished— and within each category, numerical scores were assigned ranging from 1 (low) to 10. Workers receiving an unacceptable rating were subject to dismissal, and workers had to be rated as "competent" or above in order to qualify for regular salary increases. Ratings were obtained for all workers employed six months or longer. Actual ratings of workers at the time of the study ranged from Fair–1 to Distinguished–3. Workers were not evenly distributed throughout the categories and the following breakdown was established for research purposes:

High competence: Commendable–1 to Distinguished–3 (twenty-one workers)

Medium competence: Competent–7 to Competent–10 (twenty-eight workers)

Low competence: Fair–1 to Competent–6 (twenty-one workers).

29. Gouldner has made a similar distinction between, in his terms, "utilitarian" and "voluntaristic" views of deviance. (See Alvin W. Gouldner, *Patterns of Industrial Bureaucracy* [New York: Free Press, 1954], pp. 232–33).

30. As has been pointed out by many others, Roethlisberger and Dickson made this same assumption in an analysis of worker complaints in their study of the Hawthorne plant. (See F. J. Roethlisberger and William J. Dickson, *Management and the Worker* [Cambridge, Mass: Harvard U. P., 1941.]) On the basis of this assumption, a counseling program was established which permitted workers to air their grievances and discuss their problems. By accepting the premise that worker complaints reflected individual psychological maladjustments rather than objective working conditions, management was relieved of the necessity of changing the worker's plant environment.

31. A related discussion of the dysfunctions of psychiatric interpretations is contained in Alfred M. Stanton and Morris S. Schwartz,

The Mental Hospital (New York: Basic Books, 1954), pp. 146–50, 200–6.

32. See Amitai Etzioni, *A Comparative Analysis of Complex Organizations* (New York: Free Press, 1961), pp. 4–6, 255–61.

33. See William J. Goode, "Community within a Community: The Professions," in *American Sociological Review*, 22 (April, 1957), 194–200.

34. Rapaport, *op. cit.*, p. 71.

35. Wilensky and Lebeaux, *op. cit.*, p. 179.

36. Everett C. Hughes, *Men and their Work* (New York: Free Press, 1958), p. 135.

37. This and other proposals for the reassignment of functions are discussed in Wilensky and Lebeaux, *op. cit.*, p. 294. Agency policy required that client eligibility for financial assistance was to be established before the case was accepted for service by the agency and was to be reinvestigated at periodic intervals thereafter.

38. The "Employee's Handbook" in use in County Agency made this equation explicit: "It is possible for a worker's performance to be considered 'fair' or 'unacceptable' if his rating on quantity is low even though his 'quality' rating is high in relation to the cases he does work on consistently. The Agency must require a basic minimum of caseload coverage; failure to meet this minimum will cause the total caseload to suffer, even though a relatively small number of cases may be satisfactorily handled."

39. In fact, this "administrative" requirement undoubtedly helped to protect clients from worker partiality by insuring that they would receive roughly equal attention.

40. In County Agency the size of the caseload varied with the type of client. The typical Old Age Assistance worker carried approximately 160 cases; the Aid to Dependent Children worker, 110 cases; and the Child Welfare worker, fifty cases. Workers in the Intensive Unit, a small group of workers assigned the most difficult ADC cases, carried approximately forty cases.

41. Miriam McCaffery, "Criteria for Student Progress in Field Work," in *Principles and Techniques in Social Casework: Selected Articles, 1940–1950*, ed. Cora Kasius (New York: Family Service Association of America, 1950), p. 175.

42. Elizabeth Chinchester, *et al.,* "Field work criteria for second-year casework students," in *ibid.,* p. 236.

43. *Ibid.,* p. 244.

44. At the time of the study a single son or daughter who earned more than $225 per month was expected to contribute to parents the excess up to a given amount; for a married couple, the support minimum was set at $300 per month. Most County Agency workers regarded these minimum support levels established by the state to be unrealistically low.

45. Goss, *op. cit.*

46. Sytz, *op. cit.,* pp. 239, 243. (Italics in original.)

47. Wilensky and Lebeaux, *op. cit.,* p. 243.

48. Talcott Parsons, *The Social System* (New York: Free Press, 1951), pp. 434–35.

49. Forty-eight per cent of the (eighty-four) workers responding "strongly" favored the hiring of specialists, while an additional 45 per cent stated that they would "probably" favor it.

50. Some data in support of this assertion are reported subsequently.

51. In this sense, agency workers were also "free" to ignore the demands of their superiors: they could always resign.

52. Note that there is an attempt made here to differentiate between the skillful handling of the case and the actual results obtained. Hughes (*op. cit.,* p. 96) argues that this kind of distinction is made by most professions and provides an illustration from the field of social work: "This profession is said to make a distinction between successful and professional handling of a case. The layman thinks of success as getting the person back on his feet, or out of trouble. The social worker has to think of correct procedure, of law, of precedent, of the case as something which leaves a record. She also appreciates skillful interviewing, and perhaps can chuckle over some case which was handled with subtlety and finish, although the person never got "well" (whatever that would be in social work)."

53. Blau and Scott, *op. cit.,* pp. 42–58.

CHAPTER FOUR

Semi-Professionalism and Social Work: A Theoretical Perspective*
▲ Nina Toren

COLUMBIA UNIVERSITY

*T*HE PURPOSE OF THIS CHAPTER IS TO apply a sociological–analytical framework to social work literature pertaining to the position of social work as a profession and its influence upon the relationship between social workers and the authority system of the organizations in which they are employed.

The first part of the paper is concerned with the characteristic attributes of professions in general and with the attempt to locate social work along a continuum of professionalization. The second part deals with the functions and dysfunctions of a bureaucratic framework for professionals,

* The preparation of this paper was supported by Grant (WA) CRD 280-6-175, Department of Health, Education, and Welfare. The author gratefully acknowledges the valuable comments of Professor Amitai Etzioni and Professor Terence K. Hopkins on an earlier draft of this paper.

semi-professionals, and, specifically, for social workers. In the third part the developments and modifications of the ideology and practice of social work are examined in order to expose the complex nature of this profession and the diverse interdependencies between social workers and organizations. The last part extends the analysis of the distinct relationships between social workers and organizational control concerning, in particular, the problems created by supervision and the ways through which it is exercised.

Social Work as a Semi-Profession

The nature of the professions and the process of professionalization have been dealt with extensively in recent sociological writings.[1]* The various descriptions differ as to the number of attributes by which professions are defined and in regard to the relative importance given to each. However, most writers agree that the core characteristics which distinguish the professions from other occupations are that they are based on a body of theoretical knowledge, that their members command special skills and competence in the application of this knowledge, and that their professional conduct is guided by a code of ethics, the focus of which is service to the client.

In view of the proliferation of professions in modern society, it is difficult and misleading to talk about the professions as a whole. Rather, the extent of professionalization of an occupation should be measured by applying the general criteria used to define the professions. In this connection, two points should be noted. First, it is possible to distinguish among different types or degrees of each element, for example, the type of knowledge on which the profession is based, or the degree of public recognition enjoyed by its members. Second, different attributes of professionalization may have developed to varying degrees, so that a profession may rank higher in

* Notes to this chapter begin on p. 185.

respect to one characteristic and lower in respect to another. Thus, for example, although the service ideal is strongly emphasized in social work its knowledge base is still in the process of crystallization, upgrading, and integration.[2] These two distinctions have to be taken into account if we intend to rank an occupation on a continuum of professionalization.

Measuring the degree of professionalization, particularly in respect to the type of knowledge upon which a profession is based, Carr-Saunders has differentiated four major types of professions in modern society.[3]

a. The *established professions*—law, medicine and the Church share two basic attributes; their practice is based upon the theoretical study of a department of learning; and the members of these professions feel bound to follow a certain mode of behavior.

b. The *new professions*—are those which are based on their own fundamental studies such as engineering, chemistry, accounting and the natural and social sciences.

c. The *semi-professions*—replace theoretical study by the acquisition of technical skill. Technical practice and knowledge is the basis of such semi-professions as nursing, pharmacy, optometry and social work.

d. The *would-be professions*—require neither theoretical study nor the acquisition of exact techniques but rather a familiarity with modern practices in business, administration practices and current conventions. Examples of this type are hospital managers, sales managers, works managers, etc.

In addition to the criteria of commitment to an ethical code (this is explicitly mentioned only in reference to the old-established professions) and the type of knowledge base, a structural variable is introduced: namely, the degree to which members of different professional groups are independent or salaried workers. According to Carr-Saunders, the members of the older professions were originally independent practitioners; a certain proportion of members of the new professions have always been employed; and nearly all members of the semi-professions and would-be professions are salaried. The author apparently regards the transition from the independent practitioner to the salaried professional worker as a major factor undermining the professional code of ethics.

The characteristics of a semi-profession can be described more clearly by comparing it with an ideal-type, such as the model of professions provided by Greenwood, which consists of five components:[4]

1. A basis of systematic theory.
2. Authority recognized by the clientele of the professional group.
3. Broader community sanction and approval of this authority.
4. A code of ethics regulating relationships of professionals with clients and colleagues.
5. A professional culture sustained by formal professional associations.

The term *semi-profession* indicates that the profession in question is located somewhere along the middle of the continuum of professionalism—that is, between the full-fledged professions and those occupations which are professions in name only but do not, in fact, possess any of the attributes characterizing the professions.

An occupation will be classified as a semi-profession if it lacks one or more of the professional qualities pointed out above; or if—which is empirically more frequent—one or more of these qualities are not fully developed. Thus, a semi-profession may lack a systematic theoretical knowledge base, and hence entail a shorter period of training for its members; it may not command a monopoly of control over its members, the criteria for their recruitment, training, licensing, and performance; its code of ethics may be vague or inconsistent; and the professional association may be divided, inefficient, or powerless.

Attempting to answer the question of whether social work is a profession, or to determine the extent of its professional character, different observers come to different conclusions, depending upon their general viewpoint and on the different degrees of importance they ascribe to various professional traits. Many writers on this subject open their discussion of the problem by citing Flexner, who wrote, in 1915, that social work could not qualify as a full-fledged profession because it was not founded on a body of scientific knowledge.[5] Most of them also agree that since that time social work has gone a long way on the road toward professionalization.[6] Greenwood, for example, after presenting his model of the professions, comes to the conclusion that

> Social work is already a profession; it has too many points of congruence with the model to be classified otherwise. Social work is, however, seeking to rise within the professional hierarchy, so that it, too, might enjoy maximum prestige, authority and monopoly which presently belong to a few top professions.[7]

As he sees it, social work possesses the main attributes characterizing a profession, but they are as yet less highly developed and integrated than in the established professions; therefore, social work still ranks relatively low on the continuum of professionalism.

Carr-Saunders, whose typology of the professions was described earlier, classifies social work as a semi-profession, as he ascribes primary importance to the autonomy of the professional practitioner. He writes,

> Social workers and school teachers, for example, have a dual responsibility to the employer as well as the client. But the employer lays down the limits to the service which can be rendered and to some extent determines its kind and quality. As a result, a social worker who is, say, a probation officer is far from free to treat a person committed to his charge in a manner indicated by his professional training and experience.[8]

While Greenwood is referring to the relatively lower degree of development of the main professional components in social work, Carr-Saunders emphasizes the lack of professional autonomy because of organizational pressures.

It is our contention that, as far as typologies go, social work at present should be classified as a semi-profession, although for somewhat different reasons than those provided by the authors quoted thus far. The phenomenon of uneven professionalization has already been mentioned; although the attributes of a profession are interdependent and hence tend to cluster around a certain point on the professional continuum, they may sometimes be less well integrated because of differences in the rates or directions of their development. This problem has been noted by students of the process of professionalization.[9] Considering social work, Boehm writes,

> in social work, technical features, skills and techniques are relatively identified; its value system is well articulated, but its theory is less well developed than are its other features.[10]

This means that the knowledge base of social work is still, to a large extent, drawn from experience—i.e., generalizations inferred from many specific cases—and that a great deal of intuition is required in the application of this knowledge. At the same time, the methods and particularly the service orientation of social work have attained a higher level of development and crystallization.

Of course, the upward mobility of social workers to a more "established" professional status is, in part, inhibited by a "shortage" of "authority recognized by the clientele of the professional group," and "broader community sanction and approval of this authority."[11] Social work also does not have as yet a strong inclusive professional association in which membership is a necessary prerequisite for the right to practice. However, these features are to a considerable degree the consequences of the fact that social workers have been unable until now to prove "exclusive competence" based on special training and knowledge in the treatment of their clients. Only a relatively small number of those practicing social work (16 per cent) have had full two-year graduate training, and only one-third of the employed social workers are members of the National Association of Social Workers. Moreover, casework—i.e., therapeutic interviewing, which is the most "scientific" technique of the profession—is not the monopoly of social work but is used by other professional practitioners as well.

The discrepancy between the present development of theoretical knowledge and the value system of social work is the main factor contributing to its semi-professional status. Nowadays, it is difficult to claim full-fledged professional standing on the basis of a commitment to help people in need and a concern for humanitarian and social reform. As stated by Dollard,

> The difficulty which has plagued social work in its development as a profession is that the social worker's dedication is to a degree shared by all good men and women. . . . Hence we all resist and resent the notion that the task of the social worker requires a peculiar combination of temperament, intelligence and experience.[12]

To be granted the rights and rewards of an established profession—autonomous control, high prestige, and high income—social work will have to show that its members command esoteric knowledge and skills which enable them to accomplish their task much more efficiently and with better results than "any other enthusiastic amateur," as is the case, for example, in the medical profession.

The general conclusion that can be drawn from our discussion at this point is that to claim and to be awarded an established position (particularly in the sense of professional autonomy), the profession must demonstrate a certain congruence between the two core elements—systematic knowledge and professional norms. If a profession ranks high on only one of these dimensions and low on the other, it will not be accredited full professional status either by the public or by social scientists. A profession may be based on a great amount of systematic knowledge but lack a collectivity-oriented code of ethics, as in the case of engineering specialists and other kinds of technicians. Or, it may be committed to a service ideal but lack a theoretical knowledge base, as in the case of social work, nursing, and librarianship.

It should be mentioned here that the above analysis does not account for the differentiated subdivisions of social work, for example, public welfare, family counseling, child welfare, and psychiatric casework. Some of these units command a more systematic body of knowledge than others and some are organized in different structures from others. Our analysis, therefore, is a generalization of the concrete complexity of the profession and should be considered as such.

Another problem is that any classification of a profession is, by definition, more or less temporary. Professions, even the established ones, develop and change. Many developments and modifications have taken place in social work since the days of the charity organization; new changes are taking place now, so that the categorization of social work as a semi-profession is limited to the present time period.

It is usually taken for granted that members of a semi-profession and their leaders seek to achieve full professionalization so as to gain the accompanying rewards. However, in a review of social work literature, resistance to full professionalization, and a tendency toward deprofessionalization can be detected.[13] The source of this counter-trend is the idea that social work should retain some of its original and unique qualities. The writers who give expression to this tendency base their argument on two major issues: first, that "over-professionalization" in social work will cause the loss of its basic "humanitarian" values, and second, that the profession will be drawn away from its commitment to social reform. This was eloquently expressed by Nathan Cohen: "Social work without service would be lame, but without values would be blind."[14]

Obviously, the ideals of social reform and the welfare of individuals are interrelated; however, some emphasize one or the other as being in danger of neglect as a result of professionalization.[15] Carr-Saunders, for example, deplores the decline of the true professional spirit in modern times;

referring to social workers at the beginning of the century, he says,

> They were in effect general practitioners. In their place we now find specialist social workers of many kinds, such as probation officers, hospital social workers, psychiatric social workers, and others. . . . As a consequence of the trend toward specialization, the professional man no longer takes a comprehensive interest in his client. He feels that he has no general responsibility for those who come under his care, and the personal relationship between practitioner and client is weakened.[16]

Others, too, are convinced that social work could not and should not desert its personal and humanitarian involvement:

> It can never reach the point of scientific objectivity usually characterized by such terms as "impersonal" and "descriptive". It will always have an element of the subjective, the personal, and the emotional.[17]

The universalistic–specific orientation characterizing the professional's attitude is seen here from its negative side as infringing upon personal interest and total responsibility, which are fundamental to the "helping professions."

The second issue—the effect of professionalization on the goals and values of social reform—is probably the more visible and the more stressed in debates among social workers on the future of the profession. Some view the process of professionalization in social work as a two-edged sword. On the one hand, more knowledge and better training will eventually enhance the status of social work as a profession, but on the other hand, this process is regarded with apprehension because of the growing emphasis on methods and techniques at the expense of participation in wider social action and policy-making. Bisno observes that,

> In assuming the rightness and naturalness of this trend [striving for more prestige by way of professionalization] we have tended to ignore the question of the price to be paid for the higher status and whether it is "worth" it. Does it imply a weakening of the *social* in social work?[18]

He argues that if the trend of emphasizing methods and techniques continues, three consequences will follow:

> First, a continuing de-emphasis on controversial social action which has broad social implications; second, a related lessening of attempts to influence social policy and the acceptance of the role of technician-implementer; and third, change in the ideology of social work that will lessen the gap between its system of ideas and that of the dominant groups in society.[19]

In short, a displacement of goals is likely to occur in which means (techniques and methods) will take the place of goals (social reform).[20]

This discussion has attempted to point out some of the factors underlying our classification of social work as a semi-profession, as well as the limitations of the classification. It has, we hope, indicated the need for a more detailed examination of the properties of the profession, their interrelations, and their various trends of development. But first let us outline the relationship between professions and bureaucratic organizations in general, and some of the typical traits this relationship assumes in the case of a semi-profession, that of social work in particular.

Semi-Professions and Bureaucracy

One of the problems most often discussed in the sociology of professions is the relationship between the professions and bureaucratic structures. This is not surprising in view of the fact that these two patterns of activity and organization are becoming increasingly interwoven. The process is sometimes described as the "bureaucratization of the professions," or, as the "professionalization of bureaucracies." To quote Wilensky:

> it is not that organizational revolution destroys professionalism, or that the newer forms of knowledge . . . provide a poor base for professionalism, but simply that

all these developments lead to something new. The culture
of bureaucracy invades the professions; the culture of
professionalism invades organizations.[21]

It is important to bear in mind that certain general
principles of the professions as well as of bureaucracies are
rooted in the same developmental trends of modern Western
culture: the growing division of labor, specialization, and
rationalization. Thus, Parsons in his analysis of the professions
in modern society concludes that the occupational sphere in
general (the professions, business, and bureaucratic administration) shares the common elements of rationality, functional
specificity, and universalism.[22]

Professionals in various fields acknowledge the fact that
nowadays it is almost impossible to carry out professional
work independent of large and complex organizations, e.g.
research institutes, hospitals, business firms, welfare agencies,
schools, and so on. Various types of resources, and their
management in organizations are vital to the conduct of high
quality professional work. The student–professional in
medicine, nursing, social work, teaching, and the like is
partly trained in bureaucratic frameworks (hospitals, agencies,
schools). The graduate student in social work, for example,
becomes familiar with agency structure through field training,
which is an integral and important part of his professional
education. This means that the student undergoes a process of
anticipatory socialization to the role of professional in a
bureaucratic organization. Also, in his later encounter with
the agency's rules and regulations, as a full-fledged professional, he may discover that in some areas the organization's
requirements are in fact compatible with his professional
ideology and standards; for example, the norm of treating the
client with a certain amount of detachment and without
emotional involvement coincides with the bureaucratic dictum
of *sine ira et studio*.

Nevertheless, bureaucratic rules and authority are, more
often than not, viewed as infringing upon the professional's
freedom to apply his knowledge and skills according to his
judgment and convictions.[23] The literature on this subject

stresses the contradictions and inherent conflicts between bureaucratic organizations and the professions rather than their points of congruity.[24] This may be so for a variety of reasons; but the most important is the distinctive control structure of the professions, which is fundamentally different from bureaucratic control exercised in administrative organizations. Professional control is characterized by being exercised from "within" by an internalized code of ethics and special knowledge acquired during a long period of training, and by a group of peers, which is alone qualified to make professional judgments. This type of authority differs greatly from bureaucratic authority, which emanates from a hierarchical position.[25] Gross writes,

> A strong sense of competence is important because authority rests upon it. The professional in the last analysis has nothing else on which to base his authority. His authority is not charismatic, not based on tradition, nor on the occupancy of a formal position.[26]

The suggestion that professional authority is based solely upon knowledge and competence—even though this is so only "in the last analysis"—needs further qualification. First, the authority of the *established* professions, as the term itself implies, does rest to some extent on tradition. We may even detect some "magical" elements in the exercise of professional control, e.g., the doctor's treatment of patients with "awe-evoking" instruments whose function is not always scientific. Second, to some degree the professional's authority *is* charismatic, that is, based on the "extraordinary qualities of a person."[27] This can be demonstrated by comparing the performances of professionals with similar training, skills, and positions, who, nevertheless, exert diverse powers of personality. (A good example would be provided by observing the performances of different lawyers in court.) Finally, there is no doubt that the professional's authority is frequently combined with a high hierarchical position in the organization in which he is employed. We do not intend to deny that professional authority is based mainly on knowledge and competence, but wish to point out that "professional authority" and "bureaucratic authority," as such, are ideal types. In reality, there are other components involved in the professional's authority especially when he is engaged in service to people (the scientist in industry does not have "clients" in this sense). Furthermore, these other elements—traditional, charismatic, and official—come to the front specifically under those circumstances in which knowledge and technical skills are inadequate.[28]

Here we would like to deal briefly with two questions: What is the position of the semi-professions, particularly of social work, in regard to bureaucratic control? And, is a bureaucratic framework always dysfunctional for the conduct of professional work, or does it, under certain conditions, have some positive contribution?

Semi-professions—such as teaching, nursing, librarianship, and social work—are sometimes called "heteronomous professions."[29] However, these two concepts are not merely synonymous: they pertain to different elements in the characterization of the professions. Semi-professionalism denotes that the profession does not rest on a firm theoretical knowledge base; the period of training involved is relatively short; members cannot claim monopoly of exclusive skills; and the special area of their competence, i.e., their function, is less well-defined as compared with the full-fledged established professions. Heteronomy, on the other hand, means that members of the profession are guided and controlled not only from within—that is, by internalized professional norms, expert knowledge, and the professional community—but also by administrative rules and by superiors in the organizational hierarchy.

At first sight, the relationship between semi-professionalism and heteronomy seems clear and logical. Inasmuch as professional authority rests basically on expert knowledge and technical competence, and because the semi-professions entail a shorter period of training, it follows that their members have less knowledge and less intrinsic commitment to professional norms. In short, they are less well "socialized" to perform their role without outside supervision. They will also be less able to insist on complete freedom from control, whether by the public, special groups of laymen, or their administrative superiors.

Closer scrutiny, however, may reveal that the assumption of the intimate association between semi-professionalism and heteronomy, and between full-fledged professionalism and autonomy, is not a one-to-one relationship. To a large extent this assumption is a result of comparing every profession, explicitly or implicitly, with the stereotyped image of the independent physician in private practice. But we may raise the question of whether the doctor working in a state or municipal hospital or clinic is really completely autonomous in his daily conduct, or whether the lawyer employed by a large law firm is free from control by his superiors. The answer to these questions is obviously that members of established professions are sometimes controlled by their senior colleagues and their peers, but not by nonprofessionals, at least not in the making of decisions and in the performance of tasks within their special sphere of competence. It is true that teachers, nurses, social workers, librarians, and other members of semi-professions are subjected to bureaucratic rules and regulations more than physicians, lawyers, and scientists. Nevertheless, it is interesting to note that *direct* supervision in the semi-professions is always carried out by senior or ex-professionals who have risen from the ranks— the school principal, the head nurse, the social work supervisor, and the like.

It has also been noted that even semi-professionals are not controlled to the same degree in the performance of all their different tasks and their various role relationships. Lortie writes that

> Conventional concepts of hierarchical control usually assume that superordinate–subordinate linkages are marked by uniformity on all matters, i.e., that all of a superordinate's wishes carry equal initiatory power over his subordinate's actions. Yet, . . . it appears that decision areas are subjected to differential definition, and that variable

zoning exists in which, within the *same* dyad, initiatory power varies by topic.[30]

Thus, for example, the teacher is more autonomous vis-à-vis the school's principal with regard to in-class affairs than in respect to administrative matters, such as record-keeping. Similar differential zoning of control can be found in social work and other semi-professions. In particular, the actual encounter between practitioner and client is usually not observable (this includes the human relations professions which do not enjoy the right of privileged communication) and therefore not directly controllable. Exclusion from visibility allows the semi-professional a great degree of autonomy in his contact with the client, but it also incurs the disadvantages of being judged by results rather than by the effort and skill invested in the process.

All this is not to deny the greater autonomy of the established professions, e.g., medicine and law, but to emphasize that instead of labelling any profession as heteronomous, autonomous, or otherwise, we should ask: Which aspects of the professional's daily conduct are controlled, by whom, and how? If this is specified, the description of any profession becomes more complex and realistic and less ideal-typical.

In social work, less autonomy than that which is granted to the established prestige professions is indicated by certain objective attributes of the profession. There is as yet no legal regulation in the form of licensure, which restricts practice to those who hold a license (as in medicine), or certification, which restricts the use of title to those who have a certain training (as in public accounting),[31] or privileged communication with clients, which exempts the practitioner– client verbal interchange from any outside interference, including that of the courts (as in the practice of law).

Other factors, in addition to those directly associated with less scientific knowledge and exclusive skills, may be involved in the greater susceptibility of semi-professions to bureaucratic control. The elementary fact in this connection is that most social workers are employed by bureaucratic organizations—

public or voluntary agencies, schools, hospitals, prisons, and so on. Social work did not start out as a free profession with independent practitioners; private practice in social work is only a recent development and for the time being quite marginal. Hence, the distinction between "locals" and "cosmopolitans" is somewhat obscure (in the sense of the employed social worker orienting toward an "outside colleague community" as a reference group and target of aspiration). Moreover, within the same organizational setting, certain structural properties of semi-professions, as compared with full-fledged professions, influence the degree of autonomy granted to their members. The main factors in this respect are the proportion between the sexes among those comprising the profession and their class and ethnic origins. It seems that these variables correlate with the type of knowledge and the degree of the socially legitimated autonomy that a profession commands. Simpson and Simpson, for example, argue that the fact that semi-professions are more given to bureaucratic supervision is closely related to the prevalence of women in nursing, elementary school teaching, social work, and the like. They write,

> The public is less willing to grant autonomy to women than to men. Women's primary attachment is to the family role, and they are therefore less intrinsically committed to work than men and less likely to maintain a high level of specialized knowledge . . . [and] less likely than men to develop colleague reference group orientations. For these reasons and because they often share the general cultural norm that women should defer to men, women are more willing than men to accept the bureaucratic controls imposed on them in semi-professional organizations, and less likely to seek a genuinely professional status.[32]

Social work is thus identified in the mind of the public as a feminine occupation; the helping, nurturent functions of the social worker are associated with the traditional roles of women. It has also been noticed that in the professional literature there is a tendency to refer to a social worker of indeterminate sex as "she" rather than "he."[33] All of this constitutes a threat to the male identity as defined in our society—i.e., as being dominant, active, achieving, and so forth—and partially explains the fact that less than a third of all practicing social workers are men.[34] The relation among the existing sex ratio and heteronomy and the generally low prestige of social work is circular and cumulative: social workers are accorded less autonomy on the job, in part because the majority of them are women; on the other hand, because of more bureaucratic constraints and less prestige, the profession finds it difficult to recruit more men into its ranks.

The stratificational origin of social workers affects and is affected by autonomy and status in a similar manner; it is at the same time a cause and a consequence. The majority of social workers have always come from middle-class families, and in the past few decades they have been increasingly recruited from lower social strata. This process may have a negative influence on the profession's prestige. If social work is identified as a low-class occupation it will deter people from higher classes or with upper-mobility aspirations from choosing social work as a career.[35]

The attributes of semi-professions that have been mentioned so far are likely to make their members more vulnerable to control by the organizations of which they are a part. However, it seems that the very nature of some of these professions, particularly those dealing with human beings, is incompatible with bureaucratic standardization. One of the main features of a bureaucratic organization is that the work of its members is directed by a set of universalistic rules and generalized procedures. This can be maintained only if the work to be done is specific and routine; the human relations professions, and especially social work, are neither. First, the orientation toward the client is diffuse or holistic, approaching him as an entirety and taking account of all his needs—physical, psychological, and social; secondly, each client is unique—there will always be special circumstances and exceptions to the rule.[36] These two basic attitudes are expressed in the phrasing of the "Working Definitions of Social Work Practice" prepared by a committee for the Commission on Social Work

Practice of the National Association of Social Workers in 1956.[37] Considering the "values" of social work, it says: "(4) There are human needs common to each person, yet each person is essentially unique and different from others." And in the definition of "knowledge," we find:

> The practice of the social worker is typically guided by knowledge of: (1) Human development and behavior characterized by emphasis on the wholeness of the individual and the reciprocal influences of man and his total environment—human, social, economic and cultural.[38]

Our tentative conclusion is that social work as well as other semi-professions incorporates diverse attributes, some of which are conducive to organizational regulation and control, such as a relatively short training period, no developed theoretical knowledge base, feminization, recruitment from the lower classes, and so on. Other attributes, however, such as dealing with people and some of their most severe problems, are inherently incompatible with bureaucratic principles and make rigid categorization of clients and routinization of relationships with them extremely difficult.

The other question that was raised earlier concerns the positive functions of a bureaucratic setting for the conduct of professional work. We do not refer here to the financial and organizational resources needed to discharge appropriate services to clients, which can ordinarily be commanded only by an organization and not by an individual professional, but to the special structure of control in bureaucracies and its effects on the professional. Some kind of strain, or even conflict, between line and staff seems to be unavoidable. However, sociologists have recognized that conflict may sometimes have positive functions for the parties engaged in it.[39] Gross writes,

> Conflict can be a way of creatively solving problems if it takes place in a context in which it is institutionalized and in which the rules make certain the conflict is a fair one with the sides being permitted to make their case as strongly as possible.[40]

He argues, further, that a certain type and degree of organizational control of professionals will result in improvement of professional service to clients. It has also been pointed out recently that the relationship between bureaucracy and professionalism is not necessarily a battle in which one will eventually dominate the other, but that through mutual adaptations new structures may emerge. Kornhauser, dealing with the position of scientists in industry, concludes that

> the tension between the autonomy and integration of professional groups, production groups, and other participants tends to summon a more effective structure than is attained where they are isolated from one another or where one absorbs the others.[41]

In the human relations and helping professions, and specifically in social work, the bureaucratic framework has still other functions for professional performance. It is true that rigid adherence to administrative regulations and categorization of clients in terms of abstract criteria are typical of what Merton calls "displacement of goals," or a "ritualistic orientation" which often interferes with the very goals the professional wants to achieve.[42] However, organizational rules and procedures sometimes serve as a restraining factor on a too-deep emotional involvement in the client's troubles, especially on the part of the young, idealistic, and inexperienced social worker.

Another function of the organizational setting for the holistic–helping professions is to make their services more impartial and fair. Formal impersonal rules are a yardstick for comparing and evaluating different clients' problems and needs. The positive functions of the bureaucratic organization for social work were commented on by Wilensky and Lebeaux:

> Bureaucracy tends to minimize urgency, which may be counted a disadvantage. But the gains associated with it are clear: reliability, continuity, fairness.[43]

A less conspicuous function of organizational prescriptions, which has nevertheless been noticed in family service agencies, is the use of administrative limitations as a defense against clients' demands that either cannot be satisfied or, in the social worker's opinion, should not be met.[44] An extreme example of such use (or abuse) of bureaucratic regulations would be the case in which the social worker tells her client: "Personally I would like to help you, but I am restricted by the agency's policy. . . ." The social worker is a typical man (or woman) in the middle: pressures in opposite directions are exerted on him by the organization on the one hand, and by the client on the other. It is not surprising, therefore, that under this strain he will sometimes justify his activities by claiming mere compliance with bureaucratic rules.[45]

Thus it seems that the effects of the organizational framework on the social worker's role are not totally detrimental and do sometimes contribute to better service for clients. However, in practice, the problem still remains to achieve an optimal balance between ritualism, rigid adherence to rules, and indifference and complete freedom, *ad hoc* resolutions, and personal involvement.

The Dilemma in Social Work and Its Nature

A more detailed and substantial analysis of the relationship between social work as a profession and the organizational structure can be illustrated, to a certain extent, by what is in this context called the "dilemma" in social work. This dilemma or duality is a result of different trends that have evolved in the history of social work and are incorporated in it today, though to different degrees in its various subfields.

Two basic orientations toward the achievement of social welfare can be found in the literature. Meyer writes:

> In its history, social work has long had a double focus:
> on social reform, on the one hand; and on facilitating
> adjustment of individuals to existing situations, on the other.

These two themes reappear in various forms: as environmental manipulation or promotion of psychological functioning; as concern with people through mass programs; or as casework with persons "one by one." Social workers have been conscious of these two approaches to social welfare and have often sought to reconcile them. Mary Richmond, symbol of the case by case approach, is reported to have said to Florence Kelley, symbol of reform in the grand style: We work on the same program. I work on the retail end of it, but you work on the wholesale.[46]

As we shall see later, this duality turns into a dilemma when a *zero-sum* attitude is taken, as it often is, regarding the two general approaches: that is, if one is adhered to or exercised at the expense of the other.

Both the social reform and the one-by-one approaches are rooted in the same ultimate values and goals—the promotion of human welfare. The first was dominant in social work until World War I, and attempts to promote welfare mainly by changing man's economic and social environment. The other, the individual-focused approach which developed in the second decade of this century, tries to achieve improved social functioning by changing the individual's inner world—his perceptions, attitudes, commitments, and behavior—and consequently enhance his adjustment to the environment. This orientation, emphasizing the individual case and neglecting issues of broad social reform, was related to a change in the basic perceptions of social work:

> From viewing the case as a product of impersonal forces
> in the social and economic environment, social work came
> to the image of the case as a product of unconscious impulse, needing restoration to an unchanged environment
> by self-mastery.[47]

The shift was by no means complete. Since World War II, a trend of revision became visible; voices of warning were raised against the flight from reform caused by the drive toward professionalism.[48] The debate on the relative weight to be given to each orientation is still going on, as was recently expressed at the ninety-fourth annual forum of the

National Conference of Social Welfare, held in Dallas on May 27, 1967. Charles Y. Schottland, dean of graduate studies in welfare at Brandeis University and former commissioner of Social Security, said,

> We need to place less emphasis on psychotherapy—that is, person-to-person case work methods—and begin putting more stress on broad social policy. . . . In short, we must make an impact on the physical planners, the people who run things, as well as the individual unwed mother and the individual delinquent.[49]

Few if any of the leaders or the rank-and-file social worker would suggest giving up the accomplishments of wider knowledge, training, and competence. However, the tendency is to achieve some kind of synthesis by broadening the perception of narrow professionalism, and by incorporating it within the former concern with social reform.

The basic ideological duality of society and individual, reform and therapy, situation and motivation, casework and welfare, or whatever other terms we use, is also discernible on the structural level. The development of a profession is usually accompanied by a more precise definition of its sphere of competence and responsibility, e.g., the identification of social work as dealing with casework instead of the welfare of mankind. Within this limited area, a process of further specialization and differentiation takes place.[50] In social work, the differentiation between public and private agencies has grown especially during and after the great depression, with the former assuming the burden of financial assistance, and the latter concentrating on the treatment of psychological, intra- and interpersonal problems. Specialization along these lines cuts across the public and private sectors exemplified by such programs as family counseling, child welfare, vocational rehabilitation, probation, public health, and so forth. Each of these programs has its own purposes, techniques, sponsors, and clientele.

The implications of inter-agency specializations are that some subfields are more professional than others. For example, longer training and higher qualifications, a more theoretical and scientific basis of knowledge are required in family counseling or corrections than in public assistance agencies. This also means that workers in public welfare agencies enjoy lower prestige, receive lower salaries, and have less autonomy than those in more specialized agencies. This, in turn, affects recruitment by directing the better trained social workers toward the more professional agencies, by social and self selection. In *Social Workers in 1950*, a report prepared by the Bureau of Labor Statistics of the U.S. Department of Labor and published by the American Association of Social Workers, the following information is provided: Of the estimated total of 74,240 persons in the United States in social work positions in 1950, only 16 per cent had completed the full two-year graduate curriculum. (According to the same source, in 1960, 75 per cent of the estimated 116,000 social welfare positions in the United States were occupied by persons without graduate degrees.) Public assistance workers who made up 41 per cent of the total number of social workers (in 1950), were mostly without professional training. Only 4 per cent of them had two or more years in graduate social work schools, whereas other programs had higher percentages of trained personnel (two or more years of graduate studies). For example: work with physically handicapped—8 per cent; group work—13 per cent; child welfare work, institutional—23 per cent; family services—42 per cent; and psychiatric social work in clinics—83 per cent (the highest percentage of professional workers in any one program).

The dilemma of reform and welfare versus casework on the ideological and structural levels has its repercussions on the role level, that is, on the orientation and performance of the individual social worker. The growing emphasis on the personality-focused therapeutic approach was accompanied by a transition "from preoccupation with reform to preoccupation with technical professionalism." Wilensky and Lebeaux remark,

> a professional absorbed in the technical side of his work, aiming at full use of his skills and training, preoccupied

with that competent, efficient performance of which his professional colleagues would approve—this person does not have the time, energy, or inclination necessary for social reform, for dedicated attention to the broader public purpose.[51]

The tendency of the social worker to identify his tasks as casework instead of public welfare is part of the process of professionalization.[52] It is an attempt to base the role on scientific knowledge and methods acquired by distinctive training, and thus to protect it from encroachment by anybody without proper training. By comparison, it is much more difficult to monopolize social welfare or to give it a scientific base. It is realized that,

We lacked then [in the pre-World War I period when social work was committed to social reform], and lack today any adequate scientific base that would make possible professionalization of a social action approach.[53]

On the lowest, most concrete level, welfare can be conceived of as relief dispensation which is basically an administrative function that does not require special knowledge or training. On a higher level of operation, social reform concerns political and legislative action for which

social workers as now trained are less equipped as reformers by school curricula than lawyers, labor leaders, politicians, public administrators, and others who know the political-social map and how to find their way around it.[54]

The conflict between the organization and the profession, in terms of the dilemma we have described, is most apparent and most strongly felt in the role of the trained social worker in public welfare agencies. This role entails an inherent conflict between the task of eligibility investigation and financial dispensation on the one hand, and intensive, therapeutic casework on the other. The conflict has been reconciled, theoretically, by pointing out the interdependence between the two tasks—eligibility decisions almost always involve the establishment of some personal relationships and casework;

on the other hand, Charlotte Towle has described the value
in casework of "the giving of money."[55] Empirically, this
role conflict could be solved by separating financial assistance
from professional casework and performing each in special
units and different roles. But, the Social Security Act amendments of 1962 established a new policy: welfare agencies
were not only to dispense financial aid to the needy, as before,
but in addition were to provide social services designed to
restore the indigent to self support, strengthen the family life
of recipients, and prevent dependency. Although the law's
intention is to integrate financial aid and psychological help in
one and the same role, it has not provided the necessary
resources for its implementation. The new policy implies, for
example, that agencies would have to recruit more professionally trained social workers. But if changes in recruitment
and allocation of trained personnel have occurred since the
1962 legislation, they have not been far-reaching enough to
satisfy many professionally conscious social workers. It is
claimed that of the few workers in public welfare agencies
with graduate social work education, a large percentage is
assigned to supervisory and administrative positions, resulting
in feelings of inadequacy and dissatisfaction. The authors of an
article on this problem write,

> Public assistance may need trained administrators and
> supervisors, but what happens to the trained *caseworker*?
> He may emerge from school convinced that his talents lie
> in the world of the casework relationship. He may also feel
> that full integration of his knowledge and skills demands
> concentrated work with clients for an extended time.
> When he returns instead to supervision, resultant frus-
> tration is often responsible for his decision to obtain case-
> work experience elsewhere.[56]

"Elsewhere" means other agencies with different purposes,
utilizing professional skills and dealing with a different type
of clientele. Thus, talent, training, and competence are
drained off to the more professional agencies, and public
welfare is left staffed mostly by nonprofessional, bureaucratic-
like personnel.

The great difficulty in carrying out casework because of organizational pressures was one of the pertinent issues in the "work-in" declared in 1967 by the Social Service Employees' Union in New York City. One caseworker with the City Welfare Department told a reporter:

> You know, the basic frustration of the caseworker is that you can only help your client's material needs. What they really ought to have is help in getting rehabilitated, in taking a big step along the way toward becoming better citizens. But you have sixty cases to take care of and a mountain of paper work. The department sets up no program of effective rehabilitation. And it seems to have an attitude like a vindictive parent. It's tough to do the kind of job you'd like to do.[57]

Thus, it is not surprising that professional social workers try to get rid of their administrative tasks. It has been suggested recently that the traditional eligibility investigation by the social worker should be replaced by a declaration of eligibility by clients themselves. This is designed to free the social worker from paper work and red tape, so that he may devote his time and energy to more intensive rehabilitative casework.

Proposals of this nature are based also on professional–ethical arguments. The strain in the social worker's role arises not only from the lack of appropriate organizational resources (e.g., time), or of having to perform different tasks with relation to different role-partners, namely, managing one's role-set.[58] The incompatibility between the practitioner's various tasks frequently appears in the same role-relationship, that is, with one client. In his encounter with the client, the social worker commands several types of *power*, or means that he can use to elicit compliance on the client's part. He has *utilitarian* power in the form of financial assistance that he can either give or withhold from the client; he has *normative* power by way of personal influence and activation of commitments; and he has *coercive* power, i.e., physical means of control through his ability to initiate court proceedings.[59] In using these different types of power, the social worker is faced with a professional and moral problem. From this point of view it is clear that he should not use his economic or coercive power to persuade the client to behave or not to behave in a certain manner. For example, the client must not be made to feel that he has to change his behavior or interpersonal relationships in order to be eligible for financial assistance. The immanent problems of the situation were presented by McEntire and Haworth:

> Many of the problems of dependency are completely interwoven with financial need. . . . To draw the conclusion, however, that the same worker who determines the client's financial need should also offer therapeutic service means that assistance applicants are to be treated differently from other people who receive money from public sources. It also implies the possibility that an applicant's financial need may be judged according to his acceptance of or response to services offered—if not formally, at least in various subtle ways inherent in the relationship between caseworker and client. Furthermore . . . to combine the two in the same job is wasteful of scarce professional time.[60]

A fair decision about eligibility and receiving of financial assistance is the client's right; to try to help him by means of other services may be the worker's right, but it is not clear whether the acceptance of these services is the client's duty or is subject to his own free choice. In regard to this problem, the semi-professional status of social work is apparent. In the well-established professions, particularly in medicine and law, the professional will decide, according to his own judgment, what his client's real needs are and how they will best be served. Not so in social work, in which the goals and techniques of the profession are much more given to control and criticism by outside groups, including the wider public.

The use of coercive power by the social worker raises similar problems. The threat or the actual use of force will surely evoke the client's hostility, and in any case, its intended effects will not be longlasting.[61] Aside from this, the ability of the social worker to trigger court action is somewhat dubious, as he is not at liberty to decide in which cases to use this authority; his records and testimony are liable to be subpoenaed by the court's decision. In this matter, again, the social worker's position is different from that of full-fledged professionals who have successfully obtained the right of privileged communication, the classic example in this respect being the clergy.[62] Nevertheless, the actual encounter and interaction between social worker and client is relatively invisible, that is, hidden from the public eye and from any other observer. It so happens that the practitioner, under certain circumstances, will employ utilitarian or coercive power to motivate the client to comply with his demands.[63] Such occasions have been observed during a study on family service agencies in Israel (see note 44). For example, a mother of several young children, who asked the social worker to help her find employment, was told that small children need their mother, and therefore the social worker would not comply with her request. Other cases have been observed in which the social worker promised instrumental help on condition that the client complied, for example, by bringing a child for psychiatric examination, attending a course for vocational training, and so on.[64]

We may assume that most of the clients of public welfare agencies seek concrete immediate services and help, and not to be analysed and questioned; still, ". . . far too many applicants believe that acceptance of services for which they feel no impelling need is the price they must pay in order to get financial aid."[65] Apart from this, the main organizational resources provided for the worker are those related to his right to investigate and determine eligibility.

It seems, then, that the organization as well as the clientele of public welfare are not really interested in the more professional services of the social worker; if the professionally oriented worker wants to practice therapeutic casework this is, more or less, his own problem.

We have delineated what seems to us to be a central dilemma in the profession of social work and have traced its manifestations on different levels. First, on the level of ideology and *Weltanschauung*, there is the controversy between the ideas of social reform and individual rehabilitation. Second, on the organizational level, the phenomenon of differentiation and specialization of agencies according to the two functions of welfare and therapy, or intervention for change. Third, on the level of the social worker's role, the role conflict between the more routine task of eligibility determination and administering financial assistance, and bringing about changes in people's norms and behavior. And finally, the dilemma is discernible in the basic unit of interaction between the social worker and his client in the form of alternation and manipulation of instrumental and normative sanctions.

It must be admitted that our analysis, particularly on the role and interaction levels, is limited in its application, as it pertains mainly to professionally trained social workers in public welfare agencies. It may be assumed, for example, that in "purely professional" agencies such as psychiatric clinics, the confrontation between financial assistance and intervention for change will be not as conspicuous or not present at all. A second qualification to be noted is that the conflict between the profession and the organization cannot be defined in terms of therapeutic treatment versus relief dispensation only. On the one hand, organizational goals cannot be reduced to the administrative and economic aspects of welfare; on the other hand, the professional approach cannot be equated with casework alone. We have tried to show, however, that one type of organization–profession conflict can be traced to the dual focus inherent in the profession itself.

Supervision in Social Work

Autonomy, as we have seen before, is one of the main features characterizing the established professions; that is, the professional community determines its own standards of training, recruitment, and performance. Once the professional becomes a recognized member of this community, he is relatively free from lay control and evaluation; the profession "becomes a monopoly in the public interest."[66]

By comparison, the semi-professions are characterized by lower degrees of such self-determination; they are more exposed to control by administrative superiors and lay boards. "Supervision" is the institutionalized, built-in mechanism through which the attitudes and performance of social workers are controlled.

We argued earlier that it would be fruitful to specify which areas of the social worker's role are controlled, by whom, and in what manner supervision is implemented. Regarding the first question, that of differential authority in different role-sectors, it seems that of the two tasks distinguished earlier, that of financial aid is more strictly controlled than that of casework. In general, when tasks are more complicated and can be defined in advance only in broad terms, more authority will be delegated to the professional, since the details of performance have to be left to his own discretion. Eligibility determination and checking is a routine and standardized procedure and therefore easily prescribed and regulated by bureaucratic rules. Aside from this, the simple fact that management and allocation of money which comes from public sources—federal, state, local—is involved by definition implies that these sectors will want to control the principles of its distribution. Boehm remarks,

> In no other profession is the distinction between financial probity and professional prowess more difficult to establish. No other profession is less free than social work from being directed by the laity or from being deprived of self-determination regarding the nature of its professional functions and the manner in which it discharges them.[67]

The allocation of material goods is something which is indeed unique to social work; here the professional helps the client by giving him something which is not the professional's own. In other professions, or even semi-professions, the main resources at the disposal of the professional are internalized—specific knowledge and competence guided by a commitment to the ideal of service. It is true that as the indirect result of professional help the client of the physician, lawyer, psychiatrist, teacher, or scientist may profit materially, but in none of these cases is this the main or direct function of the professional. The point is that resources which are acquired by the professional in the course of socialization and training, such as knowledge, skills, and a professional code of ethics, will be less controllable by outside agencies than the dispensation and manipulation of external resources such as money or other material goods.[68]

The second question concerning supervision is: Who has authority over the professional in the conduct of his work and to whom is he accountable for his performance? The distinction usually made in this respect is that between control by colleagues and the professional community, and by extra-professional individuals and groups.[69] However, the picture of supervision in social work is much more complex. The questions of what is supervised, in what manner, and by whom are interdependent and must be discussed simultaneously. If the social worker's adherence to the policy and regulations of the agency is to be controlled, it can be done by checking his performance against a set of abstract laws and prescriptions. If, however, his capacity to help people is to be supervised, another type of control is needed. The practitioner carrying out casework is engaged in a helping process which, to a greater or lesser degree, involves his values, intellect, and emotions. This kind of work can be supervised, if at all, only through a personal relationship between supervisor and supervisee.

The use of different methods of supervision, personal or impersonal, depends to a large extent upon the goals one wants to achieve by their application. It is generally agreed that supervision in social work has a dual function—educational and administrative. The administrative function of the supervisory process is essentially the control of a subordinate (the worker) by a superior (the supervisor) in the organization's hierarchy. This includes the supervisor's right to plan the worker's job (caseload and so on), to coordinate it with the work of others and with the over-all objectives of the agency program, and to check the worker's performance against a manual of regulations or other institutionalized procedures.

The contents and methods of the educational function of supervision are more complicated and less well defined. Supervision developed initially as a master–apprentice relationship in the charity organizations in a period when social work practice preceded formal training.[70] Knowledge was based largely upon experience and was transmitted in a practical *ad hoc* manner. The new worker was supposed to be learning by doing, under the watchful eye and guiding hand of the more experienced practitioner. During the first two decades of this century—a period in which the first schools of social work were established—tutorial teaching in agencies was systematized and formalized. Its main goal was to help the trainee and inexperienced worker to bridge the discrepancy between theoretical knowledge and actual performance, and to achieve intellectual and emotional integration of what he had learned in school. Tutorial instruction in agencies was concomitant with classroom teaching. Beginning in the Twenties, with the emergence of the psychoanalytic school and the shift of emphasis from social reform to casework, the philosophy and techniques of supervision were modified. Attention was focused on the therapeutic function of the supervisor—that is, on his task in helping the worker develop awareness and understanding of his motivations and feelings in an attempt to resolve his personality conflicts. All this was, of course, not an end in itself but was designed to advance the learning process of the trainee and to enable him to carry out more effective casework with his client.[71] During World War II, supervisory methods and definitions underwent yet another change. Emphasis shifted from the intra-psychic focus to the educational function of supervision.[72] This transition was influenced by the progress in educational theory and analyses of organizational structures. Towle writes,

> We must be clear about the essential difference between re-educational help in social work education and therapy.
> A teaching situation differs from a psychotherapeutic session, in its heavy reliance upon the student's capacity

to experience change in feeling and thereby change in thinking through an intellectual approach. In professional education, both in classroom and in field work, the initial approach or attack is upon the intellect.[73]

This does not mean that the trainee's feelings, especially those engendered by interaction with the client and with the supervisor, are not taken into consideration. Towle herself points out that

> Supervision is a process in the conduct of which the supervisor has three functions—administration, teaching and helping. This mid-position has significance in the performance of each of these functions, and notably in helping.[74]

These three elements of supervision are interrelated. The student or new social worker needs help because of the inevitable strains created by the process of learning, by his confrontation with the actual demands of practice (which include his encounter with the client, the agency, and the supervisor), and by the special nature of the profession. In turn, the learning process is facilitated by a positive–supportive relationship between supervisor and supervisee. The manifest goal of the educational process is to help the practitioner become more competent and autonomous, to achieve effective integration of knowledge, so as to be capable of rendering better service to clients.

In reality, the administrative and teaching functions of the supervisor often conflict. When we allude to the supervisor as representing the agency's policy and regulations and as holding the supervisee accountable for his performance, and so forth, we basically refer to the authority vested in a higher rank within the organization. When we refer to the teaching function of the supervisor, we mean the transmission of knowledge from the experienced to the inexperienced, the teaching of skills, positive identification, and the like—in short, something similar to professional authority. The immanent incongruity of these two types of authority has been recognized in social work literature: as Scherz says,

"Administrative leadership requires the use of one kind of authority; casework practice requires another."[75]

The debate about the effectiveness and advisability of this combination of administrative authority and the teaching–helping functions in one role has been going on in social work literature for more than a decade. One of the main arguments is that the administrative authority held and exercised by the supervisor interferes with the learning process of the supervisee. This argument derives from the conception that teaching is really the primary task of the supervisor, whereas his administrative duties are considered less important and somewhat distasteful. Scherz critically observes,

> As a teacher, the supervisor has been in conflict about discharging various administrative duties, including evaluation of workers, since these seem to intrude like a foreign body into the benign teacher–learner relationship.[76]

However, from an opposite point of view, which has been somewhat neglected, the question may be raised as to whether the personal–expressive relationships of teacher–learner do not infringe upon the maintenance of bureaucratic controls by the supervisor. By now, it is an accepted proposition in sociology that roles in groups tend to differentiate along an axis of control–support, or authority–friendliness, and—in more general terms—along the instrumental–expressive axis.[77] If an individual has authority over another, the relationship between them will be characterized by restraint, respect, and the reduction of their interaction to the necessary minimum to carry out the common task in which they are engaged. On the other hand, the relationship between equals is characterized by intimacy, mutual liking, and the increase of interaction beyond that required for task performance.[78]

The supervisory role as it has been traditionally defined in social work includes both the nurtural and the demanding functions.[79] This introduces ambiguities into the relationship and creates problems of orientation for both the supervisor and the supervisee. The supervisor cannot exercise authority and give psychological support at the same time; the supervisee cannot acknowledge his duty to obey the supervisor and at the same time feel at ease in his company.[80] Miller has attacked the idyllic picture which is usually presented of supervisor–supervisee relationships:

> it would help a great deal to give up the sentimental sham that the worker–supervisor relationship exists between equals, or between professional colleagues who happen to have different functions and responsibilities. This kind of well-meaning distortion obscures the power and authority inherent in the supervisory functions.[81]

The potential sources of strain in the supervisor–worker relationship become clearer when we consider the main techniques of supervision: reviewing of records written by the worker, private conferences with him, and evaluation of his performance. These various techniques are interconnected: the weekly conference is based upon records of interviews with clients submitted by the practitioner; evaluation, in turn, is based upon both reviewing of records and case discussions.

Ideally, evaluation is an ongoing process which is to some degree a joint enterprise of supervisor and supervisee (student or practitioner), and which is periodically summarized in writing by the supervisor and submitted to either school or agency. The worker's skills and competence in performing his role are appraised—e.g., his capacity to establish and sustain helpful relationships with clients; his understanding and use of social work methods; the degree to which he has developed self-awareness and professional attitudes, and so forth. In addition, the worker's administrative abilities may be evaluated, but this is of only secondary importance, as evaluation is primarily regarded as an educational technique. Nevertheless, insofar as evaluation serves as a basis for promotion and salary changes (or for graduation in the case of students), the immanent conflict in the task is obvious. It is not easy to draw clear boundaries between the two tasks involved in evaluation. Austin notes that supervisors have tended to confuse the evaluation process and report by introducing educational concerns. An educational appraisal actually is quite a different matter from evaluation which carries a rating responsibility and implications for promotion or dismissal. There is ample experience to demonstrate that no matter how able the supervisor is in his teaching role, mixed feelings are aroused which affect the learning situation of the supervisee when the teacher is also the sole evaluator.[82]

The various supervisory techniques outlined above have a basic common feature: they attempt to supervise a set of relationships and activities which are not directly observable. Merton points out that the effective exercise of control requires superiors to be in a position to observe actual performance of subordinates so as to gain knowledge of their prevailing norms.[83] However, in some structures—for example, the social agency—individuals in positions of authority, accountable for their subordinates' behavior and having the authority to mold it, are unable to observe the relevant activities. In cases like this, in which visibility is restricted by the practitioner's obligation to his clients, the supervisor has to rely chiefly on the worker's attitudinal conformity.[84]

Professions, in general, try to assure conformity on the part of their members by careful screening of new recruits and by a prolonged training process in which the proper attitudes and norms are inculcated. Another method of controlling invisible performance is by evaluating its product and sanctioning the individual according to the proximity of the product to the expected norm. This, of course, creates the need for clear criteria of evaluation, which are very difficult to establish in the human relations professions. Ohlin describes the problem thus:

> An extreme situation requiring a high degree of ideological conformity would exist if there were no clear criteria for evaluating successful work and the central activities of the job could not be observed or watched. There is no other profession which approximates this condition more closely than social work itself.[85]

But, even if these conditions were present in social work—that is, strong value commitment of practitioners and definite criteria of evaluation—some kind of control of ongoing activities would still be necessary, because the emphasis, particularly in casework, is not only on results but also on the ways by which they can and should be attained.

The most original and distinctive feature of the supervisory methods of social casework is the attempt to re-enact the unobservable interaction between worker and client, and thus to allow the supervisor to evaluate and regulate the worker's performance. This creates many problems, the most obvious of which is the reliability of the worker's recording. The interaction with the client is sometimes strained, and the practitioner may be emotionally involved no matter how much self-awareness he has gained; further, reports to the supervisor serve as the basis of evaluation and the worker may try, therefore, to conceal his problems or failures.

In view of the numerous problems created by the prevailing supervisory practice in social work, some of which have been described, it is understandable that the system has been strongly criticized by members of the profession. Almost every book or paper written in the past two decades that deals with social work supervision points out its dysfunctions and puts forward some suggestion for change and modification. Supervision is criticized on many grounds. It is claimed, for example, that emphasis on supervision impedes full acceptance of social work as a profession. Other professionals—physicians, psychiatrists, scientists, lawyers—are not subjected to persistent, routine review; they conduct their work independently, and society accords higher status to autonomous practitioners. Another argument is that supervision is too costly—that the time and money spent for it could be used for more important purposes. Referring to the Hill and Ormsby cost study in the Family Service of Philadelphia, Wilensky and Lebeaux show that a total of 52 per cent of all expenditures for casework services was spent on "maintaining communication" within the bureaucratic structure. This includes: case recording (32.15 per cent); supervisory conferences (13.17 per cent); and case consultations (5.77 per cent). Only 42 per cent was spent for direct contact with clients.[86] Additional problems of supervision have been pointed out, e.g., the "cultural lag" between the older, experienced supervisor and the younger, recently trained supervisee[87] and the inadequacy of supervisory practice initially developed in casework for other fields of social work, i.e., group work and community organization.[88]

The most crucial problems, however (with which much of the criticism of supervision is concerned), are those of role definition and role relationships of supervisor and worker. Thus, Austin summarized the negative consequences of the existing supervisory system in four points:

1. The assimilation of knowledge and the internalization of standards by the worker are weakened by an emphasis on extreme controls.
2. The caseworker's professional contacts within the agency are too limited.
3. The assignment of two major functions—teaching and administration—tends toward a concentration of power in one person.
4. The dual function leads to an overly complex assignment for the supervisor.[89]

Is the supervisor an administrator or a teacher? What kind of role conflict does the combination of these two functions in one role create for the supervisor? To what degree is the experienced worker independent? Is he subjected to the supervisor's bureaucratic control, or to his professional authority as well? All these are questions inherent in the debate about supervision that was launched by Babcock's article in 1953, in which the value of continuous supervision for the experienced caseworker was questioned.[90] Analyzing the phenomenon of "work inhibition" among social workers, she points to traditional supervision as one of its sources:

> In many agencies, the social worker never becomes an independent person within the framework of agency administration. He must either remain a caseworker under

supervision or try to become a supervisor. The opportunity to become an independent professional person within the agency, one who may or may not ask for consultation with the administration director or with the casework consultant as he feels he needs it, is rare. The gratification that comes from taking total responsibility for a task at hand is usually not attainable.[91]

The long-term goals of supervision, like those of any socialization process, are to develop the skills of the inexperienced worker, deepen his knowledge and understanding, and lead him, finally, to assume full responsibility as an independent professional. If, however, the supervisee is not allowed, by continuous close supervision, to grow up, the result will be that of general dissatisfaction with his work. Wax goes so far as to state,

> Agency executives have but one course. If the profession wants to keep its professionals, it must treat them as professionals. Lifelong supervision is a vestige of the sub-professional past. Social workers do come of age. They can be proud of their training and confident of their skill. They must be accorded the respect, responsibility, and autonomy to which the professional is entitled.[92]

Imposed supervision, and special types of supervision, also affect the worker's relationships with different role-partners, i.e., his supervisor, his clients, and his colleagues.[93] If the net balance of consequences of supervision for the practitioner's role-performance is negative, then the very purpose of supervision, which is to render better service to clients, is not achieved.

Still, it is reasonable to ask: Why is supervision in social work so much debated and so criticized? After all, even in the most respected of professions, medicine, the intern is supervised by the resident, and the resident by the staff physician, and so on. The major factors involved in the resistance to and dissatisfaction with supervision in social work are precisely those attributes which distinguish it from, and are not shared by, supervision in other professions. The first is a quantitative element and pertains to the duration of supervision. There is as yet no formal time limit to the process, and the supervisor–trainee relationship carries over into the supervisor–practitioner relationship. This is not the case in other professions, in which, once the independence of the fully trained member is established, he may consult more experienced colleagues, if he feels it necessary, but is not obligated to report to them at fixed intervals and in a prescribed manner. The second factor characteristic of social work supervision, and one which contributes to the growing opposition to it, is a qualitative one. It has been mentioned before that the relationship between supervisor and supervisee is perceived as *personal* with expressive overtones. Whereas the student physician is guided and controlled by different specialists according to the problem at hand, the social work trainee has an individualized–diffuse relationship with only one supervisor. The relationship is diffuse in so far as the student's personal problems are probed and discussed—his feelings, conflicts, projections, and the like. Again, this kind of psychotherapeutic technique is not part of supervision in medicine or in other professions and is applied, if at all, only in extraordinary cases.[94] The special character of supervision in social work derives from the nature of the profession itself: because the social worker has to deal with personal and psychological problems of the client, he must first be aware of and understand his own motivations and emotions. The prolonged and total nature of supervision is somewhat reminiscent of the silver cord by which a possessive mother ties the child to herself. Discussions of the problem in the professional literature, therefore, use such terms as "maturity," "growing up," "emancipation," and "independence." The third attribute that differentiates social work supervision from professional control is the administrative function of the social work supervisor. An integral part of his role is to see to it that the worker adheres to the regulations prescribed by the community and the organization, which are sometimes incompatible with professional ethics or the humanistic enthusiasm of the young practitioner. In contrast, an experienced physician, for example, when controlling the work of an inexperienced doctor, represents the profession or a specialty within it, but not the administrative structure.

The modifications suggested in the traditional supervisory system are related to the foregoing points of criticism. The major changes proposed are "termination" and "separation." Termination signifies the assumption of autonomy by the practitioner after a stipulated number of years of supervised work, the proposals in this respect ranging from two to seven years of "internship," or "as best designed to meet the worker's developmental needs."[95] The second recommendation is to differentiate the administrative from the teaching function, now combined in the supervisor's role. These two recommended changes are overlapping in certain aspects because it is the educational function of the supervisor which most social workers propose to limit, and not his administrative tasks. Alternative plans and experiments have been carried out, such as supervision of experienced workers by a group of peers,[96] and the establishment of administrative supervision with professional consultation available at the worker's request.[97] Thus, it is hoped to avoid the dysfunctions of traditional supervision for the professional role:

> When the responsibility for continued growth is transferred to the worker himself, we can expect that his own motivation, creativity, and interests, supplemented by available consultation, group meetings and opportunities for leadership within and outside the agency, will ensure his continued professional development.[98]

These are some of the theoretical and practical arguments for modifying the traditional supervisory pattern as they appear in the professional literature of social work.

In addition, the perceptions and attitudes toward supervision of the rank and file students and workers should be considered. Data on these problems can be obtained only by systematic research.[99] Interest and research in the subject have been growing constantly and have shown the sphere of orientations to supervision to be very varied—different

attitudes are held by different groups of social workers to
different types of supervision. Thus, for example, we would
like to advance the hypothesis that the attitudes of social work
students and the attitudes of social workers to organizational
controls (administrative regulations) and to personal control
(supervisory procedures) will progress in opposite directions
in the course of time. This seems theoretically plausible and
is also indicated by the data. The social work student, as he
advances through his years of training, becomes less critical
of his supervisor but usually manifests strong resistance to the
agency's rules and constraints. On the other hand, the experienced social worker tends to become less hostile to
organizational demands and regulations; at the same time,
however, as he advances in years of practice, he is likely to
grow more resistant to close personal supervision. The first
part of the hypothesis, i.e., the student's decreasing criticism
of supervision in subsequent years of training, is supported by
the study by Rose, in which he found that intensity of this
criticism is in part a function of the phase of learning in which
the student is involved.[100] In regard to the worker's attitude
to bureaucratic regulations, Blau found, in a study of a public
welfare agency, that the more experienced workers were
more adjusted to the organizational procedures and incorporated the official limitations in their thinking, whereas the
new workers felt that these rules interfered with the implementation of the "service ideal".[101] These and other studies
may guide social workers in planning changes in the existing
pattern of supervision, help them to decide when to terminate
which type of supervision and to determine what other
mechanisms of control can be employed more effectively.

Scott, in his study of a public welfare agency, examined
the influence of the degree of professionalism of both supervisor and supervisee on the worker's attitude to supervision.[102]
He found that when asked in general to evaluate the practice
of persistent routine supervision, half the respondents said
that it was a "good arrangement," the other half stated that it
had both "advantages and disadvantages," but none felt that
it was "not a good arrangement." The degree of acceptance

of the supervisory system in the agency was found to vary with the professional orientation of both workers and supervisors: (a) professionally oriented workers with longer formal training and stronger contact with the profession (the "cosmopolitans," in Gouldner's terminology), were more critical of the system than non-professionally oriented workers; and (b) workers supervised by professionally oriented supervisors were less critical of the system than workers serving under less professionally oriented supervisors.

A National Association of Social Workers study of the problem reveals that social workers react differently to the various functions of supervision.[103] Most social workers believe that supervision should change, according to the needs and progress of the supervisee, from a phase of direction and teaching to one of more permissive consultation; evaluation was seen as a legitimate part of the supervisor's role; and none of the respondents objected to the supervisor's administrative authority and responsibility. These findings support the demand to limit the teaching role of supervision that was raised in the literature. They indicate that lack of autonomy in the performance of the professional core functions, rather than the exercise of bureaucratic authority by the supervisor, creates strains in the supervisor–supervisee relationship. Moreover, it seems that trained social workers are willing to concede administrative authority to their supervisors as part of the limitations imposed by the organizational framework; however, they resent and resist the teaching function of the supervisor, which is perceived as encroaching upon their professional judgment, responsibility, and competence.

At the same time, we may assume that social workers would accept some degree of control of their professional conduct provided it were basically defined and perceived as professional, e.g., the authority of the chief surgeon over his assistants. There are no available data to bear out this assumption in respect to social workers, but some support can be found in the study conducted by Goss of a hierarchically-organized group of physicians.[104] She found that the hierarchical structure did not conflict with the individual professional autonomy, as expected, for the professional norms of the group did not require autonomy in every sphere of activity—

> but only that he will be free to make his own decisions in professional matters as opposed to administrative concerns. Nor even in the professional sphere, did the norms rule out the possibility of supervision; so long as supervision came from a physician and took the form of advice, it was within normatively acceptable bounds for physicians. Thus one of the organizational mechanisms for reconciling hierarchical supervision of professional activity with maintenance of individual authority in that sphere would appear to be the conception of supervision as a *formal advisory or consultation relationship*.[105] [Italics in text.]

In conclusion, the autonomy of professionals within a bureaucratic framework is threatened only insofar as the organizational structure interferes either with the development and application of professional knowledge or with the service orientation, i.e., with the professional commitment to place the client's interests above all others. If one or the other of these core qualities is impaired by organizational rules and procedures, the balance and consistency between them is disrupted, and in this lies the real danger of bureaucratization which employed professionals may face. Semi-professionals are in this respect in a disadvantageous position relative to full-fledged professionals who possess esoteric knowledge and skills, high prestige in society, and the powerful backing of their professional associations.

All this is generally known, yet further empirical research should provide us with more accurate data concerning the attitudes of social workers toward the diverse functions of different types of control and the consequences for the profession–organization relationship and cooperation. Such knowledge may also suggest various ways in which the existing structure and functions of roles within social welfare agencies could be differentiated and reconstructed.

Notes

1. See for example, Alexander M. Carr-Saunders and P. A. Wilson, *The Professions* (Oxford: Clarendon, 1933), Part III; Everett C. Hughes, *Men and their Work* (New York: Free Press, 1958), Chapters X and XI; Harold L. Wilensky, "The Professionalization of Everyone?" in *American Journal of Sociology*, 70 (September, 1960), 33–50; William J. Goode, "Encroachment, Charlatanism, and the Emerging Professions: Psychology, Sociology and Medicine," in *American Sociological Review*, 25 (December, 1960), 902–14; Ernest Greenwood, "Attributes of a Profession," in *Social Work*, 2 (July, 1957), 45–55; Howard S. Becker, "The Nature of a Profession," in *The Sixty-first Yearbook of the National Society for the Study of Education*, ed. Nelson B. Henry (Chicago: U. of Chicago, 1962), Part II. For studies on specific aspects of professionalization and of different professions see Kenneth S. Lynn and the Editors of Daedalus (eds.), *The Professions in America* (Boston: Beacon, 1967); Howard M. Vollmer and Donald L. Mills (eds.) *Professionalization* (Englewood Cliffs, N.J.: Prentice-Hall, 1966).

2. See, for example, Wilensky, *op. cit.*; Alfred Kadushin, "The Knowledge Base of Social Work," in *Issues in American Social Work*, ed. Alfred J. Kahn (New York: Columbia U. P., 1959), pp. 39–79; and Alfred J. Kahn, "The Nature of Social Work Knowledge," in *New Directions in Social Work*, ed. Cora Kasius (New York: Harper, 1954), pp. 194–214.

3. Alexander M. Carr-Saunders, "Metropolitan Conditions and Traditional Professional Relationships," in *The Metropolis in Modern Life*, ed. Robert M. Fisher (Garden City, N.Y.: Doubleday, 1955), pp. 279–87.

4. Greenwood, *op. cit.*, p. 45.

5. Abraham Flexner, "Is Social Work a Profession?" in *Proceedings of the National Conference of Charities and Corrections* (Chicago, 1915), pp. 576–90.

6. For discussions dealing with social work's position as a profession, see, for example, Werner W. Boehm, "The Nature of Social Work," in *Social Work*, 3 (April, 1958), 10–18, and "Relationship of Social Work to Other Professions," in *Encyclopedia of Social Work*, ed. Harry L. Lurie (New York: National Association of Social Workers,

1965), pp. 640–48; John C. Kidneigh, "Social Work as a Profession," in *Social Work Yearbook,* ed. Russell H. Kurtz (New York: National Association of Social Workers, 1960), pp. 563–72; Nathan E. Cohen, "Social Work as a Profession," in *Social Work Yearbook* (1957), pp. 553–62.

7. Greenwood, *op. cit.,* p. 54.

8. Carr-Saunders, "Metropolitan Conditions," p. 283.

9. See, for example, Goode, *op. cit.*

10. Boehm, "Relationship of Social Work," p. 644.

11. See the list of components of Greenwood's model.

12. Charles Dollard, Proceedings of the First Annual Trustees Reception of the New York School of Social Work, *Bulletin of the New York School of Social Work* (Columbia University, September, 1952), p. 4.

13. *Deprofessionalization* is used here in a similar manner to Eisenstadt's *debureaucratization*; both terms signify a process that leads in the opposite direction of the ideal type of professionalization and bureaucratization, respectively. See S. N. Eisenstadt, "Bureaucracy, Bureaucratization, and Debureaucratization," in *Administrative Science Quarterly,* 4 (1959), 302–20; and Elihu Katz and S. N. Eisenstadt, "Some Sociological Observations on the Response of Israeli Organizations to New Immigrants," in *Administrative Science Quarterly,* 5 (1960), 113–33.

14. Cohen, *op. cit.,* p. 559.

15. This is related to the basic duality in the values and goals of social work, with which we shall deal in the section on the dilemma in social work.

16. Carr-Saunders, "Metropolitan Conditions, . . . " p. 283.

17. Cohen, *op. cit.,* p. 559. An analysis of the special character of the social worker–client relationships can be found, for example, in Mary J. McCormick, "Professional Responsibility and the Professional Image," *Social Casework,* 47 (December, 1966), 635–41.

18. Herbert Bisno, "How Social Will Social Work Be?," *Social Work,* 1 (April, 1956), 17.

19. *Ibid.*, p. 18.

20. This problem is noted in many discussions about the nature of the profession: see Greenwood, *op. cit.*; Alvin L. Schorr, "The Retreat to the Technician," in *Social Work*, 4 (January, 1959), 29–33; and Harry L. Lurie, "The Responsibilities of a Socially Oriented Profession," in *New Directions in Social Work*, pp. 31–53.

21. Wilensky, *op. cit.*, p. 150.

22. Talcott Parsons, "The Professions and Social Structure," in *Essays in Sociological Theory* (New York: Free Press, 1957), pp. 34–49.

23. Referring to professionals in bureaucracies, Scott pointed out four areas of role-conflict:

    1. The professional's resistance to bureaucratic rules.

    2. The professional's rejection of bureaucratic standards.

    3. The professional's resistance to bureaucratic supervision.

    4. The professional's conditional loyalty to the bureaucracy.

W. Richard Scott, "Professionals in Bureaucracies—Areas of Conflict," in *Professionalization,* ed. Vollmer and Mills, p. 265.

24. Robert K. Merton, "Role of the Intellectual in Public Bureaucracy," in *Social Theory and Social Structure* (New York: Free Press, 1957), pp. 207–24; Joseph Ben-David, "The Professional Role of the Physician in Bureaucratized Medicine: A Study in Role Conflict," in *Human Relations*, 11 (1958), 255–74; William J. Goode, "Community within a Community: The Professions," in *American Sociological Review*, 22 (1957), 194–200; Alvin W. Gouldner "Cosmopolitans and Locals," in *Administrative Science Quarterly*, 2 (1957–58), 281–306, 444–80; Peter M. Blau and W. Richard Scott, *Formal Organizations: A Comparative Approach* (London: Routledge and Kegan Paul, 1963), pp. 60–74; William Kornhauser, *Scientists in Industry: Conflict and Accommodation* (Berkeley: U. of California Press, 1962); Fred H. Goldner and R. R. Ritti, "Professionalization as Career Immobility," in *American Journal of Sociology*, 72 (March, 1967), 489–502; Peter M. Blau, Wolf V. Heydebrand, and Robert E. Stauffer, "The Structure of Small Bureaucracies," in *American Sociological Review*, 31 (April, 1966), 179–91.

25. See Parson's discussions of the differences between bureaucratic and professional authority in Max Weber, *The Theory of Social and*

Economic Organization, trans. A. M. Henderson and Talcott Parsons, ed. Talcott Parsons (New York: Oxford U. P., 1947), "Introduction," note 4, pp. 58–60.

26. Edward Gross, "When Occupations Meet: Professions in Trouble," in *Hospital Administration,* 12 (Summer, 1967), 40–59.

27. Amitai Etzioni discusses the development and form that charismatic elements assume in a variety of organizational positions in *A Comparative Analysis of Complex Organizations* (New York: Free Press, 1961), pp. 201–9; see also, Robert L. Peabody, *Organizational Authority* (New York: Atherton Press, 1964), pp. 117–31.

28. This problem is analysed by Parsons in reference to the role of physician, in Talcott Parsons, *The Social System* (New York: Free Press, 1951), pp. 447–54.

29. See W. Richard Scott, "Reaction to Supervision in a Heteronomous Professional Organization," in *Administrative Science Quarterly,* 10 (June, 1965), 65–81. The term *heteronomy* is borrowed from Weber (*op. cit.,* p. 148): "A corporate group may be either autonomous or heteronomous, . . . Autonomy means that the order governing the group has been established by its own members on their own authority, . . . In the case of heteronomy, it has been imposed by an outside agency."

30. See Chapter 1, p. 1.

31. Voluntary registration exists at present in the State of California. The National Association of Social Workers recently proposed a national voluntary registration plan as a step toward legal regulation.

32. See Chapter 5, p. 196.

33. Harold L. Wilensky and Charles N. Lebeaux, *Industrial Society and Social Welfare* (New York: Free Press, 1965 [paperback]), p. 323.

34. *Social Workers in 1950* (New York: American Association of Social Workers, 1952).

35. For a detailed analysis of the various factors responsible for the relatively low status of the profession see Alfred Kadushin, "Prestige of Social Work—Facts and Factors," in *Social Work,* 3 (April, 1958), 37–43.

36. These two characteristics, in their extreme form, conflict with the aforementioned principles of specifity and universalism.

37. "Working Definition of Social Work Practice," in *Social Work*, 3 (April, 1958), 2–6.

38. *Ibid.*, p. 3.

39. Georg Simmel, "Conflict," trans. Kurt H. Wolff, in *Conflict and the Web of Group Affiliations* (New York: Free Press, 1955), pp. 13–123; and Lewis Coser, *The Functions of Social Conflict* (New York: Free Press, 1956).

40. Gross, *op. cit.*, p. 50.

41. Kornhauser, *op. cit.*, p. 197.

42. Robert K. Merton, *Social Theory and Social Structure*, pp. 195–206.

43. Wilensky and Lebeaux, *op. cit.*, p. 243.

44. These observations are based on a study carried out by the author in Israel in 1964–65.

45. "I am just following orders" is the typical justification of the bureaucrat faced with an over-demanding or complaining client. Ideally, the professional's ultimate legitimation of his actions is that he is doing the thing that, to the best of his knowledge, will best serve the client's needs.

46. Henry J. Meyer, "Professionalization and Social Work", in *Issues in American Social Work*, ed. Alfred J. Kahn, pp. 319–40.

47. Wilensky and Lebeaux, *op. cit.*, p. 325.

48. See the discussion of this problem in the first part of this paper.

49. The *New York Times*, May 28, 1967.

50. A classic example in this respect is the development of medicine during the past two centuries. The process of "segmentation" in the medical profession is described in Rue Bucher and Anselm Strauss, "Professions in Process," in *American Journal of Sociology*, 66 (January, 1961), 325–34; see also, Abraham Zlozower, *Career Opportunities and the Growth of Scientific Discovery in 19th Century Germany* (Jerusalem: Hebrew University, 1966).

51. Wilensky and Lebeaux, *op. cit.*, p. 330.

52. See D. G. French, *Statistics on Social Work Education 1957* (New York: Council on Social Work Education, 1957), p. 16; more time is devoted to the subject of human growth and development in the curriculum of social work schools than to the history of social reforms and the structure of welfare services; and most students choose casework as their specialization.

53. Kadushin, in *Issues in American Social Work*, p. 56.

54. Wilensky and Lebeaux, *op. cit.*, pp. 329–30.

55. Charlotte Towle, *Common Human Needs* (New York: National Association of Social Workers, 1965 [rev. ed.])

56. Jane K. Thompson and Donald P. Riley, "Use of Professionals in Public Welfare: A Dilemma and a Proposal," in *Social Work*, 11 (January, 1966), 23–24.

57. The *New York Times*, June 25, 1967, article by D. Stetson, "Welfare Workers, They Say They Can't Do Their Job."

58. This term was conceived by Merton in Robert K. Merton, "The Role-Set: Problems in Sociological Theory," in *British Journal of Sociology*, 8 (1957), 106–20.

59. This three-fold typology of power was formulated by Amitai Etzioni in *A Comparative Analysis of Complex Organizations*, pp. 3–22, and *Modern Organizations* (New Jersey: Prentice-Hall, 1964), pp. 58–67. Parsons introduced a similar typology of the ways by which compliance can be achieved: (a) "inducement" (situational–positive), the typical means employed in this case is "money"; (b) "deterrence" (situational–negative), by means of power; (c) "persuasion" (intentional–positive), by means of "influence"; and (d) "activation of commitments" (intentional–negative), by means of "general commitments"; see Talcott Parsons, "On the Concept of Influence," in *Public Opinion Quarterly*, 27 (1963), 37–62.

60. Davis McEntrie and Joanne Haworth, "The Two Functions of Public Welfare: Income Maintenance and Social Services," in *Social Work*, 12 (January, 1967), 22–30.

61. The consequences of control by physical means is an important issue in studies of custodial institutions such as prisons, correctional agencies, and mental hospitals. See, for example, Charles R. Tittle

and Drollene P. Tittle, "Structural Handicaps to Therapeutic Participation: A Case Study," in *Social Problems,* 13 (Summer, 1965), 75–82.

62. Our discussion does not imply that there are no professional and moral problems involved in the use of normative power. Much has been said and written about the imposing of middle-class values on lower-class clients by teachers, social workers, and others. This and related problems of persuasion will be discussed in another context.

63. The resources that the social worker has at his disposal in the situation are numerous and include, besides decision on eligibility for welfare payments, institutionalization of children, hospitalization, referral to other service organizations, and so forth.

64. In this study the researcher was actually present at the worker–client interview. An intensive study of the modes of "bargaining" between officials and clients in service organizations in Israel has been conducted by Katz: see Elihu Katz and Brenda Danet, "Petitions and Persuasive Appeals: A Study of Official–Client Relations," in *American Sociological Review,* 31 (December, 1966), 811–21.

65. Mary E. Burns, "What's Wrong with Public Welfare?" in *Social Service Review,* 30 (June, 1962), 116.

66. Gross, *op. cit.,* p. 47.

67. Boehm, *op. cit., Encyclopedia of Social Work,* p. 644.

68. The distinction between internal and external resources is independent of the degree of functional importance or scarcity of resources. However, it is worth noting that in contrast to material goods, the fund of knowledge does not diminish in the process of its application.

69. See, for example, Leonard Reissman, "A Study of Role Conceptions in Bureaucracy," in *Social Forces,* 27 (1949), 305–10; Gouldner, *op. cit.*; and Goode, "Community within a Community."

70. See Charlotte Towle, *The Learner in Education for the Profession* (Chicago: U. of Chicago, 1954); Lucille N. Austin ,"An Evaluation of Supervision," in *Social Casework,* 37 (October, 1952), 375–82, and, "The Changing Role of the Supervisor," in *Smith College Studies in Social Work,* 31 (June, 1961), 179–95; Margaret Williamson, *Supervision, Principles and Methods* (New York: Woman's Press, 1950); Robert D. Vinter, "The Social Structure of Service," in

Issues in American Social Work, pp. 242–69; Mary E. Burns, "Supervision in Social Work," in *Encyclopedia of Social Work* (1965), pp. 785–90.

71. It should be mentioned that supervision originally developed in the field of casework, and although it was later taken over by group work and community organization, it never gained the same importance in these specialities as it did in casework. Strong criticism is directed by group workers against the adoption of supervisory methods used in casework because of the different contents and form of group work services. See Irving Miller, "Distinctive Characteristics of Supervision in Group Work," in *Social Work,* 5 (January, 1960), 69–76.

72. Burns, *op. cit.*

73. Charlotte Towle, "The Place of Help in Supervision," in *Social Service Review,* 37 (December, 1963), 405.

74. *Ibid.,* p. 403.

75. Frances M. Scherz, "A Concept of Supervision Based on Definitions of Job Responsibility," in *Social Casework,* 39 (October, 1958), 442.

76. *Ibid.,* p. 437.

77. See, for example, Robert F. Bales, *Interaction Process Analysis* (Cambridge, Mass.: Addison-Wesley, 1950), pp. 153–54; Talcott Parsons and Robert F. Bales, *Family, Socialization and Interaction Process* (New York: Free Press, 1955), pp. 259–306.

78. This analysis is based on Homans' hypotheses concerning the interrelationships among activity, sentiment, and interaction. If one of the interacting parties has authority over the other, i.e. he gives orders to which the other defers, then ". . . the more frequently one of the two originates interaction for the other, the stronger will be the latter's sentiment of respect (or hostility) toward him, and the more nearly will the frequency of interaction be kept to the amount characteristic of the external system." G. H. Homans, *The Human Group* (London: Routledge and Kegan Paul, 1962), p. 247.

79. These two functions tend to be assigned to two different positions: that of "High Status Authority" and that of "High Status Friend." See Morris Freilich, "The Natural Triad in Kinship and

Complex Systems," in *American Sociological Review,* 29 (August, 1964), 529–39.

80. Relatively little attention has been focused in social work writings on the problems created for the supervisor himself by the traditional definition of his role. In addition to the problem of having to maneuver bureaucratic authority and a more colleagual–advisory relationship with the supervisee, the supervisor is subject to orders and pressures from his superiors, and may in turn take a more or less autonomous stand toward them.

81. Miller, *op. cit.,* p. 76.

82. Lucille N. Austin, "Supervision in Social Work," in *Social Work Yearbook* (1960), p. 584.

83. Merton, *Social Theory and Social Structure,* pp. 336–57.

84. See Rose Laub Coser, "Insulation from Observability and Types of Social Conformity," in *American Sociological Review,* 26 (February, 1961), 28–39.

85. Lloyd, E. Ohlin, "Conformity in American Society Today," in *Social Work,* 3 (April, 1958), 58–66. Another problem associated with such invisible relationships is the transmission of the knowledge and experience gained in them to others; as Freud once told his students, ". . . in the strictest sense of the word, it is only by hearsay that you will get to know psychoanalysis." (Sigmund Freud, *The Complete Introductory Lectures on Psychoanalysis,* trans. and ed. J. Strachey [New York: W. W. Norton, 1966], p. 18.)

86. Wilensky and Lebeaux, *op. cit.,* pp. 241–42.

87. Burns, *op. cit.*

88. Miller, *op. cit.,* and Arthur L. Leader, "New Directions in Supervision," in *Social Casework,* 38 (November, 1957), 462–68.

89. Austin, "An Evaluation of Supervision"; also Scherz, *op. cit.*

90. Charlotte Babcock, "Social Work as Work," in *Social Casework,* 34 (December, 1953), 415–22. Dr. Babcock, a psychiatrist, based her analysis on her experience with 60 social workers as patients in consultive and therapeutic interviews.

91. *Ibid.,* p. 421.

92. John Wax, "Time Limited Supervision," in *Social Work,* 8 (July, 1963), 43.

93. The repercussions of authoritarian supervision on the worker's orientation to the client and on the worker's performance are examined in Blau and Scott, *op. cit.,* pp. 150–59.

94. Although some writers insist that the supervisor's goals are educational, a great part of the supervisory process, especially the conference with the worker, have a therapeutic character.

95. See Ruth E. Lindenberg, "Changing Traditional Patterns of Supervision," in *Social Work,* 2 (April, 1957), 45; Esther Schour, "Helping Social Workers Handle Work Stresses," in *Social Casework,* 34 (December, 1953), 423–28; Reva Fine, "Some Theoretical Considerations Basic to Supervisory Technique," in *Social Work,* 1 (January, 1956), 67–71; Wax, *op. cit.*; and Leader, *op. cit.*

96. Ruth Fizdale, "Peer Group Supervision," in *Social Casework,* 39 (October, 1958), 443–50.

97. The separation of teaching and administrative functions in social work in the U.S. Army was examined by Donald A. Devis, "Teaching and Administrative Functions in Supervision," in *Social Work,* 10 (April, 1965), 83–89.

98. Leader, *op. cit.,* p. 468.

99. See, for example, Scott, "Reactions to Supervision . . ."; Sheldon D. Rose, "Students View Their Supervision: A Scale Analysis," in *Social Work,* 10 (April, 1965), 90–96; and "Opinions on Supervision: A Chapter Study," by the Western New York Chapter, National Association of Social Workers Committee on Social Work Practice, in *Social Work,* 3 (January, 1958), 18–25.

100. Rose, *op. cit.*

101. Peter M. Blau, "Orientations Toward Clients in a Public Welfare Agency", *Administrative Science Quarterly,* 5 (1960), pp. 341–61.

102. Scott, "Reactions to Supervision. . . ."

103. "Opinions on Supervision . . . ," NASW Committee on Social Work Practice.

104. Mary E. W. Goss, "Influence and Authority among Physicians in an Out-Patient Clinic," in *American Sociological Review,* 26 (February, 1961), 39–50.

105. *Ibid.,* pp. 49–50.

CHAPTER FIVE

Women and Bureaucracy in the Semi-Professions* ▲

Richard L. Simpson ·

UNIVERSITY OF NORTH CAROLINA AT CHAPEL HILL

Ida Harper Simpson

DUKE UNIVERSITY

SEMI-PROFESSIONAL ORGANIZATIONS ARE more bureaucratic than professional ones.[1]† Instead of the control by autonomous groups of colleagues which one finds in the law firm or the university, a predominantly bureaucratic control pattern is evident in

* The original data on teachers are from research performed pursuant to a contract with the United States Office of Education, Department of Health, Education, and Welfare. The Institute for Research in Social Science, University of North Carolina (Chapel Hill) administered the project and made its facilities available. Many people participated in this research; special thanks are due to Myra Bass, Angell G. Beza, Joy R. Gold, Charles C. Gordon, Colin K. Loftin, Donald K. McBride, and Charles R. Wingrove. Ed McCranie tabulated the findings on our teacher sample, as a National Science Foundation undergraduate research participant at the University of North Carolina (Chapel Hill). In writing this chapter we are indebted to Ray Carpenter of the School of Library Science, University of North Carolina (Chapel Hill), and Herbert A. Carl of the Library Services Branch, United States Office of Education, for bibliographic suggestions, and to Amitai Etzioni, Ann C. Maney, and Daniel A. Plummer for valuable comments on an early draft.

† Notes to this chapter begin on p. 247.

nursing services, schools, libraries, and social work agencies.[2]

We shall argue that one reason for this pattern is the prevalence of women in the semi-professions. In 1960, women constituted 98 per cent of all nurses in the United States, 86 per cent of elementary teachers and of librarians, and 64 per cent of social workers. Only in secondary teaching, among the main semi-professional occupations, were there fewer women —47 per cent—than men.[3] After noting briefly some characteristics which distinguish semi-professional from professional organizations, we shall suggest some forces underlying the differences and try to show how the concentrations of women in the semi-professions strengthen these forces.

In comparison with professional employees, semi-professionals lack autonomy: they are told what to do and how to do it. They are more accountable for their performance: employees must account to their superiors, and the organization (or, in the case of nursing, the semi-professional sector of the organization) must account to an outside authority such as a lay board (or, in the case of nursing, to physicians). Semi-professionals are subject to numerous rules governing not just their central work tasks, but extraneous details of conduct on the job.

In addition, there is in semi-professional organizations a great emphasis on hierarchical rank with duties differentiated by level. Activities in direct pursuit of the organizational goal occur mainly at the lower levels. As one goes up the ladder, administrative tasks tend to replace the semi-professional ones.[4] This situation is in marked contrast to that of professional organizations, where distinguished professors continue their research and where eminent physicians treat patients. One result is that the performance of the primary tasks loses prestige among semi-professionals, while supervision and administrative activities concerned with maintaining and representing the organization become the most rewarded ones. Such a reward system encourages the stress on rules and hierarchical accountability. It reduces dispositions toward employee autonomy.

Forces creating these characteristics of semi-professional

organizations arise from the lesser knowledge and training of semi-professionals than of professionals.[5] Three such forces may be identified as lack of mandate, necessity for bureaucratic control, and weak orientation toward autonomy.

The professional person claims a mandate to define his work and the conduct of others toward it.[6] The public grants him this claim in recognition of his superior knowledge and its relevance to decisions about the work. The public does not grant such a mandate to semi-professionals, because it does not feel that they have any just claim to specialized esoteric knowledge. For this reason boards of lay citizens control public schools in ways in which they do not control public hospitals, and analogous situations prevail with respect to other kinds of semi-professional organizations. Similarly, the administrative heads of semi-professional organizations exercise bureaucratic control over their subordinates; partly because they themselves do not recognize in their subordinates the kind of knowledge that would exempt them from such control, and partly because as administrative heads they are held more strictly accountable to the public than are the heads of professional organizations. Control over the work of semi-professionals is possible because they lack the weapon—knowledge—with which professionals resist control.

Some degree of bureaucratic control over semi-professionals may be necessary as well as possible. Where specialized knowledge is slight, intrinsic commitment to tasks is likely to be low. The kinds of occupational ideologies and colleague reference group orientations that are built upon specialized knowledge and strong work commitment in the professions do not readily develop when these prerequisites are lacking. The colleague reference groups of professionals set standards of work, enforce norms, and reward good performance through the colleague prestige system. A major source of professional sanctions is thus placed outside any particular organization, in the professional community.[7] In the community of professionals it is task performance, not organizational position, that brings the main rewards. Lacking such an extra-organizational orientation, semi-professionals are likely to derive their chief rewards from organizational position, not from performance. With less intrinsic performance motivation than professionals have, they may require more conventional bureaucratic surveillance.

Moreover, semi-professionals do not seem strongly inclined to demand autonomy or resist bureaucratic control. The motive which drives professionals to seek autonomy is strong intrinsic commitment to specialized knowledge and skills, together with confidence in their ability to exercise these skills. Professionals feel that they know the best way to do things and that they therefore should not be told what to do. Semi-professionals are less attached to the principle of autonomy, and less confident of their ability to claim it or use it. Without strong reference group orientations to colleagues, they are less likely than professionals to see the generalized colleague group as a source of norms, and therefore more willing to accept an administrative superior as such a source. The same absence of colleague reference group orientations limits the task-oriented moral solidarity which might unite semi-professionals in opposing control from above. Without a well-developed prestige system built around the performance of tasks, they accord prestige on the basis of official position, and defer to their official superiors.

The predominantly female composition of the semi-professions strengthens all of these forces for bureaucratic control in the organizations in which they work. The public is less willing to grant autonomy to women than to men. A woman's primary attachment is to the family role; women are therefore less intrinsically committed to work than men and less likely to maintain a high level of specialized knowledge. Because their work motives are more utilitarian and less intrinsically task-oriented than those of men, they may require more control. Women's stronger competing attachments to their family roles and (as we shall show) to their clients make them less likely than men to develop colleague reference group orientations. For these reasons, and because they often share the general cultural norm that women should defer to men, women are more willing than men to accept the bureaucratic controls imposed upon them in semi-professional organizations, and less likely to seek a genuinely professional status.

In the remainder of this chapter we shall examine literature about semi-professional women and their work orientations, and the effects of these orientations on their work organizations. In some instances we shall also give original data, from a 1963 classroom-administered questionnaire survey of 2,685 students in 15 predominantly white colleges and universities in North Carolina, and from a 1962 mail questionnaire survey of 7,501 teachers in predominantly white public schools in two southern states.[8]

Entry into the Semi-Professions

Strong enthusiasm for their intended careers does not appear to be typical of either the men or the women who enter the semi-professions. Easy upward mobility and, for women, the availability of a temporary haven before marriage are not uncommon among the reasons for entering these occupations.

Upward Mobility

The majority of semi-professionals have moved up from family origins below their present status. Mason reports that 62 per cent of the men and 49 per cent of the women starting to teach in the fall of 1956 were from blue-collar or farm backgrounds.[9] If we assume that teachers whose fathers were clerks, salesmen, blue-collar workers, or farmers had been upward mobile, 61 per cent of these teachers had moved up.[10] Several studies suggest that a still higher percentage of nurses is upward mobile.[11] The origins of teachers and nurses are lower than those of medical students, college social science faculty members, independent attorneys, or dental students.[12]

Librarians and social workers appear to come from somewhat higher backgrounds than teachers or nurses. The fathers of 55 per cent of a national sample of librarians studied by Bryan were in professional, entrepreneurial, and managerial occupations.[13] Two-thirds of the Detroit social workers studied by Polansky, Bowen, Gordon, and Nathan were in these occupations, but their sample was confined to a professionally active elite.[14] White found substantially lower backgrounds than in the Polansky sample among Western Reserve University social work students in the early 1950's,[15] and Lebeaux found progressively lower backgrounds among professionally trained Detroit social workers over the past few decades.[16] In social work as in teaching, upward intergenerational mobility is more common among men than among women, but it is evident in both sexes.[17]

There is some evidence that many upward-mobile semiprofessionals have chosen their occupations primarily as an easy way up, rather than because of intrinsic appeal. White notes that social work schools in 1949 were subsidizing 68 per cent of their students,[18] a higher percentage than was subsidized in other professional schools. Edwards found that a high proportion of Negro public school teachers in Washington, D.C. had entered teaching as a second-choice occupation not requiring education beyond the bachelor's degree.[19] Rosenberg found that the less-well-to-do college students tended to choose salaried professions and semi-professions, whereas those from well-to-do families were more likely to choose business, law, or medicine.[20] Of 60 student nurses in the Boston Psychopathic Hospital studied by Kandler, 44 had taken up nursing because they could not attain their first choice of career; 23 of these 44 had entered nursing school because they could not go to college.[21]

Late Occupational Choice

Many of the people entering these occupations make their decisions late in their college education, or even after college.

(Nursing is an exception, because nurse training starts in the first post-high school year.) Davis reports that more college students transfer their majors *into* than out of education;[22] this suggests that decisions to teach are often made late in the college career. Late career decisions are especially common in social work and librarianship, where jobs can be had without formal training or certification. Half of all social workers in 1960 had taken no graduate work, and 30 per cent lacked bachelor's degrees.[23] Leigh indicates that in all but the largest libraries, it is common to find people without full professional qualification doing professional-level work; he cites a survey showing that only 40 per cent of the professional-level staffs in a sample of 60 libraries in 1947 held postgraduate library degrees, and that some at this level lacked any formal training at all in librarianship.[24]

Because one need not have a library degree to become a librarian, and perhaps because librarianship is less socially visible and has a less clear public image than the other semi-professions, this field has an especially high proportion of late deciders. About half the children's librarians studied by Wheeler had worked in other fields before becoming librarians.[25] Bryan found among public librarians that about two-fifths had worked a year or more in other occupations before entering library work, and that the median age at which the professional-level librarians in her sample had chosen library careers was 24.5 years among the men and 22.2 years among the women.[26] Parker indicates that it is common for teachers lacking prior experience or training to be made school librarians, and that many people drift rather aimlessly into library work.[27]

Occupational Motivation

Whatever their career choice processes may be, it does not appear that semi-professionals typically base their decisions on scholarly attraction to the intellectual content of their intended work. Reports have described students going into teaching as average or below in academic performance,[28] and a similar pattern appears to prevail in librarianship and social work. A feeling of inadequacy to succeed in other fields was the second most frequent reason given for their occupational choices by the public librarians Bryan studied; 16 per cent named this as their main reason for being librarians.[29] Wolfle includes elementary teaching and librarianship among the occupations that absorb college graduates "of only moderate ability."[30] Bemoaning the low quality of the people their field attracts is endemic among leaders of the library profession.[31] White sees the problem among social work students as one of effort more than of ability; 58 per cent of the social work students he studied had been academic underachievers during their undergraduate years, as compared with only 37 per cent of undergraduates generally.[32] Lack of scholarly zeal is more pronounced among the men entering these occupations than among the women, but is apparent among both sexes.[33]

The main intrinsic appeal of the semi-professions is to the heart, not the mind. All of these occupations attract individuals who want to work with people and to be of service.[34] These are values that appeal more to women than to men, though the men entering these occupations are more characterized by such values than are men entering other fields.[35] But women can satisfy their desires for service through family life, regardless of their occupations or of whether they work at all; even strong humanitarian motives, therefore, are usually insufficient to create strong vocational commitments among women. Rosenberg found that three times as many men as women expected their careers to represent their major life satisfaction.[36] Well over 90 per cent of women undergraduates expect to marry not long after graduation (if not before),[37] fewer than half want to work all or most of their lives, and fewer than a fourth want to work continuously if they have children.[38]

The ascendancy of the female sex role over the scholarly or career role is clearly portrayed by Davis, who reports that while women college students in a national sample were more

likely than men to be high academic performers, even the
female high academic performers were only slightly more likely
to indicate future plans for graduate or professional study
than were male low performers. Women at all achievement
levels were considerably less likely than men to be motivated
toward work careers, and those women who planned postgraduate study significantly overchose "female" occupations.
(The male low performers tended to choose occupations that
did not involve further study.)[39]

For a woman to become highly work-committed, an
atypical value orientation and unusually potent personal
influences on her decision seem to be required. Rosenberg
found that the 12 per cent of college women in his sample
who were highly career-committed were more like men than
non-career-committed women in the values they expressed;
they were less inclined to stress people-oriented values.[40]
Simpson and Simpson report a similar finding, and they found
also in comparing career-oriented and non-career-oriented
undergraduate women that the career-oriented were more
likely to have received advice about occupational choice and
to have utilized representational models, such as teachers or
people in their intended occupations.[41] When women do
become committed to the work world, this commitment does
not, however, necessarily lessen their concern with their
female status; in some ways it seems to heighten it. Career-
oriented college women are more concerned than the non-
career-oriented about combining work with family life;[42]
their concern probably indicates the difficulty they anticipate
in pursuing a consistent career line while meeting family
responsibilities.

If not many women are deeply concerned with work
careers, it is not because they do not expect to work at all
after college. Davis found that fewer than 5 per cent of college
senior women in the spring of 1961 did not plan to work
after they graduated.[43] A survey of the June, 1957, women
college graduates found 76 per cent employed full-time,
17 per cent looking for work or attending school, and only
7 per cent entirely outside the labor force. (Of those who

were working, 59 per cent were teachers, 7 per cent were nurses, 2 per cent were social workers, and a negligible percentage were librarians).[44] If nearly all women today work but only a small minority expresses long-range occupational commitments, the inference seems clear that most women entering the semi-professions lack the kinds of interests that would be conducive to professionalism in these occupations.

Nor does the undergraduate life of college women seem to socialize them into orientations favorable to professionalism. Undergraduate life seems to have the opposite effect. Alice Rossi has observed that the ambitious freshman girl tends to scale down her aspirations during college so that she "seems uncommitted to anything beyond early marriage, motherhood and a suburban home," or else she lowers her aspirations from a professional or research field to pursue a practical vocation in a feminine occupation.[45] Rosenberg has also concluded that college dampens women's occupational ambitions more often than it creates them; he found more coeds, as they went through college, shifting toward than away from a preference for housewife as a full-time vocation.[46] Table 5-1 shows that among the North Carolina undergraduate women we studied who were preparing to teach, preference for lifelong work in education did not increase during college and was, if anything, lower among seniors than among freshmen (25 per cent versus 29 per cent).

Perhaps a clearer indication of the absence of professionalizing forces in the training of semi-professional women is the relative lack of vocational commitment stemming from

Table 5-I. Of Undergraduate Women Who Planned to Teach, Per Cent Who Preferred Lifelong Careers in Education by Academic Year in College

Academic Year	PREFER LIFELONG CAREERS	
	%	N
Freshmen	29	133
Sophomores	22	160
Juniors	29	179
Seniors	25	146

interaction with fellow students or from apprenticeship relations with teachers in the intended field. Becker and Carper have shown that research apprenticeship to professors and contacts with fellow students build up strong vocational commitment among graduate physiology students, many of whom had no intention of being lifelong physiologists when they started graduate work.[47] This did not happen to any marked extent, if at all, among undergraduate education majors. Among the North Carolina women preparing to teach, a student was slightly more likely to want lifelong work in education if she knew an education professor well as a person, if she spent much social time or ate many meals with fellow education majors, and if two or all of her three best friends were education majors; but none of these influences made a difference of more than 5 per cent in the likelihood that the student would express a lifetime commitment to teaching.

Family, Work, and the Discontinuity of Careers

Home Versus Job

Regardless of their initial orientations toward work careers, married women workers are apt to find that the family role competes with the work role. In this competition, work tends to come out second. The culture defines woman's responsibility to home and family as her primary one. When home and work obligations conflict, the home has to take precedence. Women's self-images are built chiefly around their family roles, whereas men's are conditioned more by occupational roles. Moreover, women have more household tasks than men have. Such household duties as men have can usually be routinized, scheduled, and, if necessary, postponed when work obligations intrude, but a woman cannot so easily postpone cooking dinner, nor can she schedule the times when her children will need her attention.

It is clear that many working wives perceive considerable conflict between their domestic and work roles. Hoffelder's study of 4,039 married women teachers in North Carolina found that 46 per cent of them reported "serious" or "some" conflict between "your work as a teacher and your household responsibilities."[48] (The remaining 54 per cent reported "very little conflict" or "no conflict at all.") As one would expect, role conflict was most serious among young mothers of pre-school children. More than 60 per cent of the women in their twenties with pre-school children felt "some" or "serious" role conflict, as compared with fewer than 30 per cent of the women over fifty with no children in the home.[49]

Hughes, Hughes, and Deutscher note that for the kind of nurse whom Habenstein and Christ term the *utilizer*—one who works solely for the money, and for whom the work role is in effect an instrumental extension of the family role—there is no problem of divided allegiance between home and work,[50] though there may be conflicting time demands. For nurses whose commitment to nursing goes beyond its monetary rewards, there may be an emotionally-felt conflict between the two roles, but the home usually comes first. Theriault collected some statements from such nurses in New Hampshire: "I would not want to retire . . . , it would be a great waste of experience"; "I wouldn't say I could give up nursing completely, I don't think I could do it";—but, "My home comes first"; "I would never sacrifice my family for my work."[51]

Discontinuous and Part-Time Careers

Some of Theriault's nurses said that marriage had forced them to stop work, or to work only part-time. They were describing a situation common among married women, including those with specialized semi-professional or professional training. Women today make up a larger percentage of the labor force than ever before. In April, 1960 about one-third of American workers were women.[52] But a woman's work history remains closely tied to her status as a home-maker, and as her family life cycle changes, her work partici-pation is altered.

The most general pattern of female employment in the United States, according to Esther Peterson, is for the woman to work about four years after finishing her education, quitting work either when she marries or when her first child is born. After the youngest child enters school, the mother has an almost even chance of returning to work.[53] This pattern is revealed in the age distribution of female workers. The peak years of their employment are 18–19 and 45–49 years of age, with 47 per cent of the women in these age groups in the labor force. In the age group from 25 to 34, only 35 per cent of the women work.[54] These differences indicate that young children impose a major restriction on female participation in the labor force. While 56 per cent of the women workers in 1962 were married,[55] only about 37 per cent had children under 18.[56] Only 19 per cent of the mothers with children under 3 were in the labor force in 1962, as contrasted with 29 per cent of those with children aged 3 to 5 and none younger, and 45 per cent of those with children aged 6 to 17 only.[57]

Part-time employment is another adaptation to the female role that sets many women's work lives apart from men's. In March, 1962 there were 8.8 million working mothers of children under 18 in the United States, but fewer than a third of these were full-time, year-around workers. Age of children strongly affected the amount of time they worked. Among working mothers living with their husbands, the percentage employed only part-time or part of the year was 66 per cent of those with children 6 to 17 years old only, 73 per cent of those with children 3 to 5 but none younger, and 87 per cent of those with children under 3.[58]

Semi-professional women are no exception to these patterns, and the disinclination to pursue continuous work careers which we have noted among students preparing for semi-professional work remains after they begin working.

Mason reports that 80 per cent of the men in a national sample of first-year teachers in 1956 expected to remain continuously employed as teachers or school administrators until retirement, but only 25 per cent of the women had this expectation.[59] The difference was mainly because of the anticipation by 58 per cent of the women that they would withdraw from work temporarily during the early years of family life but return later; the combined percentage of women who expected to leave education for other occupations (6 per cent) and to become homemakers and not return to work (12 per cent) was less than the percentage of men (20 per cent) who expected to leave education.

Many nurses and librarians also begin their careers with the anticipation of leaving them. Stewart and Needham found that about 60 per cent of the general duty nurses and 75 per cent of the operating room nurses in ten Arkansas hospitals expected, and only 45 per cent of general duty nurses wanted, to be active in nursing five years later.[60] Reissman's findings on New Orleans nurses are similar.[61] Of the unmarried women library workers in Bryan's study, 39 per cent said that they would like to marry and leave library work.[62] But Habenstein and Christ report that most of the Missouri nurses they studied planned to come back to work when their youngest children were in school.[63]

It is thus evident that semi-professional women typically neither expect nor desire to work continuously until old age. Census data on the age distribution of women in these fields show that their performance bears out their expectations, and that they are like other women and unlike men in the discontinuity of their work histories.

The 1960 age distributions of males in these occupations approximated the distribution for males in all professional and semi-professional occupations combined, with two exceptions that are more apparent than real (see Table 5–2). An unusually high percentage of male elementary teachers (43) was in the 25–34 age group, and an unusually high percentage of male librarians (27) was 24 or younger. The relative youth of male elementary teachers reflects their tendency to move quickly

Table 5–2. Age Distribution of Males and Females in Semi-Professions
and in All Professions *

| | PER CENT IN AGE GROUPS | | | |
| | 14–24 | 25–34 | 35–44 | 45 Years |
Occupation and Sex	Years	Years	Years	and Older
All Professions				
Males	9	32	27	32
Females	16	21	21	42
Librarians				
Males	27	26	23	25
Females	14	14	20	52
Nurses				
Males	9	27	25	39
Females	15	25	24	36
Social Workers				
Males	8	34	24	34
Females	9	19	22	50
Elementary Teachers				
Males	10	43	24	24
Females	12	20	20	49
Secondary Teachers				
Males	7	38	25	30
Females	12	19	21	48

* All professions includes the occupations termed semi-professions. This holds for all tables
based on the U.S. Census.
Data Source: U.S. Census of Population, 1960, Final Report PC(2)-7E: Characteristics of Professional Workers, Table 3.

into administrative positions or, failing this, to leave the field
of education; few men spend their lives as classroom elementary teachers. The young male librarians undoubtedly included
many college and high school students working part-time with
sub-professional duties.

In contrast to men, semi-professional women, other than
nurses, had an older age distribution in 1960 than did women
in all professions and semi-professions combined (Table 5–2).
Female teachers and social workers had low percentages in
the 24-and-under age group; nurses, most of whom begin
work after only three years' training beyond high school, and
librarians, who in this age group include students working
in sub-professional capacities, had about the same percentages
of their women in the ages 24 and under as did all professions
combined. About the same percentages of women in these
semi-professions as of women in all professions were in the

25–34 and 35–44 age categories, except that nurses were somewhat over-represented in these ages and librarians were under-represented in the ages 25–34. The most striking difference between the semi-professions' and all professions' age distributions was in the 45-and-older category. In all professions combined, 42 per cent of the women were 45 and older, but the percentages of older women ranged from 48 per cent to 52 per cent among secondary and elementary teachers, social workers, and librarians. Nurses, only 36 per cent of whom were 45 and older, were an exception to the general pattern.

These figures suggest that nurses, who are over-represented relative to all professional women in the child-rearing years but under-represented in the older years, have more continuous work careers than other semi-professional women. It also appears that female librarians, whose overconcentration in the older ages would be even greater than Table 5–2 shows if the figures excluded part-time student workers, are especially prone to enter or re-enter the labor force after the age of 45. The age distributions of women in all of these occupations, including nursing, are older than those of male professionals, and reveal clearly the tendency of women to stop working during the child-rearing years.

Another way to look at female career discontinuity is to examine the sex composition of workers of different ages in these occupations in 1960. Table 5–3 shows this. Among

Table 5–3. Per Cent Female in Different Age Groups of Semi-Professionals and of All Professionals

Occupation	PER CENT FEMALE IN AGE GROUPS			
	14–24 Years	25–34 Years	35–44 Years	45 Years and Older
All Professionals	51	29	33	44
Librarians	76	76	84	93
Nurses	99	97	97	97
Social Workers	67	50	61	72
Elementary Teachers	88	74	84	93
Secondary Teachers	59	31	43	58

Data Source: U.S. Census of Population, 1960, Final Report PC(2)-7E: *Characteristics of Professional Workers*, Table 3.

professionals as a whole, social workers, and elementary and
secondary teachers the percentage of employed workers who
were women dropped sharply from the under-25 to the
25–34 age group. This drop was not visible among librarians,
but it seems likely that if student library workers with no
plans for library careers could be removed from the under-25
category, the female percentage in this category would rise
and some drop-off in the female percentage would then appear
in the 25–34 group. Nearly all nurses regardless of age were
women, but even in this field the percentage of men in the
25–34 group (2.6) was nearly twice that in the youngest
group (1.4). In the semi-professions other than nursing, and
among professionals as a whole, the percentage of women rose
from ages 25–34 to ages 35–44, and rose further from ages
35–44 to ages 45 and up. Women in the semi-professions
constituted about as high or higher a percentage of all workers
in the oldest group as in the youngest. Again we see evidence
of women stopping work to have families, then going back to
work in middle or later life. (The extremely high female
percentage among older elementary teachers is due partly to
the movement of men into administrative positions; men who
become administrators in the occupations other than teaching
do not change to a different Census occupational category.)

In every age category, women social workers and librarians
in 1960 were less likely to be married than were nurses,
elementary teachers, or secondary teachers (Table 5–4).
Nurses in every age group had the smallest percentage of
single (never married) women; and they had the highest
percentage of married women in the main child-rearing ages
(25–34) and by far the smallest increase in the percentage of
married women from the 25–34 to the 35–44 group. These
data underscore the earlier conclusion that nurses' work
histories are less discontinuous than those of other semi-
professional women, and they suggest that the most discontinuous careers may be those of social workers and librarians,
with elementary and secondary teachers intermediate in career
discontinuity.

One can only speculate about the reasons for these differ-

Table 5–4. Marital Status of Female Semi-Professionals and All Female Professionals in Different Age Groups

Occupation and Age Group	Single	MARITAL STATUS (PER CENT)	
		Married, Spouse Present	Widowed, Divorced, Separated
All Professionals			
14–24 Years	66	31	4
25–34 Years	31	61	8
35–44 Years	19	68	13
45 Years and Older	26	51	23
Librarians			
14–24 Years	80	19	1
25–34 Years	39	52	9
35–44 Years	28	59	13
45 Years and Older	34	42	24
Nurses			
14–24 Years	55	42	4
25–34 Years	25	67	8
35–44 Years	15	70	15
45 Years and Older	21	49	30
Social Workers			
14–24 Years	60	36	5
25–34 Years	41	49	10
35–44 Years	26	58	16
45 Years and Older	26	45	29
Elementary Teachers			
14–24 Years	56	40	3
25–34 Years	32	61	7
35–44 Years	17	73	10
45 Years and Older	24	58	19
Secondary Teachers			
14–24 Years	56	40	4
25–34 Years	33	61	6
35–44 Years	17	73	10
45 Years and Older	36	47	17

Data Source: U.S. Census of Population, 1960, Final Report PC(2)-7E: *Characteristics of Professional Workers*, Table 3.

ences. Conceivably they might mean that nurses are the most committed to their work, and social workers and librarians the least committed. Another hypothesis would explain the differences in career discontinuity on the basis of economic need to continue working after marriage. Our earlier discussion suggested that nurses' social backgrounds may be the lowest, and social workers' and librarians' the highest, among these women.[64] Most nurses are not college graduates, while many social workers and librarians have done graduate work.

On these grounds one might surmise that social workers and librarians marry men of comparatively high status, with high incomes, who can support families without the added income of working wives, and that nurses stand lowest in these respects.[65] Still a third possibility is that social workers and librarians are more likely to remain single than other semi-professional women, and nurses less likely, and that the marital status distributions of women in the various occupations and age categories reflect this rather than indicating differing propensities to stop work after marriage. If nurses are the least educated of these women, while many social workers and librarians have entered their occupations through the approved graduate school route, we would expect most nurses to marry and relatively many social workers and librarians to remain single, since women's chances of marriage diminish with increasing education.[66] In the case of librarians, Bryan's finding that the median age at which library work had been chosen was 22.2 years among the professional-level female librarians in her sample and 23.2 among the sub-professionals[67] suggests that many of these women might never have become librarians at all if they had married.

Regardless of the differences among these occupations, it is clear that family life reduces career continuity in all of them. Another indication of this is the extent of part-time employ-

Table 5–5. Part-Time Employment * among Female Workers in Different Occupational and Age Groups

	PER CENT WORKING PART-TIME IN AGE GROUPS			
Occupation	14–24 Years	25–34 Years	35–44 Years	45 Years and Older
All Professionals	29	28	27	26
Librarians	66	19	23	28
Nurses	16	28	23	16
Social Workers	16	14	11	12
Elementary Teachers	25	28	28	29
Secondary Teachers	19	22	23	22

* Part-time employment is defined as working 34 hours or less each week.
Data Source: U.S. Census of Population, 1960, Final Report PC(2)-7E: *Characteristics of Professional Workers,* Table 4.

ment. Table 5–5 shows the percentages of the employed women in different age and occupational groups in 1960 who worked thirty-four hours a week or less. (We define part-time work as thirty-four hours or less because the full federal government work week for some semi-professionals was thirty-five hours.) In the ages of heaviest child-rearing responsibility, part-time work was most prevalent in the occupations where the highest percentages of women were married: nurses aged 25–34 and teachers aged 35–44. At these same ages the least married groups, social workers and librarians, were least likely to be working part-time, though librarians aged 35–44 differed only negligibly in this respect from nurses and secondary teachers.

The availability of part-time work in the different fields probably affected these figures as much as the differing family situations of the women in them did. Unavailability of part-time social work jobs may explain why social workers of all ages had low rates of part-time employment. But by the same token, part-time work is readily available in libraries: nearly two-thirds of the youngest female librarians and more than a fourth of the oldest worked part-time. Given the ease of finding part-time library work, the low rates of such employment among women librarians aged 25 to 44 support the view that variations in part-time employment result not only from its varying availability, but also from differences in the family situations of women in these occupations.

The data we have been discussing actually underestimate the lack of vocational commitment among women trained in these fields, for the figures leave out those women who never work at all in the occupations for which they have been trained. Corwin reports that "one-third of the people trained to teach never enter teaching, and three out of five trained teachers are not in the profession at any one time."[68] Charters' study of University of Illinois graduates qualified to teach found that over a ten-year period, 40 per cent of them did not teach at all; of those who entered teaching, half dropped out within two years; and 12 per cent of the graduates produced 50 per cent of the man-years of teaching done by these graduates.[69]

Factors Offsetting Low Career Commitment

A number of factors can somewhat increase the interest of semi-professional women in their work and the continuity of their careers. One such factor is marriage to a colleague in the same field. In the elite sample of professionally active social workers studied by Polansky, Bowen, Gordon, and Nathan, 27 of the 47 married social workers were married to other social workers.[70] The husbands of 23 per cent of the married women starting to teach in 1956 were teachers or other educators.[71] About a fourth of the married psychiatric nurses in the North Carolina hospitals studied by Martin and Simpson were married to psychiatric attendants, who in these hospitals performed some quasi-nursing functions.[72]

Such a marriage seems to reduce the feeling of separation between work and home. From data given by Mason it can be inferred that teachers' husbands who were themselves educators were more favorable toward their wives' continuing to teach than were other husbands.[73] If this is generally true of husbands working in the same fields as their wives, it seems almost certain to have some effect in keeping the wives at work and increasing their vocational interest. Weil found that a positive attitude of the husband was the most important factor in married women's decisions to work.[74] The North Carolina married women teachers studied by Hoffelder felt substantially less role conflict if their husbands preferred that they work, or left the decisions to them, than if their husbands preferred that they not work;[75] and analysis of a 10 per cent sample of these teachers indicates that the ones who felt no role conflict were the most likely to be planning lifetime work careers, to have changed from an initially unfavorable to a currently favorable career orientation, and to have maintained their initial career orientation if it was favorable.[76]

Professional success, high status, and extensive training also increase women's vocational commitment. Studying successful women executives, Margaret Cussler found that some of them would now choose work over marriage if they had to make a choice, though none had felt this way to begin with.[77] Deutscher, who studied nurses in Kansas City, reports that school nurses and nursing administrators, who were the best paid and most educated kinds of nurses, had the highest rates of participation in professional activities.[78] Weil found that women with high educational attainment and specialized training, who had worked before marriage in technical, managerial, or professional jobs, were more inclined than other women to work after marriage.[79] At a given level of husband's income, a woman's propensity to work is greatest if she is highly educated.[80]

Economic Need Versus Low Motivation

Despite the positive effects of these factors on the work commitment of some women, it remains generally true that semi-professional women are far less committed to work careers than are most men of comparable attainments. The main reason why some mothers stay at work in these occupations is the same reason why mothers stay at work in other occupations: economic pressure. We have seen that most semi-professional women do not have lifelong vocational hopes when they start to work, and that many experience acute conflicts between the demands of job and family. Therefore they tend to quit work when they become mothers, unless financial pressures force them to stay on the job.

A fairly mild economic pressure is often enough, however, to keep them at work. Relatively few of them would face utter destitution if they stopped work. The pressure is more often the desire to maintain a standard of comparative luxury, to help the family move into a larger house, or to save toward the children's college education. This is a change from the not too distant past. Smuts has shown that until recent decades, only severe pressure—such as that caused by widowhood, abandonment, or an incapacitated and dependent husband—was enough to keep women gainfully employed.[81] Work for women is no longer considered a tragedy; it is an acceptable alternative, but it is not the first choice for many.

It is true that educated women whose husbands' incomes are high often re-enter the labor force after their children are beyond early childhood, and many of these appear to be motivated by a wish for self-expression apart from economic considerations.[82] But the need for self-expression which these women say they feel appears to be occasioned more by the boredom of finding themselves with an empty nest than by strong identification with the world of work. Fully professional women, who are strongly identified with their work, generally manage to lose less work time because of motherhood than is usually lost by semi-professional women with high-income husbands. Jessie Bernard has described the efforts of academic women to keep working despite the demands their families make on them.[83] A study of 1,240 women graduates of seven large eastern medical schools found that 82 per cent of the married women went into and remained in full-time practice and 90 per cent engaged in some form of medical activity.[84]

The relation of work continuity to financial need is apparent among semi-professional women. Hughes, Hughes, and Deutscher report that, "There is evidence in Kansas City of a tendency for nurses who marry men of higher occupational status than their fathers to leave the labor force."[85] Mason found that the occupation of the father had little relation to career commitment among men, but that among women beginning to teach, 70 per cent of those with white-collar fathers and only 59 per cent of those with blue-collar fathers expected to leave teaching within five years.[86] He does not give information on the relation of husband's occupation to career commitment, but it seems probable that some of this difference reflects the tendency of women from blue-collar backgrounds to marry lower-income husbands.

The predominantly utilitarian motives for work among semi-professional women are evident, too, in the reasons they give for choosing one job rather than another. Asked to name the single most important reason for having changed to their current teaching positions, 63 per cent of our sample of women teachers who had changed positions indicated "reason not connected with the position itself," rather than "professional advancement," or, "to get a position I liked better." Only 26 per cent of the men answered in this way. Similarly, Hughes, Hughes, and Deutscher, summarizing several studies of nurses, conclude that few nurses choose specialties because of intrinsic preference for them. Nurses take whatever jobs are most readily available, regardless of what nursing specialties these may be in, or they select jobs for reasons of pay, hours of work, easy journey to work, and the like.[87] Habenstein and Christ report what might seem to contradict this generalization. They say that many nurses prefer specialties and work settings where patients recover rapidly and visibly, and where they can get to know the patients; for example, many dislike surgery because the patient is unconscious and no personal bond is established.[88] This indicates that nurses may have job preferences based on sociable and service motives, but it does not suggest commitment to professional skills.

Thus we see that career motivation is not deeply ingrained in most semi-professional women, and that they tend to embark on their careers with the full expectation of leaving when they marry and have children. Many who stay despite conflicting family demands do so reluctantly, and even those who prefer to work after marriage may be hampered in the amount of attention they can devote to their work. In these ways a woman's family situation makes it improbable that she will develop a strong professional commitment, or, in the unlikely event that she had one to begin with, that she will be able to maintain it. Apart from the low motivation of the woman herself, one might surmise that an organization staffed mainly with such people would not have an atmosphere favorable to professionalism among its other employees.

Employee Turnover in Organizations

For the organizations in which women work, their interrupted careers make it hard to keep a stable work force. Various studies of public school systems at different times and places

indicate annual teacher turnover rates ranging from about
11 per cent to about 17 per cent for school systems; within
individual schools, the turnover is higher.[89] Turnover is about
the same among men and women teachers, but for different
reasons. Men more often change teaching jobs or leave
teaching for administrative posts, whereas women more often
stop work altogether.[90] Turnover is especially high in rural and
small-town districts, since teachers tend to move to larger
communities. Community size differences in turnover rates
are more pronounced among men than among women, but
they exist among both sexes.[91]

Annual personnel losses in libraries and social work
agencies appear to be as high or higher as the losses in schools.
Bryan found that the smallest libraries (like the smallest school
systems) had more turnover of professional-level personnel
than the larger libraries. Turnover of professional librarians
in the two largest of her five library-size categories in 1947
were 13 and 12 per cent; the rate jumped to 29 per cent in
the smallest libraries.[92] A California study found 35 per cent
turnover of social caseworkers in a one-year period.[93]

Turnover rates of men and women in libraries and social
work agencies, as of teachers, do not differ greatly, according
to the previously cited studies, but the reasons for male and
female turnover are not the same. Women tend to leave jobs
for family reasons; men, for professional advancement.[94]
Moreover, one should not infer from the similarity of male
and female turnover rates that turnover would be as high as
it is if all semi-professionals were men. It seems likely that
much of the turnover of men is made possible by that of
women: men may leave for better jobs that have been vacated
by women interrupting their careers.

Turnover appears to be highest by far among young
employees with little experience in their fields or tenure in
their jobs, as one would expect from the fact that the women
are leaving to marry and have children, and the men in order
to establish themselves professionally. The study of caseworker
turnover in California found that 30 per cent of the separated
caseworkers responding to a questionnaire had worked in the

field less than a year, 82 per cent had worked in the field less than five years, and over 91 per cent had worked less than five years in the agencies they left.[95] A national study found that in 40 public assistance agencies in 1954 the caseworkers entering and leaving positions both had a median age of 30, whereas the median age of all caseworkers in these agencies was 38.[96] More than 32 per cent of the people leaving their jobs in these agencies was between 25 and 29 years old; the authors attribute the heavy turnover of these people to marriage, children, promotion to supervisory positions, and leaving for better positions.[97]

The fact that young, inexperienced workers account for so many of the departures is no doubt a saving feature for the organizations where they work. It means that despite high turnover, an experienced cadre of older workers remains. A study of teacher turnover found, for example, that teaching experience in the same district ranged from a median of 13.0 years in the largest urban communities to 5.5 years in the smallest districts.[98] It is not clear how long the average teacher stays at a particular school, however, since these figures refer to experience in school districts, not in individual schools. Becker found much movement between schools in the Chicago school district; the tendency was to begin in a slum school and try to move to one in a middle-class neighborhood.[99] The rural and slum schools have the most difficulty in retaining experienced staffs.

Employee turnover has effects on organizations. Later in this chapter, we shall suggest that one of its effects is to increase the bureaucratization of semi-professional organizations.

Discrimination Against Women

The low motivation and discontinuous work histories of women raise questions about the prevailing assumption that women are discriminated against in occupations where they compete with men. To what extent is women's relative lack of success in obtaining the most desirable jobs the result of discrimination against them? The picture is less clear than it might appear on the surface. It is easy to demonstrate that men get more than their proportionate share of the best jobs in the semi-professional fields, as in other occupations, and it is plain that individual women are often the victims of discrimination in hiring and promotion. But a case can be made that women's lack of occupational success is not always due to discrimination, and that when discrimination does occur, there may be valid grounds for it from the organization's standpoint.

Sex Differences in Income and Advancement

Table 5–6 compares incomes in 1959 of men and women with differing amounts of education and of different ages, in the various semi-professions and in all professions and semi-professions combined. Except in the under-25 age group, where part-time workers made the male income distribution spuriously low in some of the occupations, at all ages and educational levels larger percentages of men than of women earned more than $4,000. Much of the difference represents greater concentration of men in administrative positions, but not all of it does. A *Monthly Labor Review* study of 1960 incomes in social work showed that the median income for men was $820 higher than for women. Men in each separate type of position earned more than women; the difference was $470 among caseworkers and among supervisors. The 1960 salary differentials were not given for executives, but in 1950 the difference was $1,250.[100] Similarly, Bryan reports salary differentials in favor of men at each rank in library work.[101]

These figures do not prove, however, that sex discrimination takes the form of different salaries for genuinely similar work. Smuts has concluded, after extensive research, that this kind of discrimination is now rare.[102] The main reason for the apparent differences is that over-all rank categories, such as *superivsor* and *executive*, conceal an enormous amount of variation in the work actually done, and men tend to get the

Table 5–6. Per Cent of Workers in Different Occupations
Whose Incomes Were $4,000 and Over, by Age and Sex

OCCUPATION AND AGE	Education and Sex (per cent)					
	LESS THAN FOUR YEARS OF COLLEGE		FOUR YEARS OF COLLEGE		FIVE OR MORE YEARS OF COLLEGE	
	Males	Females	Males	Females	Males	Females
All Professionals						
14–24 Years	34	11	43	30	36	36
25–34 Years	82	28	85	47	79	62
35–44 Years	91	33	94	52	93	71
45 Years and Older	83	41	90	64	91	80
Librarians						
14–24 Years	5	3	18	23	22	36
25–34 Years	41	25	54	50	70	66
35–44 Years	83	30	79	56	90	77
45 Years and Older	64	33	72	60	90	82
Nurses						
14–24 Years	21	14	15	21	49	28
25–34 Years	46	25	62	40	57	51
35–44 Years	65	30	96	57	95	66
45 Years and Older	59	37	82	61	96	87
Social Workers						
14–24 Years	18	10	14	24	15	26
25–34 Years	73	38	67	57	84	64
35–44 Years	75	38	90	67	97	79
45 Years and Older	75	53	94	69	96	85
Elementary Teachers						
14–24 Years	20	13	36	33	52	50
25–34 Years	56	22	69	47	87	64
35–44 Years	62	20	79	51	93	72
45 Years and Older	65	47	77	66	93	80
Secondary Teachers						
14–24 Years	28	24	40	29	43	44
25–34 Years	64	24	71	44	87	68
35–44 Years	83	22	86	50	95	73
45 Years and Older	79	44	87	68	96	83

Data Source: U.S. Census of Population, 1960, Final Report PC(2)-7E: *Characteristics of Professional Workers,* Table 7.

best supervisory and executive positions. Bryan found that
among women librarians, salaries were actually higher for
middle administrators than for top administrators; her explanation is that women often become middle administrators in
the largest libraries where salaries are highest, but they seldom
become top administrators except in small libraries.[103] Social
work salaries of women also followed such a pattern in 1950,
with supervisors earning more than executives; male executives, on the other hand, earned considerably more than male
supervisors.[104] The reason is presumably the same as in library
work: women normally become executives above the supervisory level only in small social agencies, where salaries tend
to be low.

Apart from salaries and from the tendency to appoint
women to top positions mainly in small, ill-paid organizations,
even the gross statistics on sex distribution in administrative
and lower-level positions show that men have a marked
advantage. In Bryan's sample of librarians, 15 per cent of the
men but only 4 per cent of the women held top administrative
positions; and the men in such positions averaged five years
younger than the women, an indication that promotion for
the men had been more rapid.[105] Among women social
workers in 1960, 59 per cent were caseworkers and 15 per
cent were executives, nearly a four-to-one ratio, whereas
male caseworkers outnumbered male executives by a ratio of
only 41 per cent to 29 per cent, or less than three to two.[106]
A 1955–56 survey found that 38 per cent of the elementary
school principals in small urban districts (population 2,500–
5,000) and 62 per cent of those in large districts (population
500,000 or more) were women, although well over 80 per
cent of elementary teachers were women.[107] At the secondary
school level, where women constituted nearly half the
teachers, only 9 per cent of the junior high school principals
and 5 per cent of the senior high school principals were
women.[108] A woman school superintendent is a still greater
rarity. In nursing, where nearly 98 per cent of all workers
are female, women have a clear path to executive positions;
but even here, as Hughes, Hughes, and Deutscher note, they

have little hope of reaching the summit of hospital administration.[109]

The Belief in Male Superiority

A basis for discrimination is the widely held cultural belief that "women should not be in authority over men of roughly the same social class and age."[110] This norm is so strong among industrial workers that, as Caplow puts it, "the idea of placing a woman foreman over a male crew is regarded as intrinsically ridiculous."[111] In restaurant kitchens studied by Whyte, male kitchen workers objected strenuously to taking food orders from waitresses unless physical barriers separated the two groups and prevented face-to-face contact.[112]

This feeling exists among semi-professionals, though perhaps in weaker form than among blue-collar workers. There is no objection to women administrators in nursing, for their subordinates are either women or men of considerably lower social status, such as orderlies. Similarly, women are considered acceptable as chief librarians in small libraries or as middle-level executives in larger libraries; here their subordinates tend to be either women or part-time men for whom the situation is temporary. In elementary schools and in smaller social work agencies there are likely to be few if any men, or chiefly men serving brief apprenticeships on the way to administrative positions, so that here, too, a woman may be considered acceptable as an executive. But secondary schools, large libraries, and large social agencies—in short, those semi-professional organizations with sizable numbers of male career employees—tend to bar their top positions to women. An added barrier against women in these latter organizations is that in general, the larger the organization, the greater the extent to which its top executives' duties involve representing the organization in the community political arena. The same beliefs that keep women from exercising authority over men make them seem unsuited for political infighting against male antagonists.[113]

Table 5–7. Perceived Teachers' Respect for Different Male and Female Teachers by Sex and Teaching Level of Teacher Respondents

TYPES OF MALE AND FEMALE TEACHERS, AND PERCEIVED RESPECT	Sex and Teaching Level of Respondents			
	ELEMENTARY TEACHERS		SECONDARY TEACHERS	
	Males	Females	Males	Females
High School Algebra Teacher				
Male More Respected	49%	28%	61%	27%
Same Respect for Both	50	68	37	67
Female More Respected	1	4	2	5
(N)	(125)	(3,744)	(1,231)	(2,346)
Fifth Grade Teacher				
Male More Respected	21%	5%	22%	4%
Same Respect for Both	44	48	31	42
Female More Respected	34	48	48	54
(N)	(126)	(3,758)	(1,226)	(2,343)
Teacher Ambitious to Be Elementary Principal				
Male More Respected	68%	51%	74%	48%
Same Respect for Both	27	44	22	44
Female More Respected	6	6	4	8
(N)	(124)	(3,744)	(1,231)	(2,340)

* Numbers within parentheses are N's on which percentages are based.

Women themselves often share these norms or feel uncomfortable if they violate them. Cussler reports that women executives with male subordinates may feel awkward in everyday situations that point up the incongruity of their sex roles with their organizational positions. Such simple problems as deciding who should initiate coffee breaks, or who should pick up the check at lunch, can cause embarrassment.[114] Table 5–7 shows attitudes supporting sex discrimination among the school teachers we studied. They were asked whether they thought that "most teachers would have more respect for" a man or a woman who taught high school algebra; who taught the fifth grade; who was ambitious to become principal of an elementary school. Both the elementary and the secondary teachers of both sexes attributed more respect to the male algebra teacher and to the female fifth grade teacher, though many felt that the sex of the teacher did not matter.

Table 5–8. Education of Males and Females of Different Ages in the Semi-Professions and All Professions

OCCUPATION AND AGE	Education and Sex (per cent)					
	LESS THAN FOUR YEARS OF COLLEGE		FOUR YEARS OF COLLEGE		FIVE OR MORE YEARS OF COLLEGE	
	Males	Females	Males	Females	Males	Females
All Professionals						
14–24 Years	70	66	20	30	10	4
25–34 Years	38	48	28	35	34	18
35–44 Years	40	50	23	29	37	22
45 Years and Older	47	51	19	27	34	22
Librarians						
14–24 Years	87	80	8	14	6	6
25–34 Years	19	35	22	31	59	34
35–44 Years	12	38	11	22	77	40
45 Years and Older	35	43	14	20	51	37
Nurses						
14–24 Years	86	87	11	11	3	3
25–34 Years	69	84	9	11	23	5
35–44 Years	75	85	13	10	12	5
45 Years and Older	87	90	4	7	9	4
Social Workers						
14–24 Years	45	25	39	59	16	16
25–34 Years	19	21	38	42	43	38
35–44 Years	27	29	25	25	48	47
45 Years and Older	49	42	20	25	31	32
Elementary Teachers						
14–24 Years	30	37	55	59	14	5
25–34 Years	12	26	44	56	44	19
35–44 Years	7	25	27	50	66	26
45 Years and Older	17	37	28	41	55	22
Secondary Teachers						
14–24 Years	17	16	66	73	17	11
25–34 Years	7	11	41	56	52	33
35–44 Years	4	9	19	45	76	46
45 Years and Older	7	11	19	38	73	52

Data Source: U.S. Census of Population, 1960, Final Report PC(2)-7E: *Characteristics of Professional Workers*, Table 7.

Significantly, all four categories of teachers attributed far more respect to the male than to the female aspiring elementary school principal, though they favored the female as a teacher at this level. More than two-thirds of the male respondents felt that the man would be preferred as an elementary school principal. Among the female respondents, nearly half felt that the sex of an aspiring elementary principal did not matter, but very few attributed more respect to the female than to the male candidate, and more attributed greater respect to the man than saw no difference.

Some Justification for Sex Differentials

It is clear that men more often attain administrative positions and that cultural norms support this situation. The pattern is not wholly the result of discrimination, however. The data previously shown in Table 5–6 indicate that as the education of a woman increased, so did the likelihood that she was earning more than $4,000, though education was less necessary for men, many of whom were in the high-income bracket despite relative lack of education. Moreover, as Table 5–8 demonstrates, men in the semi-professions are more likely than women to have received advanced training, and this accounts for some of their concentration in executive positions. The table shows the percentages of male and female workers of different ages in the various occupations who had less than four years of college education, four years, and five or more years, in 1959. The men had higher percentages with five years of college or more in every category except the youngest librarians and the oldest social workers. Sex differences in educational background were generally least marked among social workers and most marked among nurses and elementary teachers. Among the elementary teachers, more than twice as high a percentage of men as of women reported five years' college education; no doubt much of their advanced work was in direct preparation for administrative positions. Bryan, who gives more detail for librarians than our table shows, states that in her sample the men were nearly 50 per cent more likely than the woman to have B.L.S. degrees, twice as likely to have M.L.S. degrees, and three times as likely to have master's degrees in subject fields.[115]

It is conceivable that women's relatively low vocational commitment and, if they marry, the competing demands from the family, make them less likely than men to keep up their professional skills or make the effort required for high achievement, regardless of the formal education they may receive. If so, this would make them less valuable in high-level positions. Komarovsky, reviewing Bernard's book on academic women, speaks of "women who solve the problem of multiple roles . . . by lowering career aspirations."[116] In our sample of teachers, 56 per cent of the 1,351 men responding as contrasted with 40 per cent of the 5,983 women said that they spent ten or more hours a month reading in the fields they taught.[117]

Marriage, or the prospect of it, and discontinuous work histories have additional effects that block the advancement of women. While men are being promoted or gaining experience that will equip them for promotion, many women are at home tending babies, their skills growing rusty and their knowledge lagging behind new developments in their fields. A married woman looking for jobs is confined to the labor market where her husband lives; she cannot move where the best opportunities are. (This may help to explain why women principals are more common in metropolitan than in small school districts. In a big city with many schools a woman can take a principalship in a different school without changing her residence.) Moreover, an employer knows that he runs a risk if he puts a woman in a top position. She may leave to marry, or to have children, or her husband's job may take her to a different community.[118]

That discontinuous careers account in part for woman's failure to advance within their occupations is indicated by the greater success of single than of married women. A common complaint by Theriault's New Hampshire nurses was that marriage had made it hard for them to rise in the profession.[119] Stewart and Needham found that only 32 per cent of the nursing supervisors they studied in Arkansas was married, compared with 58 per cent of general duty nurses.[120] In Deutscher's Kansas City study, 33 per cent of the nursing administrators was married as compared with 63 per cent of general duty nurses and 70 per cent of industrial nurses.[121] We lack this information for the other semi-professions but it is reasonable to suppose that single women enjoy similar professional advantages in all of them. Esther Peterson has commented that in professional and technical positions generally, single women are over-represented relative to married women; she attributes this fact to the continuity of single women's lives in the labor force, which enables them to secure the needed education and experience.[122]

We shall show later that women workers are less ambitious than men for advancement on the job and less inclined toward the kinds of competition that the struggle for advancement may require. Their lesser career commitment may make them less creative in the long-range planning needed in upper-echelon positions. We have seen that many of them share the prevailing belief that women should not give orders to men, and may not feel at ease if they have to do so. Caplow notes that in executive groups where coordination with colleagues is a key part of the job and aggression between colleagues is sometimes expected, women are hampered by norms against relaxed give-and-take and the expression of hostility in mixed-sex groups.[123] Men are apt to resent the introduction of women into their colleague groups.[124] Garceau finds that women library executives may be taken less seriously than men in the community political arena where they must represent their organizations,[125] and the same would seem true of women school officials and heads of social work agencies. For all of these reasons women may usually be, in fact, less effective administrators than men.

Thus there exists a vicious circle in which discrimination against women and the sometimes valid basis for it reinforce each other. Their competing family roles and the expectation that they will be discriminated against reduce women's performance and aspirations. They are then discriminated against partly because they are thought to lack ambition. What seems to be discrimination against the individual may often be a wise policy for the organization.

Values, Goals, and Compliance

The semi-professions are centered in organizations where the worker's autonomy is limited. Semi-professional women may be the handmaidens of a male occupation that has authority over them, as in nursing, or they may carry out policies established at higher echelons, as in school teaching with its required lesson units, or social work with its legally prescribed welfare eligibility criteria. They rarely work in solitary settings or determine their own hours of work. When they exercise authority over clients, the authority is confined to enforcing minor rules (as in library work), or is delegated to them from a superior source in the organization or the community and exercised only over people of low status or dependent condition (as in social work, nursing, and teaching). Their position is more that of petty bureaucrats than of professionals. It is therefore not surprising if their compliance patterns somewhat resemble those usually found in what Etzioni calls "utilitarian" organizations, such as business firms, even though their work involvement is partly moral rather than calculative and they work in organizations with normative goals.[126]

Their orientations on the job tend to fit this organizational position, and the predominance of women in the semi-professions accentuates such orientations. Women's values and goals make many of them tractable subordinates. Their low work commitment makes some women welcome an easy job that makes few demands, and it is easier to follow instructions than to exercise judgment. They tend to want friendly relations with co-workers and are often afraid to risk these for the sake of autonomy and power. Relatively unambitious, on the average, they are not willing to fight for advancement. They tend to be more interested in giving personal service to clients than in technical mastery of skills or in professional prerogatives to define how their skills will be put to use. Their unsure position in any situation where they might have to exercise power over men contributes to their willingness to submit to bureaucratic control. Semi-professional women do not strive to establish professional independence or collegial authority patterns.

Deference of Women to Men

The fact that so many semi-professional workers are women while the organization executives and community board members with authority over them are usually men plays a part in their readiness to submit to restrictions of their autonomy. Zander, Cohen, and Stotland found that most psychiatric social workers in hospitals they studied accepted their subordination to psychiatrists without complaint. The researchers infer that one reason for this was that the social workers were women while the psychiatrists were men, and they note that among clinical psychologists (who included enough women to make the comparison), women tended to be more accepting of their subordination to psychiatrists than men.[127]

High status can offset the tendency of women to defer to men. Southern white women assert superiority over Negro men, teachers give orders to school janitors and nurses to male orderlies, and female social workers enforce rules over male welfare recipients. Women whose community status is high are sometimes loath to defer even to men of high or moderate status. Bressler and Kephart, examining the willingness of nurses to defer to physicians, found that only 11 per cent of upper-class nurses were in the high-deference category whereas 16 per cent of middle-class and 21 per cent of lower-class nurses were.[128] Fiske found that the public librarians most likely to resist pressures from library boards were those whose families had higher community prestige than most board members.[129] But not many semi-professional women have husbands with extremely high community standing, and these few are likely to leave the labor force. In the usual situation, women of modest community status confront male superiors with more advanced education to match their greater authority. In nursing, some superiors (the nursing directors, head nurses, and nurse supervisors) are women, but the data of Habenstein and Christ show a strong positive relation between the husband's occupational status and the nurse's organizational rank.[130] This means that nurses' tendencies to defer to authority may be reinforced by their nursing superiors' higher community status.

Desire for Sociability

Women tend to have stronger desires than men for pleasant social relations on the job. They are more fearful of conflict that might endanger it, and less interested in the long-range career goals that might make the risk of conflict seem worthwhile. In Rosenberg's college student sample, 59 per cent of the women but only 39 per cent of the men named work with people as a highly important occupational value.[131] Among undergraduate students in two universities studied by Simpson and Simpson, 68 per cent of the women in contrast to 57 per cent of the men indicated that friendly relations with fellow workers on a job would be very important to them.[132]

Rosenberg identifies a "compliant personality type": people who want to be well liked (rather than independent or successful), are willing to be dominated but reluctant to dominate others, and express a positive view of human nature. Such people are "concerned with approval, acceptance, warmth, support."[133] He does not report the sex distribution of compliant and other personalities, but the occupational values most characteristic of compliant students in his sample were the people-oriented values that appealed mainly to women, so we may infer that the compliant personality was mainly feminine.[134] The intended occupational fields with the highest concentrations of these acceptance-seeking students included social work and teaching.[135]

A desire for warm personal relations and a disinclination to engage in the kinds of behavior that are helpful in acquiring independence and power in an organization are closely related and predominantly feminine traits. Experimental studies of coalition formation by Vinacke and associates indicate that men tend to bargain competitively and to be power-oriented in their coalition strategies whereas women "are less concerned with winning as such and more concerned with arriving at a fair and friendly solution of the problem."[136] Similarly, Coleman finds that high school girls are less effective participants than boys in simulation studies that require manipulative or aggressive behavior.[137]

While these differences seem rooted to some extent in the basic personalities of men and women, differences in work commitment can accentuate them. We have mentioned earlier that vocationally oriented college women are essentially the same as men in their occupational values, though the existing studies do not show whether the values followed or preceded the career decisions.[138] Zander, Cohen, and Stotland found that while most social workers sought acceptance by psychiatrists and were deferential toward them, this was less true of those with high status in their profession and commitment to it; these latter avoided contact with psychiatrists.[139]

Whyte and Henry provide evidence from the business world of the relation between sociability and compliance (though their evidence concerns men). Whyte's "organization man" is a pliable conformist whose desire for acceptance hampers his independence and creativity.[140] Henry concludes that the absence of a need for close personal relationships is an element in the independence that helps men on the way up in business. His research on the personalities of successful executives revealed that the personal ties they formed were shallow: they cut off old friends quickly and without regret when promoted above them.[141]

Holistic Versus Task Orientations

A fundamental orientation of semi-professionals is their desire to be helpful to others, to give humanitarian service. This must be distinguished sharply from the obligation to put the welfare of clients before personal gain which is regarded as a hallmark of the professions.[142] The service component in the ideal-typical relation of professional to client is, as Parsons has shown, functionally specific, instrumental, affectively neutral, and universalistic.[143] The physician, the lawyer, or the architect applies special skills to specific problems brought to him by the client. The relationship is limited and segmental, and no personal bond need be established; in the ideal case, personal sentiments are irrelevant to the relationship and might be harmful if they entered into it.

What we mean by the service orientation of semi-professionals is different from this. It is an emotionally felt humanitarian urge to give of oneself, to relate in an intensely personal way to the recipient of the service. The act of service is its own reward, an expressive act, and it establishes a diffuse particularistic tie. The humanitarian service motive is thus quite different from the professional orientation. Professional activity is sometimes expressive, but the rewards are derived more from the exercise of skills than from the response of the client, who may sometimes be seen essentially as an object to whom skills are applied. Student nurses may speak of the wonderful, friendly Mr. Brown in room 406; doctors may instead refer to him as a kidney malfunction or a hernia.[144] To distinguish the desire to give service and relate to the whole person from the professional's concern with the exercise of special skills, we shall use the terms *holistic* versus *task* orientation.

Holistic orientations are prevalent among semi-professionals. In Rosenberg's study, the three occupations with the largest percentages of students choosing them rating high in "faith in people" included social work and teaching, along with personnel work.[145] (Nursing and librarianship were not among the occupations in his study.) The relation between faith in people and choice of these occupations held when men and women were considered separately.[146] Davis reports similar findings in a national sample of students planning graduate study. The four intended graduate fields with the highest percentages of students checking "opportunity to work with people rather than things" as a value included social work, nursing, and education, along with clinical psychology.[147] In Davis' study, students aiming toward these semi-professions ranked near the bottom in the proportions who expressed interest in originality and creativity and in making money.[148]

These holistic orientations are a major source of work satisfaction among semi-professionals. According to Naegele and Stolar, "ideas of service to the point of self-sacrifice are prominent" among the librarians they studied.[149] The social workers in the elite sample studied by Polansky, Bowen, Gordon, and Nathan, rated doctors, lawyers, plant executives, school teachers, and store owners above social workers in prestige, but they ranked social workers second only to doctors in power to help people.[150] Habenstein and Christ quote a number of nurses as saying that they liked to get to know patients intimately, to know their families, and to have recovered patients come back to visit. Some of their nurses said that they disliked work in surgery because they could not get to know the unconscious surgical patients.[151] Summarizing various studies of nurses, Hughes, Hughes, and Deutscher conclude that "love of people and particularly the urge to aid the helpless is firmly established as a pervasive motive for nursing and as the greatest satisfaction found there. . . ."[152]

Theories or ideologies that would support task orientations are not well developed in semi-professional occupations. The semi-professions communicate or apply knowledge, but in general they derive the knowledge they use from others, rather than creating it themselves.[153] Moreover, the theoretical knowledge and technical tasks of semi-professionals are either ill-defined (as in teaching and librarianship), concrete rather than abstract (the nurse with her hypodermic needle), or defined by people outside the occupation (when political bodies prescribe school curricula and welfare eligibility rules, or doctors instruct nurses). Such abstract knowledge as these occupations possess is not accorded legitimacy by the public or by practitioners in the professions who have working relations with them, and sometimes not by the members of the occupations themselves.

The established training programs do not seem to have overcome these difficulties. Sometimes the tasks are taught as intrinsically holistic, as in much of the theory of elementary teaching, nursing, and social work. Professional schools have made only limited progress toward abstract or rigorous education in the semi-professions, according to some critics. Hughes maintains that professional master's degrees in these fields do not build on solid undergraduate foundations, but are watered down and involve the cultivation of methodological rituals and pseudo-skills.[154]

Studies of work and workers in these fields support such a view. Martin and Simpson asked psychiatric nurses what "patient needs" and "relating to the patient," two technical concepts in the literature on psychiatric nursing, meant to them. To some nurses these terms meant nothing, and to most of the others they meant something different from the technical meanings discussed in the literature.[155] Gates' research on education students during their practice teaching period revealed a pervasive feeling that their courses on the theory of pedagogy had not done them much good. They seemed to see no connection between educational theory and educational practice.[156]

In short, it does not appear that the training of people for these fields offers much competition for the holistic orientations they bring with them. Beyond this, the prevalence of women fosters holistic orientations. Teaching, nursing, and social work are "helping" occupations. The clients tend to be socially dependent: children, sick people, needy people. Wilensky and Lebeaux point out that the work can be seen as an extension of feminine sex roles.

> [The woman] is traditionally expected to provide care to children, the aged, the sick; to be nurturant, kind, receptive; in short, feminine. As a caseworker, though professionalism and agency procedures hold this in check somewhat, she functions in a similar way—as does the nurse or elementary schoolteacher.[157]

Holistic orientations are common among people of both

Table 5-9. Percentages of Men and Women Teachers Giving
Indicated Responses

	SEX OF RESPONDENTS	
Responses to Questions	Men *	Women *
Describe themselves as more interested in children than in subject matter	44%	59%
Strongly agree that teachers should concern themselves with students' emotional problems	42	55
Agree that understanding what lies behind students' behavior is more important than maintaining classroom discipline	35	48
Say that failing a child bothers them very much	23	32
Rank spending a lot of time working with children as the best aspect of teaching	65	73
Say that it would please them most to be told by principal, students, or parents (rather than colleagues) that they are the best teacher in school	56	63
Say that what their former principals or students (rather than colleagues) thought of applicants would influence them most if they were superintendents choosing among applicants for teaching jobs	58	67
Say that opinions of superiors, students, or parents of students (rather than colleagues) have influenced them most in sizing up their success in teaching	71	78
Strongly agree that teachers should report all infractions of faculty rules	49	58
Do not agree that teachers should put their ideas into practice even if it means breaking a few rules	57	64

* N's vary from 1,283 to 1,363 among men and 5,761 to 6,138 among women.

sexes in these fields, but more so among women. Mason found that 9 per cent more women than men (among both elementary and secondary teachers considered separately) designated "work with people" as an important occupational value.[158] Table 5-9 shows that among our southern school teachers, women exceeded men in the percentages who described themselves as more interested in children than in subject matter, who strongly agreed that teachers should concern themselves with students' emotional problems, who agreed that understanding what lies behind students' behavior is more important than maintaining classroom discipline, who were bothered very much when they had to give a failing grade, and who ranked "spending a lot of time working with children" as the best aspect of teaching. These differences held among both elementary and secondary teachers.[159]

Just as a holistic orientation is present among women, an orientation toward intellectual achievement seems relatively absent among them. Coleman's research in ten Illinois high schools found that girls, in comparison with boys, were unlikely to make As and also unlikely to make bad grades; girls' grades were bunched in the B category.[160] This suggests two patterns related to our thesis: that women tend not to be competitive in the academic sphere (therefore making few As) and that they tend to comply with organizational directives (therefore making few bad grades).

This lack of drive toward intellectual mastery, added to the holistic focus on clients and the fact that women tend to readily follow directives from above, lessens the likelihood that semi-professional women will develop an ideology of professional autonomy and colleague control. They do not have the kind of belief system that makes college professors demand academic freedom or doctors ignore rules set by hospital administrators.[161] Task orientations give rise to demands that the control of work be placed in the hands of the individual and his professional colleagues, since only colleagues are able to define the content and proper application of tasks based on esoteric skills. Holistic orientations, in contrast, can be maintained in bureaucratic settings so long as the bureaucracy does not interfere with the personal relationship of staff member to client. Sometimes the bureaucracy does intrude in this relationship. Blau shows that official requirements may deflect semi-professionals' goals away from holistic service, in a bureaucratic direction. He found that the requirement of a maximum number of job placements deflected employment counselors' goals away from counseling toward the speedy placement of applicants in the most immediately available jobs.[162] Bel Kaufman's partly fictional, partly autobiographical account of a high school teacher's experience describes instances in which the goal of order and efficiency led school administrators to thwart teachers' efforts to help students with personal problems, thus subordinating holistic orientations to bureaucratic requirements.[163] In general, however, holistic orientations are consistent with bureaucratic compliance. To gratify holistic motives, it is not necessary that the worker have full autonomy or be free from elaborate rules; it is only necessary that the controls not be such as to prevent his forming diffuse expressive attachments to clients. Usually these attachments can be formed without difficulty in a context of instrumental compliance. The situation is analogous to that of the traditional housewife, subordinate to her husband in instrumental decision-making but free in her own sphere of nurturance.[164]

Lack of Ambition

Women's lack of long-range occupational ambitions also helps to maintain their subordinate orientations in the organizations where they work. They can often gain more social approval through marriage than through upward occupational mobility. If they marry, their community status is influenced mainly by their husbands' work and by their success as mothers and hostesses. Therefore, it is not surprising if they seek "an agreeable job that makes few demands,"[165] are less ambitious than men for advancement, and tend (as we noted earlier) to drop out of work if their husbands have high status. Several studies indicate that most nurses do not want administrative positions.[166] Mason found that 51 per cent of male first-year teachers hoped to become school administrators, in contrast with 9 per cent of single women, 8 per cent of married women, and 19 per cent of widowed, separated, and divorced women. Much of the difference was due to women's expecting to leave work altogether, but even among the beginning teachers who expected to work in education continuously until retirement, 64 per cent of the men wanted to become administrators as contrasted with 43 per cent of the single women,

31 per cent of the married women, and 28 per cent of the widowed, separated, and divorced women.[167]

Lack of Occupational Communities

Another professionalizing force that is weakly developed among semi-professional women is colleague groups or "occupational communities" of a kind that foster professionalism. These women seek friendly relations with co-workers, as we have seen, but the content of the interaction in these groups is not necessarily a force for professionalism. If women compare notes on clothing styles and child rearing, this does not have the same professionalizing effect as the task-related contacts of professionally dedicated workers.

Some of the forces that make for task-oriented colleague interaction in many male work settings are weaker in predominantly female settings. High turnover of employees is not favorable to the growth of task-oriented subcultures. Where there are both men and women in the work group, social distance between the sexes reduces colleague solidarity.[168] Even in dealing with their own sex, women may have difficulty in maintaining the give-and-take of constructive colleague relations because of the conflicts of viewpoint that inevitably arise; women seem less able than men to disagree impersonally, without emotional involvement. This may reflect a desire to avoid giving offense and a tendency to think in value terms rather than intellectualizing a problem. It is also affected by the lack of some of the techniques men have for expressing aggression in approved ways—through horseplay, mock hostility, lighthearted swearing at each other, and the like.

Many semi-professional women interact off the job with work colleagues, but this interaction does not seem to lead to the kinds of occupational communities that increase professionalism.[169] Wheeler's data on children's librarians suggest that those who spent the most off-duty time with fellow librarians were not the most professionally motivated or the most active in professional associations.[170] Among the school

Table 5–10. Teachers' Responses to Questions Concerning
Professionalism and Satisfaction by Occupational Community
and Sex

RESPONSES CONCERNING PROFESSIONALISM AND SATISFACTION	Sex and Occupational Community (per cent*)			
	MEN		WOMEN	
	High Occupational Community	Low Occupational Community	High Occupational Community	Low Occupational Community
Read in their subject matter ten or more hours a month	52	57	38	41
Do not agree that teachers should avoid taking sides in community controversies	75	79	73	73
Believe that teacher participation in school policy-making is strongly desirable	43	41	38	36
Say that their current teaching position is better than most	65	61	68	61
Say that teaching is the most satisfactory career they can realistically imagine for themselves	27	24	39	36

* N's range from 415–422 for men high in occupational community, 918–924 for men low in occupational community, 1,808–1,835 for women high in occupational community, 4,070–4,139 for women low in occupational community.

teachers we studied, the women were about as likely as the men (31 per cent of each) to say that they spent more than half their social time with other teachers, but they were less inclined than men to use occupational colleagues as a reference group. Table 5–9 shows that the women were more likely to say that the favorable opinion of someone other than colleagues would please them most, that the opinion of someone other than colleagues had been the most influential in their professional self-evaluation, and that they would rely on the opinion of someone other than colleagues if they were placed in the role of a superintendent choosing among applicants for teaching jobs.

Table 5-10 shows that off-the-job interaction with occupational colleagues did not seem to make these teachers more professional. Those who said that more than half their social activities were with other teachers were designated high in occupational community. Considering a 5 per cent difference in the dependent variable as meaningful, as we have done elsewhere in presenting these data, the only effects of occupational community shown in Table 5-10 are a favorable one on the job satisfaction of women and a *negative* relation to the amount of professional reading by men. Occupational community was not related to satisfaction with teaching as a career, belief that teachers should avoid taking sides in public controversies, or belief in teacher participation in educational policy-making.

Compliant Predispositions of Women

We have shown reasons to expect that women accept subordination more readily than men. There is evidence that they do. Zander, Cohen, and Stotland found a strong sense of deference to psychiatrists among the social workers they studied. As we have noted earlier, they attributed some of this to the fact that the social workers were women. To test this hypothesis they compared attitudes of male and female psychologists, among whom there were enough men and women to make the comparison. They found few consistent differences between male and female psychologists, but those they found indicated that the men felt more professional rivalry with psychiatrists but less personal threat from them. The men had more desire for independence and greater willingness to work for it.[171]

Findings on teachers also indicate more compliance among women. Mason found that while first-year women teachers were about as likely as men to name "freedom from supervision" as an occupational value, they placed less stress on "exercise of leadership"; 13 per cent more men than women elementary teachers rated this as important, and the difference

was 7 per cent among secondary teachers.[172] Comparing the
male and female teachers we studied (Table 5–9), women
more often agreed that teachers should report infractions of
rules by colleagues, and less often agreed that teachers should
practice their ideas if this meant breaking rules.

In short, it seems clear that women's increased participation in the labor force has not led them to view work as
men do. Their discontinuous work histories and low vocational
commitment lead them to look upon their employment more
as a series of jobs than as a career. Accordingly, it does not
appear that their employment has had radical effects on their
self-images as females. They work in occupations, such as the
semi-professions we are discussing, in which they can play
feminine roles as helpers of the weak and dependent. With
this kind of orientation they submit more willingly to bureaucratic subordination than men and strive less for autonomy as
professionals. Unmarried women depart somewhat from the
patterns of working wives, but it seems that they too do not see
their work in the same way as men do. Thus, as Parsons says,
discussing submissiveness among librarians, "Sex composition
should therefore be considered both as a symptom and a
partial determinant of the pattern with which we are concerned."[173]

Effects on Organizations

The organizations that employ semi-
professionals tend to be authoritarian in administrative style.
The worker is often hemmed in by numerous rules, and left
little autonomy. Bryan reports, for example, that library
administrators typically do not explain decisions to subordinates, let alone consult them before making the decisions.[174]
In schools, the principal has no formal obligation to involve
teachers in decisions about such matters as determining the
acceptable level of student performance or developing student
discipline policies, and data reported by Gross and Herriott
suggest that many principals make little effort to do so.[175] The

subordination of teachers traditionally has extended into the community, where they may be bound by requirements governing many details of personal conduct.[176] Social work agencies tend to be highly bureaucratized, with caseworkers often supervised closely.[177] Nurses owe obedience to doctors and must observe elaborate hospital and nursing service regulations.[178]

Semi-professional employees do little to resist this pattern. Martin and Simpson found that most psychiatric nurses wanted doctors to tell them what to do.[179] More than three-fourths of the Pennsylvania nurses studied by Bressler and Kephart felt that a nurse should rise when a doctor enters a hospital room.[180] Corwin asked a sample of teachers what they would do in a series of administrator-teacher conflict situations. He found that while 19 per cent of them would overtly oppose the administrator, 28 per cent would normally do nothing to support their side of the conflict, and another 52 per cent would discreetly seek the support of colleagues.[181] Of the 9,122 teachers in a national sample studied by Greenhoe in 1937, more supported than opposed restrictions against teachers' shopping or living outside the local community, failing to attend church, teaching controversial issues, smoking in public, making political speeches, and drinking alcohol.[182] The smaller the community, the more its teachers tended to favor these restrictions. Greenhoe interprets this to mean that the larger communities were more tolerant of the behaviors in question and that the teachers' attitudes reflected their conceptions of community sentiment and willingness to be guided by it.[183]

Besides the compliant tendencies of their individual members, the semi-professions share another characteristic that fits the bureaucratic mold. To be successful one must normally become an administrator.[184] This is not so true in more securely established professions. The eminent scholar or medical specialist may be more esteemed than the university dean or the hospital administrator. Industrial scientists must become managers to reap the highest rewards, but they consider this wrong.[185] In contrast, semi-professionals themselves as well as the public usually regard the person who becomes an administrator more highly than the one who does his work well as a practitioner. There is little opportunity for purely professional recognition because there is little basis for it in distinctive skills to be judged by an audience of colleagues, there is little development of orientations to colleagues as the primary audience, and there is little feeling among clients or the public that specifically professional skills might deserve more rewards than administrators receive. Lacking a genuinely professional basis for recognition, semi-professional organizations create a proliferation of hierarchical levels which provide status badges. Each level guards its badge jealously. A result is still further reduction of professional colleague solidarity.

The high rates of employee turnover in these feminine occupations may also have bureaucratizing effects. Turnover reduces the colleague solidarity that might protect professional autonomy. If no one stays long, the staff may remain fragmented and without *esprit de corps*. If a few stay on while others come and go, a split may arise between a home guard of oldtimers and short-time itinerants who resent the power of this group.[186] Either of these situations makes it difficult for informal group norms to develop, and without these, excessive formalization of procedures may result. A work group which lacks the shared understandings that would enable it to deal with contingencies and work out informal solutions to problems must depend on rules, and so must a group divided into hostile camps. Rules are also apt to proliferate when large numbers of newcomers must be initiated too fast and too often, to make sure that work procedures are agreed upon and communicated to the newcomers. Such formalization of procedures can reduce flexibility. Blau has shown that professional orientations help workers to make informal adjustments to unforeseen organizational needs.[187] We are suggesting that the relationship works the other way too, with informal work norms being a precondition for fully professional orientations, because their absence leads to bureaucratization.

Once a semi-professional organization is set up along

relatively bureaucratic rather than collegial authority lines, the pattern is self-reinforcing and affects male as well as female employees. People expect the administrators to make the important decisions and the employees to comply, and the organization becomes inhospitable to other kinds of behavior. Employees who deviate from the prevailing compliant orientation are likely to be seen as troublemakers. Their efforts to show initiative and exercise autonomy may not be appreciated. Thus, Corwin found that teachers who scored high on a scale of "professional" ideology and low on a scale of "bureaucratic-employee" ideology tended to have exceptionally high rates of conflict with administrators.[188] One might speculate that such militant professionalizing employees usually submit after a brief struggle or change to other occupations, in either case leaving the field clear for authoritarian administrators and compliant employees.

Because semi-professionals lack the degree of specialized knowledge around which professionals build collegial authority patterns, their organizations would probably be run on partially bureaucratic lines even if they all were men. The fact that most semi-professionals are women does, however, seem to enhance these tendencies. The public is less willing to grant professional autonomy to women than to men, and, in ways we have discussed, women are less likely than men to develop attitudes favorable to professionalism, because most of them are oriented more toward family roles than toward work roles. So long as our family system and the prevailing attitudes of men and women about feminine sex roles remain essentially as they now are, this basic situation seems unlikely to change.

Notes

1. See the comparative analysis in Amitai Etzioni, *Modern Organizations* (Englewood Cliffs, N.J.: Prentice-Hall, 1964), pp. 75–93.

2. On the distinction of bureaucratic versus collegial control structures and on control by colleagues as an essential feature of professionalism, see Max Weber, "Bureaucracy," in *From Max Weber: Essays in Sociology,* ed. and trans. H. H. Gerth and C. Wright Mills (New York: Oxford U.P., 1946), pp. 236–39; A. M. Henderson and Talcott Parsons (eds. and trans.), *Max Weber: The Theory of Social and Economic Organization* (New York: Oxford U.P., 1947), p. 402, and Parsons, "Introduction," pp. 58–60; Eugene Litwak, "Models of Bureaucracy That Permit Conflict," in *American Journal of Sociology,* 67 (1961), 177–84; William A. Kornhauser, *Scientists in Industry: Conflict and Accommodation* (Berkeley and Los Angeles: U. of California, 1962), p. 13.

3. Computed from data in U.S. Census of Population 1960 Final Report PC(2)-7E: *Characteristics of Professional Workers,* Table 1. These figures refer to women in the experienced labor force. The percentages of women among those actually employed at the time of the census would be slightly lower, but still well over half the workers in all these occupations except secondary teaching.

4. William J. Goode succinctly analyzes this phenomenon in libraries in "The Librarian: From Occupation to Profession?" in *Seven Questions about the Profession of Librarianship,* Philip H. Ennis and Howard W. Winger, eds. (Chicago: U. of Chicago, 1962), pp. 16–17. It is found in other semi-professional organizations too.

5. Etzioni, *op. cit.,* pp. 87–89. For a related discussion, see Goode, *op. cit.,* pp. 10, 13–17.

6. Everett C. Hughes, *Men and Their Work* (New York: Free Press, 1958), p. 78.

7. For a discussion of professions as communities see William J. Goode, "Community within a Community: The Professions," in *American Sociological Review,* 22 (1957), pp. 194–200.

8. Neither sample was random, though both were broadly representative. Questionnaires were administered to students in all four-year universities and colleges in North Carolina which had complied with a request to send us their latest catalogs. All assistant professors listed in the catalogs were asked to administer questionnaires to students in their nine o'clock classes on a given day, if they taught at this hour. All students attending the classes of cooperating

faculty at the appointed hour completed the questionnaires. We have no reason to suspect that this procedure led to any systematic bias in the kinds of students selected. We are indebted to Snell Putney for explaining a somewhat similar procedure which he and Russell Middleton had used to obtain a sample of college students. The teacher questionnaires were sent to principals for distribution, with stamped return envelopes, to the teachers in their schools, after permission and lists of schools and teachers had been obtained from superintendents. The school systems included were selected to represent a broad geographic and economic spectrum within North Carolina, with some oversampling of large urban systems and the addition of one large city system in another southern state. The response rate for white teachers was 49 per cent. Negro and white college students and teachers were studied but data on Negroes are omitted from the presentation in this chapter.

9. Ward S. Mason, *The Beginning Teacher: Status and Career Orientations*, OE-23009, Circular No. 644 (Washington: U.S. Govt. Printing Office, 1961), p. 13. Backgrounds of elementary and secondary teachers differed very little. See also William Wattenberg, *et al.*, "Social Origins of Teachers," in *The Teacher's Role in American Society*, ed. Lindley J. Stiles (New York: Harper, 1957), pp. 13–16; and National Education Association, *The Status of the American Public-School Teacher* (Washington: NEA, 1957), p. 9.

10. Mason, *op. cit.*, p. 12.

11. Marvin Bressler and William M. Kephart, *Career Dynamics* (Harrisburg: Pennsylvania Nurses' Association, 1955), p. 116; Irwin Deutscher, "A Survey of the Social and Occupational Characteristics of a Metropolitan Nurse Complement" (Kansas City, Mo.: Community Studies, Inc., 1956), cited in Everett C. Hughes, Helen MacGill Hughes, and Irwin Deutscher, *Twenty Thousand Nurses Tell Their Story* (Philadelphia: Lippincott, 1958), p. 22; Harry W. Martin and Ida Harper Simpson, *Patterns of Psychiatric Nursing: A Study of Psychiatric Nursing in North Carolina* (Chapel Hill: Institute for Research in Social Science, U. of North Carolina, 1956), p. 14.

12. Mason (*op. cit.*, p. 13), shows these comparisons. The data he gives are from Douglas M. More, "A Note on Occupational Origins of Health Service Professions," in *American Sociological Review*, 25 (1960), 404; Paul F. Lazarsfeld and Wagner Thielens, Jr., *The Academic Mind* (New York: Free Press, 1958), p. 401; Stuart Adams,

"Regional Differences in Vertical Mobility in a High-Status Occupation," in *American Sociological Review*, 15 (1950), 231; and Bressler and Kephart, *op. cit.*, p. 116.

13. Alice I. Bryan, *The Public Librarian* (New York: Columbia U.P., 1952), p. 34.

14. Norman Polansky, William Bowen, Lucille Gordon, and Conrad Nathan, "Social Workers in Society," in *Journal of Social Work*, 34 (1953), 74–80.

15. R. Clyde White, "Social Workers in Society: Some Further Evidence," in *Journal of Social Work*, 34 (1953), 161–64.

16. Charles N. Lebeaux, "Some Factors in the Advancement of Professional Social Workers," paper presented at the annual meeting of the American Sociological Society, 1955, pp. 4–5.

17. Mason, *op. cit.*, pp. 11–13; Lebeaux, *op. cit.*, p. 5.

18. White, *op. cit.*

19. G. Franklin Edwards, *The Negro Professional Class* (New York: Free Press, 1959). See also Carter Goodwin Woodson, *The Negro Professional Man and the Community* (Washington: Association for the Study of Negro Life and History, 1934), pp. 45–49.

20. Morris Rosenberg, with the assistance of Edward A. Suchman and Rose K. Goldsen, *Occupations and Values* (New York: Free Press, 1957), p. 54.

21. Harriet M. Kandler, "Why Students Chose Nursing as a Career: Analysis of Opinions of Sixty Students," Report to the American Nurses' Association on Boston Psychopathic Studies, Metropolitan State Hospital Project, cited in Hughes, Hughes, and Deutscher, *op. cit.*, pp. 211–12.

22. James A. Davis, *Undergraduate Career Decisions* (Chicago: Aldine, 1965), pp. 17–36.

23. Bureau of Labor Statistics, "Economic Status of Social Welfare Workers in 1960," in *Monthly Labor Review*, 84 (1961), 862–68.

24. Robert D. Leigh, *The Public Library in the United States* (New York: Columbia U.P., 1950), p. 142.

25. Sara H. Wheeler, "Children's Librarians in the Northwest," in *Libraries and Librarians of the Pacific Northwest*, Pacific Northwest Library Association, Library Development Projects Reports, Vol. IV, ed. Morton Kroll (Seattle: U. of Washington, 1960), p. 146. She does not state the exact number who had worked in other fields.

26. Bryan, *op. cit.*, pp. 118, 120.

27. Ralph H. Parker, "Ports of Entry into Librarianship," in Ennis and Winger, *op. cit.*, p. 50. On drift into librarianship see also Wheeler, *op. cit.*, p. 147; and Agnes L. Reagan, Discussion of Parker, *op. cit.*, pp. 54–55.

28. Dael Wolfle, *America's Resources of Specialized Talent* (New York: Harper, 1954), p. 200, shows education ranking fifth from the bottom among nineteen fields in intelligence test scores of postgraduate students. (Dentistry, business and commerce, home economics, and physical education were lower.) James A. Davis (*op. cit.*, pp. 48–49) sheds a more favorable light on education majors; he finds them about average in undergraduate grades. The discrepancy between Wolfle's and Davis' data may reflect the lack of comparability of grades (Davis' measure) in different subjects (see Wolfle, *op. cit.*, pp. 204–5), or it may mean that graduate students excel undergraduates less in education than in other fields, or both.

29. Bryan, *op. cit.*, p. 128.

30. Wolfle, *op. cit.*, pp. 275–76.

31. Parker, *op. cit.*, p. 51; Ernest J. Reece, *The Task and Training of Librarians* (New York: King's Crown, 1949), p. 65; Agnes Lytton Reagan, *A Study of Factors Influencing College Students to Become Librarians*, ACRL Monograph No. 21 (Chicago: Association of College and Research Libraries, 1958), p. 6.

32. White, *op. cit.*

33. On librarians, see Bryan, *op. cit.*, p. 128. On teachers, see Davis, *op. cit.*, pp. 81, 87–88.

34. On teachers and social workers, see Rosenberg, *op. cit.*, pp. 18, 27, 78. On nurses, see Kandler, *op. cit.* and Ida Harper Simpson, "Patterns of Socialization into Professions," in *Sociological Inquiry*,

37 (1967), 47–54. On librarians, see Bryan, *op. cit.*, p. 129. We shall discuss service motivations of semi-professionals more extensively later in this chapter.

35. Mason, *op. cit.*, pp. 71–78; Davis, *op. cit.*, p. 80.

36. Rosenberg, *op. cit.*, pp. 48–49.

37. Irene M. Wightwick, *Vocational Interest Patterns* (New York: Columbia U.P., 1945); Mirra Komarovsky, *Women in the Modern World* (Boston: Little, Brown, 1953), p. 92.

38. Komarovsky, *op. cit.*, pp. 93–97; Richard L. Simpson and Ida Harper Simpson, "Occupational Choice among Career-Oriented College Women," in *Marriage and Family Living*, 23 (1961), 377–83.

39. James A. Davis, *Great Aspirations* (Chicago: Aldine, 1964), pp. 61–99.

40. Rosenberg, *op. cit.*, p. 50.

41. Simpson and Simpson, *op. cit.*

42. *Ibid.*

43. James A. Davis, *Great Aspirations*, p. 86.

44. *1962 Handbook on Women Workers*, U.S. Department of Labor, Women's Bureau, Bulletin No. 285 (Washington: U.S. Gov't. Printing Office, 1963).

45. Alice S. Rossi, "Equality Between the Sexes," in *Daedalus*, 93 (1964), 638.

46. Rosenberg, *op. cit.*, pp. 66–67.

47. Howard S. Becker and James W. Carper, "The Development of Identification with an Occupation," in *American Journal of Sociology*, 61 (1956), 289–98.

48. Robert Lloyd Hoffelder, "The Married Woman School Teacher: A Study of Role Conflict," unpublished M.A. thesis (Chapel Hill: University of North Carolina, 1964), p. 2.

49. *Ibid.*, pp. 20–22, 45.

50. Hughes, Hughes, and Deutscher, *op. cit.*, p. 185. Robert W. Habenstein and Edwin A. Christ, *Professionalizer, Traditionalizer and Utilizer* (second edition) (Columbia: U. of Missouri, 1963).

51. George F. Theriault, "A Study of Functions of Nurses in Eleven New Hampshire Communities," unpublished ms. (Hanover, N. H.: Dartmouth College, 1957), cited in Hughes, Hughes, and Deutscher, *op. cit.*, p. 185.

52. National Science Foundation, "Women in Scientific Careers," (Washington: U.S. Gov't. Printing Office, 1961), p. 4.

53. Esther Peterson, "Working Women," in *Daedalus*, 93 (1964), 674.

54. National Science Foundation, *loc. cit.*

55. Peterson, *loc. cit.*

56. Computed from data in *Who Are the Working Mothers?*, U.S. Department of Labor, Women's Bureau, Leaflet 37 (Washington: U.S. Gov't. Printing Office, [rev.] 1963).

57. *Ibid.*

58. *Ibid.* See also Robert W. Smuts, *Women and Work in America* (New York: Columbia U.P., 1959), p. 36.

59. Mason, *op. cit.*, p. 103.

60. Donald Stewart and Christine E. Needham, "The Operating Room Nurse—The Function of the Operating Room Nurse in Ten Arkansas Hospitals," (p. 3) and "The General Duty Nurse," (p. 27), unpublished mss. (Fayetteville: U. of Arkansas, 1955), cited in Hughes, Hughes, and Deutscher, *op. cit.*, p. 239.

61. Leonard Reissman, "Social Psychological Characteristics of the Hospital Employee," in *Change and Dilemma in the Nursing Profession,* ed. Leonard Reissman and John H. Rohrer (New York: Putnam's, 1957), p. 157.

62. Bryan, *op. cit.*, p. 37. This statistic refers to her combined sample of professional-level and sub-professional library workers, and the percentage might be lower among the professionals.

63. Habenstein and Christ, *op. cit.*, p. 76.

64. See the sources in notes 7, 8, 9, and 10.

65. Bryan found that 37 per cent of the husbands of female professional librarians were engaged in professional occupations, and data

of Habenstein and Christ show that only 13 per cent of the husbands
of nurses were professional. Bryan, *op. cit.*, p. 36; Habenstein and
Christ, *op. cit.*, Table 12, p. 133.

66. Analysis of available data shows clearly the pattern of fewer
marriages among the more educated women, though the pattern has
become less marked as a rising percentage of women has attended
college in recent years. See, for example, Metropolitan Life Insurance
Company, "Marriage and Educational Attainment," *Statistical Bulletin*
XXVI, 8 (1945), 5; Clifford Kirkpatrick, *The Family* (New York:
Ronald, 1955), p. 378; Wilson H. Grabill, Clyde V. Kiser, and
Pascal K. Whelpton, *The Fertility of American Women* (New York:
Wiley, 1958), Table 67; William Petersen, *Population* (New York:
Macmillan, 1961), p. 221. Probably, in the case of women who
attend graduate school, lack of a husband is often the reason for the
extra education and the career choice, rather than vice versa.

67. Bryan, *op. cit.*, p. 118.

68. Ronald G. Corwin, *A Sociology of Education* (New York: Appleton,
1965), pp. 5–6.

69. W. W. Charters, Jr., "Survival in the Teaching Profession: A
Criterion for Selecting Teacher Trainees," in *Journal of Teacher
Education*, 7 (1956), 253. These figures say nothing, of course, about
those who enter teaching for the first time more than ten years after
college, or about those who leave during this ten-year period, but
later return.

70. Polansky, Bowen, Gordon, and Nathan, *op. cit.*

71. Mason, *op. cit.*, p. 55. This figure and the total on which it is
based exclude student husbands, who were almost one-fourth of the
over-all total.

72. Martin and Simpson, *op. cit.*, p. 14. For information on the
kinds of functions the attendants sometimes performed, see Richard
L. Simpson and Ida Harper Simpson, "The Psychiatric Attendant:
Development of an Occupational Self-Image in a Low-Status
Occupation," in *American Sociological Review*, 24 (1959), 389–92.

73. Mason, *op. cit.*, p. 93.

74. Milred W. Weil, "An Analysis of Factors Influencing Married

Women's Actual or Planned Work Participation," in *American Sociological Review*, 26 (1961), 91–96.

75. Hoffelder, *op. cit.*, p. 11.

76. Joel F. Bennett, "Feminine Role Conflict," unpublished ms. (Chapel Hill: Department of Sociology, University of North Carolina, 1964). This relationship was partly, but not wholly, the result of the association of youth with high role conflict and with low career orientation.

77. Margaret Cussler, *The Woman Executive* (New York: Harcourt, 1958).

78. Deutscher, "A Survey of the Social and Occupational Characteristics of a Metropolitan Nurse Complement," cited in Hughes, Hughes, and Deutscher, *op. cit.*, p. 116.

79. Weil, *op. cit.*

80. U.S. Department of Labor, *Who Are the Working Mothers?*

81. Smuts, *op. cit.*

82. Betty Friedan, *The Feminine Mystique* (New York: W. W. Norton, 1963).

83. Jessie Bernard, *Academic Women* (University Park: Pennsylvania State U.P., 1964).

84. U.S. Department of Labor, Women's Bureau, *Spotlight on Women in the United States, 1956–57* (Washington: U.S. Government Printing Office, n. d. [mimeographed]. This study was done in 1945, a time when far fewer women worked than today.

85. Hughes, Hughes, and Deutscher, *op. cit.*, p. 43. The study referred to is Deutscher, "A Survey of the Social and Occupational Characteristics of a Metropolitan Nurse Complement."

86. Mason, *op. cit.*, p. 109.

87. Hughes, Hughes, and Deutscher, *op. cit.*, pp. 265–66. They cite evidence from Stewart and Needham, "The Operating Room Nurse"; Erna Barschak, *Today's Industrial Nurse and Her Job* (New York: Putnam's, 1957); Elizabeth Couey and Diane D. Stephenson, "The Field of Private Duty Nursing" (Atlanta: Georgia State Nurses' Association, 1955); and Martin and Simpson, *op. cit.*

88. Habenstein and Christ, *op. cit.*, p. 73. See also Couey and Stephenson, *op. cit.*, quoted in Hughes, Hughes, and Deutscher, *op. cit.*, p. 266.

89. For various estimates of school district turnover see Ward S. Mason and Robert K. Bain, *Teacher Turnover in the Public Schools, 1957–58,* U.S. Department of Health, Education, and Welfare, Office of Education, Circular No. 608, 1959, and *Teacher Turnover in Public Elementary and Secondary Schools,* HEW-OE, 1963 (Washington: U.S. Gov't. Printing Office); and National Education Association, *op. cit.* A rate of "nearly 30 per cent," which may refer to individual schools rather than entire districts, is indicated in *The New Copyright Law and the Public Interest,* a pamphlet prepared by the Copyright Committee of the American Textbook Publishers Institute (New York: 1965), p. 4; but no source is cited for this statistic.

90. Mason and Bain, *Teacher Turnover in Public Elementary and Secondary Schools,* p. 11.

91. National Education Association, *op. cit.*

92. Bryan, *op. cit.,* p. 199.

93. Department of Health, Education, and Welfare, Social Security Administration, Bureau of Public Assistance, "California Separation of Social Workers," (Washington: U.S. Gov't. Printing Office; August, 1956).

94. *Ibid.* Bryan's data (*op. cit.,* p. 200) suggest this also.

95. Department of Health, Education, and Welfare, Social Security Administration, Bureau of Public Assistance, *op. cit.*

96. Department of Health, Education, and Welfare, Social Security Administration, Bureau of Public Assistance, Division of Program Statistics and Analysis, *Selected Information about Personnel Entering and Leaving Casework Positions in Public Assistance Agencies, Fiscal Year 1954* (Washington: U.S. Gov't. Printing Office; July 1955).

97. *Ibid.*

98. National Education Association, *op. cit.*

99. Howard S. Becker, "The Career of the Chicago Public Schoolteacher," in *American Journal of Sociology,* 57 (1952), 470–77.

100. Bureau of Labor Statistics, "Economic Status of Social Welfare Workers in 1960," gives 1960 data. The 1950 data are from United States Department of Labor, Bureau of Labor Statistics, "Economic Status of Social Workers," in *Monthly Labor Review*, 72 (1951), 391–95. On 1950, see also Maxine G. Stewart, "The Economic Status of Social Workers, 1950," in *Social Work*, 32 (1951), 53–62.

101. Bryan, *op. cit.*, p. 88.

102. Smuts, *op. cit.*, p. 104.

103. Bryan, *op. cit.*, p. 87.

104. Bureau of Labor Statistics, "Economic Status of Social Workers."

105. Bryan, *op. cit.*, pp. 29, 32–33.

106. Bureau of Labor Statistics, "Economic Status of Social Welfare Workers in 1960." The remaining 26 per cent of the women and 30 per cent of the men were in intermediate and miscellaneous categories.

107. Women's Bureau, *1962 Handbook on Women Workers*, p. 19. The community size difference is opposite in direction to the one we have mentioned in social agencies and libraries.

108. *Ibid.*

109. Hughes, Hughes, and Deutscher, *op. cit.*, pp. 228–29.

110. Harold L. Wilensky and Charles N. Lebeaux, *Industrial Society and Social Welfare* (New York: Russell Sage Foundation, 1958), p. 323.

111. Theodore Caplow, *The Sociology of Work* (Minneapolis: U. of Minnesota, 1954), p. 239.

112. William Foote Whyte, *Human Relations in the Restaurant Industry* (New York: McGraw-Hill, 1948), pp. 66–81.

113. For a discussion related to this point, see Oliver Garceau, *The Public Library in the Political Process* (New York: Columbia U.P., 1949), pp. 114–15.

114. Cussler, *op. cit.*

115. Bryan, *op. cit.*, pp. 366–67.

116. Mirra Komarovsky, review of Jessie Bernard, *Academic Women,* in *Social Forces,* 43 (1965), 604.

117. The difference is less when elementary teachers (men, 42 per cent versus women, 33 per cent) and secondary teachers (57 versus 51 per cent) are considered separately. The combined difference exceeds the separate elementary and secondary level differences because over three-fifths of the women were elementary teachers whereas over nine-tenths of the men were secondary teachers.

118. Caplow (*op. cit.*, p. 235) notes that women's residential immobility is especially disadvantageous "on the high occupational levels, where almost all positions involve the possibility of a change of residence, and in private bureaucracies, which attach particular emphasis to experience in different parts of the organization." This applies chiefly in big business, and is not usually a factor in semi-professional organizations, which are mainly local in scope.

119. Theriault, *op. cit.*, cited in Hughes, Hughes, and Deutscher, *op. cit.*, p. 185.

120. Stewart and Needham, "The General Duty Nurse," p. 21, cited in Hughes, Hughes, and Deutscher, *op. cit.*, p. 240.

121. Deutscher, "A Survey of the Social and Occupational Characteristics of a Metropolitan Nurse Complement," p. 57, cited in Hughes, Hughes, and Deutscher, *op. cit.*, p. 241.

122. Peterson, *op. cit.*, p. 674.

123. Caplow, *op. cit.*, pp. 242–43.

124. *Ibid.*, p. 242; Katherine Archibald, *War Time Shipyard* (Berkeley: U. of California, 1947), pp. 15–39. Jessie Bernard (*op. cit.*) found that women scientists' integration into colleague communication systems was inferior to men's, though not greatly so.

125. Garceau, *op. cit.*, pp. 114–15.

126. For these distinctions, see Amitai Etzioni, *A Comparative Analysis of Complex Organizations* (New York: Free Press, 1961).

127. Alvin Zander, Arthur R. Cohen, and Ezra Stotland, *Role*

Relations in the Mental Health Professions (Ann Arbor, Michigan: Institute for Social Research, Research Center for Group Dynamics, 1957), pp. 39–81.

128. Bressler and Kephart, *op. cit.*, cited in Hughes, Hughes, and Deutscher, *op. cit.*, p. 169.

129. Marjorie Fiske, *Book Selection and Censorship: A Study of School and Public Libraries in California* (Berkeley and Los Angeles: U. of California, 1959), pp. 35–36.

130. Computed from Habenstein and Christ, *op. cit.*, p. 132. In their sample the husbands of 79 per cent of the 24 directors, assistant directors, and supervisors were in white-collar or skilled fields; but of the 58 husbands of staff R. N.s, 58 per cent were farmers or lower blue-collar workers. This difference takes on added meaning when we recall that women with high-status husbands are the most likely to drop out of nursing temporarily or permanently.

131. Rosenberg, *op. cit.*, p. 49.

132. This research is discussed in Simpson and Simpson, *op. cit.*, and in their "Values, Personal Influence, and Occupational Choice," in *Social Forces,* 39 (1960), 116–25; but these articles do not give directly comparable data for men and women on this item.

133. Rosenberg, *op. cit.*, p. 42.

134. *Ibid.* See also Davis, *Great Aspirations*, p. 34, for similar sex differences using the same questions with a different sample.

135. Rosenberg, *op. cit.*, pp. 46–47. Others were medicine, social science, and personnel. Nursing and librarianship were not included in Rosenberg's study.

136. W. Edgar Vinacke, "Sex Roles in a Three-Person Game," in *Sociometry,* 22 (1959), 343–60; the quotation is from p. 357. See also John R. Bond and W. Edgar Vinacke, "Coalitions in Mixed-Sex Triads," in *Sociometry,* 24 (1961), 61–75; and Thomas K. Uesugi and W. Edgar Vinacke, "Strategy in a Feminine Game," in *Sociometry,* 26 (1963), 75–88.

137. James S. Coleman, personal communication.

138. Rosenberg, *op. cit.*, p. 50; Simpson and Simpson, "Occupational Choice among Career-Oriented College Women." Rosenberg

maintains that more students shift their occupational choices toward fields consistent with their values than shift their values to conform with their occupational choices; but Davis, re-analyzing Rosenberg's data, finds the two kinds of shifts equally prevalent, and a study of nurses by Katz and Martin shows that explanations for career choices are often invoked after the fact, to justify the choices. See Rosenberg, *op. cit.*, p. 22; Davis, *Great Aspirations*, p. 32, note 8; Fred E. Katz and Harry W. Martin, "Career Choice Processes," in *Social Forces*, 41 (1962), 149–54. None of these authors' data bear directly on the strength of commitment to the chosen field.

139. Zander, Cohen, and Stotland, *op. cit.*, pp. 43–46, 51.

140. William H. Whyte, Jr., *The Organization Man* (Garden City, N.Y.: Doubleday Anchor, 1957), pp. 3–152.

141. William E. Henry, "The Business Executive: The Psychodynamics of a Social Role," in *American Journal of Sociology*, 54 (1949), 286–91. Whyte (*op. cit.*, pp. 155–72) contrasts the independence and autonomy of such top executives with the conformity of the organization men at lower echelons.

142. On service orientation and professionalism, see Abraham Flexner, "Is Social Work a Profession?" in *School and Society*, 1 (1915), 901–11; A. M. Carr-Saunders and P. A. Wilson, *The Professions* (Oxford: Clarendon Press, 1933), pp. 284–86; Ernest Greenwood, "Attributes of a Profession," in *Social Work*, 2 (1957), 45–55.

143. Talcott Parsons, *The Social System* (New York: Free Press, 1951), pp. 434–36.

144. Ida Harper Simpson, "The Development of Professional Self-Images Among Student Nurses," unpublished Ph.D. dissertation (Chapel Hill: University of North Carolina, 1956). This example and our analysis of the ideal-type professional orientation are truer of physicians in large hospitals and clinics than of traditional family doctors, who often establish somewhat more particularistic and diffuse relations with their patients.

145. Rosenberg, *op. cit.*, pp. 26–27.

146. *Ibid.*, p. 27.

147. Davis, *Great Aspirations*, p. 173.

148. *Ibid.*, pp. 174, 177.

149. Kaspar D. Naegele and Elaine Culley Stolar, "Income and Prestige," in *Library Journal*, 85 (1960), 2888–91. Alvin W. Gouldner makes a similar statement about social workers in "The Secrets of Organizations," in *The Social Welfare Forum, 1963, Official Proceedings*, 90th Annual Forum, National Conference on Social Welfare (New York: Columbia U.P., 1963), pp. 162–64.

150. Polansky, Bowen, Gordon, and Nathan, *op. cit.*

151. Habenstein and Christ, *op. cit.*, p. 73.

152. Hughes, Hughes, and Deutscher, *op. cit.*, p. 214.

153. See Etzioni, *Modern Organizations*, pp. 87–88.

154. Everett C. Hughes, "Education for a Profession," in *Seven Questions*, ed. Ennis and Winger, p. 41.

155. Martin and Simpson, *op. cit.*, pp. 100–103, 113–15.

156. Davida P. Gates, "The Professional Socialization of Student Teachers in North Carolina," unpublished M.A. thesis (Chapel Hill: University of North Carolina, 1964), pp. 74–80.

157. Wilensky and Lebeaux, *op. cit.*, pp. 322–23.

158. Mason, *op. cit.*, p. 75.

159. Some of these items were adapted from those used in a study of nurses by Ronald G. Corwin, to whom we are indebted for a copy of his questionnaire. Table 5–9 and the foregoing discussion omit items on which sex differences in the dependent variables were less than 5 per cent, and items on which sex differences of 5 per cent or more in the total sample were reversed among elementary or secondary teachers considered separately. On no item, however, was there a sex difference as large as 5 per cent in the direction opposite to the one hypothesized.

160. James S. Coleman, *The Adolescent Society* (New York: Free Press, 1961), pp. 252–53. See also Davis, *Great Aspirations*, p. 29, note 5, for a related finding among college students.

161. On doctors and hospital administrators, see Harvey L. Smith, "Two Lines of Authority Are One Too Many," in *Modern Hospital*, 84 (1955), pp. 59–64.

162. Peter M. Blau, *The Dynamics of Bureaucracy,* second edition (Chicago: U. of Chicago, 1963), pp. 25-26. Not all the counselors he studied had social work training, but some did. Strikingly similar conclusions were reached independently, in a study of the same kind of agency in a different city, by Roy G. Francis and Robert C. Stone, *Service and Procedure in a Bureaucracy* (Minneapolis: U. of Minnesota, 1956). It is not clear whether any of the counselors they studied were trained as social workers. See also the replication and extension of Blau's study in Harry Cohen, *The Demonics of Bureaucracy* (Ames: Iowa State U.P., 1965). There is no indication that the workers Cohen studied included trained social workers.

163. Bel Kaufman, *Up the Down Staircase* (Englewood Cliffs, N.J.: Prentice-Hall, 1964).

164. On family roles, see Morris Zelditch, Jr., "Role Differentiation in the Nuclear Family: A Comparative Study," in *Family, Socialization and Interaction Process,* eds. Talcott Parsons and Robert F. Bales (New York: Free Press, 1955), pp. 307-52.

165. Smuts, *op. cit.,* p. 108.

166. Bressler and Kephart, *op. cit.*; Habenstein and Christ, *op. cit.*; Theriault, *op. cit.* For a summary discussion, see Hughes, Hughes, and Deutscher, *op. cit.,* pp. 229-30.

167. Mason, *op. cit.,* 103. The second set of figures represents our calculations from his data.

168. Archibald, *op. cit.*; Bernard, *op. cit.*; John James, "Clique Organization in a Small Industrial Plant," in *Pacific Sociological Review, Research Studies, State College of Washington,* 19 (1951), 126-29; Stan R. Nikkel, "Characteristics of the Informal Organization: An Observational Study of the United States Committee for UNICEF," unpublished M.A. thesis (Chapel Hill: University of North Carolina, 1964), pp. 97-110. A general discussion of sex differences in clique formation, citing research in nonwork settings, is given in Gardner Lindzey and Edgar F. Borgatta, "Sociometric Measurement," in *Handbook of Social Psychology,* ed. Gardner Lindzey (Cambridge, Mass.: Addison-Wesley, 1954), p. 430. Blau and Scott, however, found no relation between sex homogeneity and work group cohesion in the welfare agencies they studied; see Peter M. Blau and W. Richard Scott, *Formal Organizations: A Comparative Approach* (San Francisco: Chandler, 1962), p. 109.

169. On the relation of occupational communities to work commitment and colleague relations on the job, see Seymour Martin Lipset, Martin A. Trow, and James S. Coleman, *Union Democracy* (Garden City, N.Y.: Doubleday Anchor, 1962), pp. 77–159, 257–60, 413–18; Joel E. Gerstl, "Determinants of Occupational Community in High-Status Occupations," in *Sociological Quarterly*, 2 (1961), 37–48; Robert Blauner, "Work Satisfaction and Industrial Trends in Modern Society," in *Labor and Trade Unionism: An Interdisciplinary Reader*, ed. Walter Galenson and Seymour Martin Lipset (New York: Wiley, 1960), pp. 350–52; Peter J. Fensham and Douglas Hooper, *The Dynamics of a Changing Technology* (London: Tavistock, 1964), p. 150.

170. Wheeler, *op. cit.*, pp. 150–51.

171. Zander, Cohen, and Stotland, *op. cit.*, pp. 39–81.

172. Mason, *op. cit.*, p. 75.

173. Talcott Parsons, "Implications of the Study," in *The Climate of Book Selection*, ed. J. Periam Danton (Berkeley: U. of California School of Librarianship, 1959), pp. 94–95.

174. Bryan, *op. cit.*, pp. 165–66. See also Kaspar D. Naegele and Elaine Culley Stolar, "The Librarian of the Northwest," in *Libraries and Librarians* . . . , p. 112; Naegele and Stolar, "Income and Prestige," *op. cit.*, p. 2891.

175. Neal Gross and Robert E. Herriott, *Staff Leadership in Public Schools* (New York: Wiley, 1965), pp. 121–22. They do not say exactly how many of the principals they studied attempt to involve teachers in decisions, but it is clear from their discussion that while many do, many others do not. Other discussions of authority in schools give an impression of less variation among principals and more thorough subordination of teachers than Gross and Herriott's data seem to indicate: Corwin, *op. cit.*, pp. 218–19; Howard S. Becker, "The Teacher in the Authority System of the Public School," in *Journal of Educational Sociology*, 27 (1953), 129–41.

176. Willard Waller, *The Sociology of Teaching* (New York: Wiley, 1932), pp. 43–66; Howard K. Beale, *Are American Teachers Free?* (New York: Scribner's, 1936), pp. 374–409; Lloyd A. Cook, Ronald B. Almack, and Florence Greenhoe, "The Teacher and Community Relations," in *American Sociological Review*, 3 (1938),

167–74; Florence Greenhoe, *Community Contacts and Participation of Teachers* (Washington: American Council on Public Affairs, 1941), pp. 40–61. Community conduct codes for teachers have been considerably relaxed since World War II but have by no means disappeared; see Lloyd Manwiller, "Expectations Regarding Teachers," in *Journal of Experimental Education*, 26 (1958), 315–54. Alma S. Wittlin, "The Teacher," in *Daedalus*, 92 (1963), 749, notes that the official code of the National Education Association requires acceptance of community control.

177. Wilensky and Lebeaux, *op. cit.*, pp. 235–38; Gouldner, *op. cit.*, p. 172; Edgar May, *The Wasted Americans* (New York: Harper, 1964), pp. 104–21; Hallowell Pope and Edgar W. Butler, "Public Social Welfare and Bureaucracy," unpublished ms. (Chapel Hill: University of North Carolina, 1965). The discussions by May and by Pope and Butler parallel the conclusions of Blau (*op. cit.*), Francis and Stone (*op. cit.*) and Cohen (*op. cit.*), that bureaucratic controls over agency personnel are often reflected in an over-bureaucratized approach to clients and their needs.

178. See the discussions of doctor–nurse authority relations in Milton J. Lesnik, *Nursing Practice and the Law* (Philadelphia: Lippincott, 1947), pp. 277–78; Eleanor C. Lambersten, *Education for Nursing Leadership* (Philadelphia: Lippincott, 1958), p. 82; Robert Guy Brown, "Problems of Social Organization in a New Psychiatric Inpatient Service," unpublished Ph.D. dissertation (Chapel Hill: University of North Carolina, 1960), p. 51; Elinor V. Fuerst and LuVerne Wolff, *Fundamentals of Nursing* (Philadelphia: Lippincott, 1964), pp. 7, 581; and William A. Rushing, *The Psychiatric Professions: Power, Conflict, and Adaptation in a Psychiatric Hospital Staff* (Chapel Hill: U. of North Carolina, 1964), pp. 113–17.

179. Martin and Simpson, *op. cit.*, p. 91. See also Brown, *op. cit.*, p. 83; and Rushing, *op. cit.*, pp. 113–14. All of these authors suggest that nurses may desire more guidance in psychiatric work, where roles are poorly defined, than in other nursing specialties, but similar orientations among nonpsychiatric nurses are shown in Reissman, *op. cit.*, pp. 148–52.

180. Bressler and Kephart, *op. cit.*, cited in Hughes, Hughes, and Deutscher, *op. cit.*, p. 168.

181. Ronald G. Corwin, "Militant Professionalism, Initiative and

Compliance in Public Education," in *Sociology of Education,* 38 (1965), 310–31; see the table on p. 320. See also the related discussions in Becker, "The Teacher in the Authority System of the Public School," and Corwin, *A Sociology of Education,* pp. 219–21.

182. Greenhoe, *op. cit.,* p. 51. Her sample of teachers was national and broadly representative though not random. More recent evidence of such attitudes among teachers, though with liberalization evident since the time of Greenhoe's 1937 study, is reported in Manwiller, *op. cit.,* and in Hugh Max Miller, "Teacher Roles and Community Integration," unpublished Ph.D. dissertation (Chapel Hill: University of North Carolina, 1964), pp. 36–37, 55–57, 89–92, 116–20, 133.

183. Greenhoe, *op. cit.,* p. 56.

184. Goode, "The Librarian: From Occupation to Profession?" pp. 16–17, discusses this situation. Some efforts are being made to modify the remunerative aspect. For example, a news item in *Phi Delta Kappan,* 47 (1965), 256 reports a plan being considered in the Detroit school system to enable a selected number of outstanding classroom teachers to earn salaries up to the maximum paid to assistant elementary school principals. This plan would create considerable overlap of teacher and administrator salary scales but would leave many administrators earning more than any teacher. Similar plans are being implemented in parts of New York State.

185. Simon Marcson, *The Scientist in American Industry: Some Organizational Determinants in Manpower Utilization* (Princeton, N.J.: Princeton University, Department of Economics, Industrial Relations Section, 1960), pp. 61–85; Kornhauser, *op. cit.,* pp. 128, 136–40.

186. For the concepts of home guard versus itinerants, see Hughes, *Men and Their Work,* pp. 129, 130, 136. Habenstein and Christ (*op. cit.,* pp. 48–58), present a good analysis of "home-guardism" in a hospital.

187. Blau, *op. cit.,* pp. 256–60.

188. Corwin, "Militant Professionalism, Initiative and Compliance in Public Education," pp. 326–28.

CHAPTER SIX

The Theoretical Limits
of Professionalization* ▲

William J. Goode

DEPARTMENT OF SOCIOLOGY

COLUMBIA UNIVERSITY

SOCIAL THEORISTS HAVE ATTEMPTED TO
explain why an industrial society is a
professionalizing one, and in fact the percentage of the
United States labor force that is *professional and technical* does
increase each decade. How far can this trend go? An exploration of the theoretical limits of professionalization should
illuminate both sets of processes that create this trend: how a
profession comes into being, and how a society facilitates or
impedes the development of professions.

Such an inquiry leads to the conclusion that many aspiring

* This paper was originally presented under the same title at the 1960
meetings of the American Sociological Association in St. Louis. It was revised
substantially and given as part of a lecture series"The Professional as Educator,"
directed by Prof. Arthur W. Foshay, at Teachers College of Columbia University
in the spring of 1968. It has been partially supported by N.S.F. Grant G.S-2180.
Louis Perin and Stanley H. Raffel have been helpful in the final preparation of
manuscript.

occupations and semi-professions will never become professions in the usual sense: they will never reach the levels of knowledge and dedication to service the society considers necessary for a profession. Such occupations include school teaching, nursing, librarianship, pharmacy, stockbroking, advertising, business management, and others.

Further, most of the occupations that do rise to such high levels will continue to be viewed as qualitatively different from the four great *person* professions: law, medicine, the ministry, and university teaching. This view will correspond to a social reality, for they *will* be less *professional* in such traits as cohesion, commitment to norms of service, percentage of members remaining in the profession throughout their lifetime, homogeneity of membership, control over professional violations, and others. In this narrower sense, then, the occupational structure of industrial society is not becoming *generally* more professionalized, even though a higher percentage of the labor force is in occupations that enjoy higher prestige rankings and income and that *call* themselves "professions." An examination of these limitations should clarify somewhat the general place of the professions in modern society.

Competition Among Occupations

All societies are systems of competition among individuals. Each person makes demands on the money, power, or prestige markets, and these are accepted or rejected. But each is also a member of a stratum, occupation, or of various groups whose members are in similar positions, making similar demands. Leaders and their followers in a given occupation work out (consciously or not) strategies and tactics for aggrandizement on the basis of whatever amateur social science engineering they can command. Whether these people are united, as in a labor union, or merely a social aggregate, their total collective failure or success in these exchanges has a continuing effect on the terms of *individual* bargaining in the next phase, and on the rise or fall of occupations.

But though mere aggregate effects are of some importance, doubtless folk sociology is correct in its ancient assertion that a united group can gain what an individual cannot, or that an individual's investment in a group may ultimately pay off. Skill and time invested in the formation of a guild might, for example, yield an occupational monopoly from which great individual advantage could be wrung. Raising the educational standards in medicine in the decade 1910–20 required the expenditure of power, money, and friendship,[1*] but that investment raised the prestige ranking of the physician, the power of the profession in legislation, and the income level of the average M.D.

Such group efforts may also fail to yield any perceptible rise. Men invested enough to organize a Swine Breeders Association, and even wrote a code of ethics for its members, but that movement—like that of hundreds of other such organizations for which codes have been written—doubtless paid off more in friendly interaction among its members than in power or prestige in the larger society.

These processes by which an occupation tries to rise constitute a set of transactions among the occupation as a collectivity, its individual members, other related occupations, and the larger society. In the stratification of occupations, as in that of individuals, each actor decides what the other is worth and finds out what it or he is worth through the outcome of a continuing set of exchanges, of demands or offers made and acceptances or rejections received. However, for the most part these evaluations are based on values and norms each already accepts, and only over time are they created within those transactions themselves.[2]

Members of an occupation give a higher prestige ranking to it than do other members of the society; thus, they try to get more deference than others will concede. They are forced to accept less money than they want, and achieve less in protective legislation than they seek. They are held in place

* Notes to this chapter begin on p. 308.

by their closest occupational kin (e.g., one of the various building trades will not rise much above the others), and by the refusal of others in the society to agree they are worth that much.

Economic supply and demand, shaped by such factors as monopoly, entrance restrictions, shifts in tastes, and the like will determine how high their incomes will be, but supply and demand operate in the markets of power and prestige as well. An occupation can command more prestige only if the society, applying its evaluative criteria, perceives the performances of the occupation to be better than before or higher than those of similar occupations. An occupation can enjoy more power if it can exchange some of its friendly relations, income, prestige, or political influence for legal privileges or controls.

Occupations that seek recognition as professions engage in transactions within all three markets—prestige, power, and income—with varying success. Most will not rise far or achieve professional status, but those that do rise *must change themselves*. (Self-advertisement may create self-delusion but will hardly persuade others.) They must be able to offer more on one or another of these markets, in order to gain more in return. In order to be accepted by the society as a profession, an occupation requires special transactions in mainly the prestige markets. If these are successful, they can be used to obtain more power and money.[3] However, merely clever transactions that yield power and money for an occupation are not sufficient to achieve acceptance as a profession.

The advantages of being accepted as a profession are obvious. However, few of even the privileged occupations can or will pay the costs of transforming themselves enough to become accepted.

Is the Professions Market a Zero-Sum Game?

Although people and occupations do compete with one another for the rewards of the total society, whether this competitive action system can be viewed as a zero-sum game depends on the time perspective. Over the relatively long time period of a generation or so, an occupational system as a whole may produce more goods, as it may also produce more prestige or power, so that a wide range of occupations (theoretically, perhaps all) may benefit: all may rise. In such a perspective, it is not true that what one occupation gains, another must lose. In a declining social system, correspondingly, all could fall. In the shorter time perspective of, say, a few months, there is by contrast only so much money, power, or prestige to be shared. If blue-collar workers succeed in raising their wages substantially, white-collar workers must lose somewhat. For example, over the past one hundred and fifty years of automation of several kinds, workers have generally assumed that each job eliminated by machinery would create that much more unemployment, and they were wrong (it was not zero-sum). But they were and are correct (because the individual has but one life, his time perspective is short) in their *fear*, for at any given time there *were* in fact only so many jobs: the worker knew personally some men who had lost their jobs to the machine (in the short run, it is zero-sum).

These facts are significant in the general processes of interoccupational competition, but more important for our specific concern with professionalization is that some of the actions by which a semi-profession seeks to improve its position (guided by its leaders' folk sociology) are likely to increase its own prestige or income as well as that of the society. To that extent, these actions are not a zero-sum game. Obtaining a monopoly will, of course, yield an economic advantage to the occupation and not to the society, but raising the competence of entrants, imposing quality controls over members' work, establishing centers for developing improved techniques, and so forth will yield greater production for the society, and very likely a modestly greater amount of prestige for the semi-profession as well.

Thus, over the longer time perspective in which a profession becomes recognized, its greater eminence is not likely to have been taken away from that of another profession, but has rather been earned independently, through transactions in which in fact it has begun to contribute more to the society.

Individual Compared With Occupational Competition

At more than one point we have compared individual mobility and that of occupations, as a way of clarifying the process of professionalization. A few additional relations should be added briefly. Metaphorically, perhaps one might say that the competition among occupations lies somewhere between the passivity of commodities on the market and the conscious activity of jobholders, but we can state the patterns more precisely.

1. An important contrast is that thousands of *individuals* have the same type of job, and thus compete directly; no two *jobs* claim exactly the same charter, so that the competition is somewhat more oblique. Many jobs have overlapped sometimes, amid charges of encroachment and incompetence. Some claim part of a task, while their competitors claim it all. Some claim the right to carry out a task, but also reserve the right to delegate it to another occupation, under supervision. A few of the overlapping jobs will remind the reader of these patterns of oblique or direct competition:

Lawyer–notary public.
Medical doctor–bonesetter–midwife–pharmacist.
Airplane pilot–engineer.
Sanitary engineer–plumber.
Plumber–steamfitter–sewer layer.
Veterinary–farrier; farrier–blacksmith; blacksmith–
    armorer.
Coppersmith–tinsmith.
Priest–psychiatrist–clinical psychologist–social worker.

2. Although a substantial percentage of *men* rise from blue collar origins to high positions,[4] almost no occupation has risen from a low rank to the top. Midwifery did not, for example, "rise" to become gynecology. Perhaps concert

artists have risen more than any other group.[5] More commonly, an occupation destined for professionalization appears at a fairly high level, and then rises somewhat, if at all.

In the mobility of occupations, the following patterns of upward movement are more likely than is the high ascent sometimes observed in individual mobility: (a) a semi-profession arises from a non-occupation, e.g., social work from individual philanthropy or "doing good to the poor"; (b) a semi-profession claims to have a special "package" of high level skills, e.g., the city planner; (c) a profession specializes in a task that another had considered partial, e.g., psychiatry; (d) a professional specialty is built on new instruments and techniques, e.g., cryogenics or laser engineering.

3. As in transactions among individuals, competition is strongest among similar or overlapping occupations, because to some extent they are substitutable: one can be chosen, the other rejected. Especially in an expanding economy, neither an individual nor an occupation is likely to push another out by simply taking over the other's work. The rising individual rarely actually rises by pushing another out of his job, but rather gets a post another man had hoped to enjoy. Similarly, the rising semi-profession is less likely to destroy another directly than to create a new package of high-level skills (social worker, marital counselor, management consultant, architect) that other occupations possess only at a lower level or only in part.

4. In a specialized technology, most occupations (of the more than 25,000 listed in the *Dictionary of Occupational Titles*) engage in few direct transactions with the society and thus are not even known to the public. They come into existence and disappear in response to changing industrial techniques. Their members feel little collective identity and make little concerted effort to rise, other than as members of a large industrial union.

5. Especially in a local market, both men and occupations can rise to high levels of income without an equal rise in power or prestige. In the early 1960s, some school building superintendents in New York City were able to earn six-figure

incomes. Mark Twain's classic foray into the sociology of occupations, *Life on the Mississippi*, describes in detail the high income and (he claims) high prestige of the steamboat pilot.[6]

Effects of Competition Among Occupations

Before examining the more specific elements in the narrower area of professionalization within the *general* pattern of competition, let us consider briefly some of the consequences of a *social structure* in which occupations freely fall or rise. First, the outcomes of the exchanges between occupation and the society alter the terms of *individual* bargaining. For example, the rising prestige and income of university professors as an occupation will affect the new contracts that are made. The new terms will also affect the cost–reward calculations of potential recruits, and so affect the flow and allocation of talent within the occupational system.

Second, like lineage or family, caste or class, organization or social institution, an occupation must expend some of its collective resources even to maintain its position. Its rank is constantly threatened. Activities may range from proposing laws to the occupation's advantage to founding schools for the improved training of recruits, from publishing encomiums of the profession to establishing higher ethical controls over members.

Third, because the individual shares in the rise of his occupation, some people must decide how much of their personal resources to invest in this *corporate* enterprise. If the individual has himself moved upward occupationally, he may foresee an added increment from such an investment. In addition, of course, the organizational efforts of the occupation may offer still more opportunities to some individuals for prestigious leadership posts and activities.

Fourth, the total effort toward maintenance of position and the jockeying for additional rewards is a large part of the total allocation of energies and resources in the society. These aims and activities determine in part the establishment of schools, licensing commissions, research agencies, and inspection units; the granting of honors and posts; legislation concerning many areas of life; changes in technology, and so on. Such goals also shape in part the inputs and outputs of social institutions and organizations of the society; they are part of the major competitive processes that constitute much of human behavior.

Fifth, the efforts of all occupations, but especially the semi-professions and professions, to rise or to maintain their positions are a *source of social change*. As is clear from the foregoing discussion, these social changes—the research that becomes the foundation of a new profession, or a useful tool for an older one; the alterations in graduate education and post-college education in industry; legislation to protect a profession against new threats or to consolidate an emerging profession in its new privileges; the distribution of manpower —all arise in part from the efforts of various occupations to increase the various rewards they obtain from the society, to gain recognition, or to protect their privileged position from other aspiring occupations, semi-professions, or professions.

A Natural History of Professionalization

If various occupations do try to rise, however—and many succeed to some extent, thus contributing to social change—how far can the process go? Various analysts have described a natural history of professionalization, the sequence of steps by which a semi-profession, through its transactions with the society, is transformed into a recognized profession, but these statements are neither empirically correct nor theoretically convincing.[7] Wilensky offers these steps:[8]

Full-time activity at the task
Establishment of university training
National professional association

Redefinition of the core task, so as to give the "dirty
work" over to subordinates
Conflict between the old timers and the new men who
seek to upgrade the job
Competition between the new occupation and neigh-
boring ones
Political agitation in order to gain legal protection
Code of ethics.

Most of these social processes are going on simultaneously, so
that it is difficult to state whether one actually began before
another. For this reason, such a sequence is both time-bound
and place-bound and thus accidental rather than theoretically
compelling. To mention but a few examples that do not fit:
the American bar, true enough, had no published code of
ethics before the American Revolution, but it was well-
educated and tightly controlled in its professional behavior;
British barristers did not establish university training schools,
but continued to train recruits through the four Inns of Court.
Medicine and dentistry did not publish a formal code of ethics
until the twentieth century, but in the 1840s men were
expelled from their associations for violating their respective
codes. Lobbying for protective legislation has been continual
in the history of occupations. The ministry still has no formal
code of ethics.

In the present era, people are likely to create a formal
occupational organization to solve problems, so that a profession emerging now is more likely than one rising a century
ago to use such an association at an early phase of its existence,
but it is also likely to develop a code of ethics rather early.
Even when a formal code is not written, a set of such ethical
understandings is likely to be widespread. At present, such a
concrete set of "steps" as Wilensky's is really a description
of the many areas in which an emerging profession must
participate in its transactions with other occupations and the
society.

Moreover, and much more fundamentally, these formal
steps miss the essential elements in professionalization. They

do not separate the core, *generating* traits from the derivative ones. Many occupations and activities have tried all or most of these steps without much recognition as professions. It is unlikely that a list of the specific historical *events* in the structuring of a profession will yield the organic sequences in its development.

The Generating Traits of Professionalism

An inclusive list of the occupations whose claims to professional status have been announced very likely would total as many as one hundred. The term is loosely used in popular language: I would hazard the guess that a majority of adults would accept the label *profession* when applied to as many as forty or more white-collar occupations.

Nevertheless, both laymen and sociologists do use various objective traits in making evaluative distinctions among these white-collar *jobs*; moreover, speakers at thousands of *professional* meetings have made hortatory and self-congratulatory references to similar traits. When tabulated, in fact, the characteristics attributed to various occupations in order to prove that they are professions show a satisfying similarity, suggesting that their foundation is a shared observation of reality.[9] The lists of traits also contain a hidden similarity, which I shall later analyze at greater length, that all of them derive from an ideal–typical conception whose closest concrete approximation is medicine and the priesthood. Ignoring variations in language, such lists report: high income, prestige, and influence; high educational requirements; professional autonomy; licensure; commitment of members to the profession; desire of members to remain in the profession; codes of ethics; cohesion of the professional community; monopoly over a task; intensive adult socialization experience for recruits, and so on. However, it seems worthwhile to abstract from such lists the core, or generating, traits, and those which are a predictable outcome of core characteristics.

It would be generally agreed, I think, that the two central generating qualities are (1) a basic body of abstract knowledge, and (2) the ideal of service.[10] Both actually contain many dimensions, and, of course, each subdimension is a continuum: with respect to each, a given occupation may fall somewhere toward the professional pole or not; and one may ask *where* along that subcontinuum any occupation may be found, even if clearly it is not to be considered a profession. Necessarily, too, at present we have no adequate measure for any of these subdimensions, and must be content with reasonable assertions about where a given type of job may fall. Let us examine each subdimension of the two core traits in turn before weighing the limits of professionalization for a given aspirant semi-profession, or for a range of professions.

Professional Knowledge

With respect to knowledge, seven major characteristics affect the acceptance of an occupation as a profession. They are:

1. Ideally, the knowledge and skills should be abstract and organized into a codified body of principles.
2. The knowledge should be applicable, or thought to be applicable, to the concrete problems of living. (Note that metaphysical knowledge, however well organized, may have no such applicability.)
3. The society or its relevant members should believe that the knowledge can actually solve these problems (it is not necessary that the knowledge actually solve them, only that people believe in its capacity to solve them).
4. Members of the society should also accept as proper that these problems be given over to some occupational group for solution (thus, for example, many do not as yet accept the propriety of handing over problems of neurosis to the psychiatrist) because the occupational group possesses that knowledge and others do not.

5. The profession itself should help to create, organize, and transmit the knowledge.
6. The profession should be accepted as the final arbiter in any disputes over the validity of any technical solution lying within its area of supposed competence.
7. The amount of knowledge and skills and the difficulty of acquiring them should be great enough that the members of the society view the profession as possessing a kind of *mystery* that it is not given to the ordinary man to acquire, by his own efforts or even with help.

The Service Ideal

The ideal of service, sometimes called a *collectivity orientation*, may be defined in this context as the norm that the technical solutions which the professional arrives at should be based on the client's needs, not necessarily the best material interest or needs of the professional himself or, for that matter, those of the society. Again, this may be defined somewhat more specifically by its subdimensions:

1. It is the *practitioner* who decides upon the client's needs, and the occupation will be classified as less professional if the client imposes his own judgment.
2. The profession demands real sacrifice from practitioners as an ideal and, from time to time, in fact. (For example, the student–professional must defer the privileges of adulthood for several years after his nonprofessional contemporaries have come to enjoy them. In each profession there are junctures or different situations in which the individual should expose himself to threats and even dangers from the larger society if he is to live up to the highest ideal of the profession: the lawyer defending the unpopular client, the military man sacrificing his life, the scientist persisting in expounding the truth against the opposition of laymen, and so on. The profession must also allocate

some of its own resources and facilities to the development of new knowledge—with the result that some of the knowledge of its practitioners becomes obsolete— and to the recruitment of the most talented youngsters available, though in fact this increases competition within the field.)

3. The society actually believes that the profession not only accepts these ideals but also follows them to some extent.

4. The professional community sets up a system of rewards and punishments such that "virtue pays"; i.e., in general, the practitioner who lives by the service ideal must be more successful than the practitioner who does not.

It is not necessary to spell out in tedious detail just how these two core, though multifaceted, elements generate the commonly recognized traits of the established professions. A brief statement should suffice.

The income of professionals averages higher than that of other occupations because their services are needed (they have the knowledge to solve a problem) and there are no alternatives. In simple supply–demand terms, they have a monopoly over a valuable product. On the prestige market, too, their product is valuable because of their dedication to the service ideal, because their education is high, and because their performances are above those of average people.[11] Professionals usually have a monopoly because they have persuaded the society that no one else can do the job and that it is dangerous to let anyone else try. They are permitted autonomy more frequently than members of other occupations (professionals, not laymen, are more likely to judge performance), both because others are not sufficiently knowledgeable, and because others cannot be trusted to be as concerned about the client's interest. The shaping of legislation, the manning of control and examination boards, and standards for licensing are all more likely to be in the hands of professionals for the same reasons. Because professionals must learn to abide by a code that is different from that of the larger society, a period of adult socialization is more necessary than in other occupations. Because the rewards are high and a period of adult socialization (in which professional commitment is inculcated) is more likely, members are less willing to leave the occupation, and are more likely to assert that they would choose the same work if they were to begin again. A code is necessary to implement such service ideals, but it is also an expectable correlate of any subcommunity.

The Aspiring Occupations

Any predictions are subject to all the hazards of peering into the future, and especially so with respect to the problem of predicting that a given occupation will not develop a sufficient knowledge base for professionalism. Speculation will, however, serve as a vehicle for discussing further the dynamics of professionalization. These estimates divide occupations into three groups: some have become professions, some will become professions, and some will not. Later, we shall want to distinguish *among* the successful ones those which are closer to the four great *person* professions.

These occupations have become professions in the last generation: dentistry, certified public accounting, clinical psychology, and certain high levels of the scientific and engineering fields, such as electronic engineering, cryogenics, aeronautical engineering, and so on.

These semi-professions will achieve professionalism over the next generation: social work, marital counseling, and perhaps city planning.[12] An unlikely category is that of various managerial jobs for nonprofit organizations, such as supervising principals and school superintendents, foundation executives, and so on.

The following occupations will not become professional: within the medical situs, none will achieve it, with the possible exception of veterinary medicine. Osteopathy is gradually being absorbed into the ordinary status of physician. Nurses have been pressing hard toward professionalism, but will not move far. Chiropractic will remain a marginal or quack occupation, as will podiatry. Pharmacy will not change its status much. Next, school-teaching will not achieve professionalism, nor will librarianship.[13] Many articles and speeches have argued that business management, public relations, and advertising are, or should be, professions, but none of these will achieve such a status.

This is not to say that all of these will retain their present positions relative to one another. Teachers will doubtless move upward in income relative to other semi-professions, and so will librarians and nurses. I am merely asserting that though perhaps all of these will move somewhat towards improving their economic and prestige positions, the journey will not be long and the movement upward not great.

Let us now examine some of the elements or factors involved in the process of professionalization, using various occupations to illustrate the process.

The Development of Professional Knowledge

On both the prestige and the economic markets, the aspiring profession must be able to offer its control over a more substantial body of codified, applicable knowledge than that controlled by other occupations.[14] However, to express doubt as to whether an occupation has a sufficient knowledge base to be accepted as a profession is likely to arouse considerable emotion among its practitioners (a test of this assertion is easy, if hazardous, to make). Any doubt expressed on this matter undermines the basic claim of any occupation to respect or pay from the society.

Such arguments are difficult to settle because three complex facts or relationships make any measurement difficult:

(1) every occupation knows *some* facts or can do some things better than a supposedly higher-level profession (TV repairman–electronics engineer; pharmacist–medical doctor); (2) admission to every occupation or profession of any importance is so hedged about with rules that the entrant must learn far more than he will typically apply in the course of his practice—with a consequent overlap in the abstract knowledge base of adjacent occupations (e.g., the physical principles relating to ultra high frequency waves are relevant to a wide range of occupations and professions); and (3) it seems at least speculatively possible to build a broadly scientific foundation for almost any job, i.e., it may be possible to develop a great deal of organized abstract knowledge applicable in any task, whether acting or typing. How much reality must there be, then, behind the public concession that the knowledge base of a given occupation is of professional quantity and quality?

Of course, how much knowledge the profession possesses is defined in part by the society itself. The witch doctor may have very little valid knowledge, but by the canons of truth of his society he may have a great deal. But we need not move so culturally distant as the witch doctor; the physician until the late nineteenth century is an equally good example. And certainly the validity of much psychodynamic knowledge of our time rests on shaky empirical grounds.[15]

Actually most professionals do not use much of their abstract knowledge and perhaps for most problems do not really apply principles to concrete cases, but instead apply concrete recipes to concrete cases. The physician learns much but utilizes relatively little of it in his normal practice. Similarly, it is not possible to obtain a journeyman's license in most of the skilled trades in large American cities without learning a great many skills and principles that are almost never used. One may almost say that practitioners are typically overtrained; on the other hand, such overtraining is a partial guarantee (because they will also forget much of what they have learned) that they can at least handle with ease the run-of-the-mill problems.

Because of this overlapping of knowledge between

subordinate and superordinate occupations, an intermediate medical occupation developed, both in Germany and in Russia, between the nurse and the full-fledged physician: the *Feldscher*, who handled many simple medical problems. In U.S. military life, too, the corpsman often has to act as the near-equivalent of a physician. Moreover, the suggestion has been made at times that one way to improve health in underdeveloped countries is to reduce the usual long training required to become a physician, as most ordinary medical problems can be solved by someone with far less training.

It might therefore be argued that professions have persuaded a gullible public that all members must command an unnecessarily large body of abstract knowledge, that practitioners do not need that much knowledge in their daily practice, and that occupations exist or could be developed which would carry out most of their tasks with a lesser amount of knowledge. A brief consideration of this knowledge overlap clarifies further the nature of the knowledge base that is believed to be required.

Although much of the knowledge demanded for entrance to any profession may not be used frequently in its daily practice, this is also true for any highly-trained occupation. Consequently, in ranking the various occupations by their knowledge, the society can consider only the amount of learning required for admission. That is, if the physician uses one-third of the knowledge he had to acquire to become a doctor, and the electrician has roughly the same experience, their actual applied knowledge ratio remains the same, and the M.D. still knows much more.[16]

In addition, just how much knowledge is required by society for acceptance as a profession is in part a function of how much the public believes is needed for crises. With reference to the major professions, the social pressures within the profession as well as the larger society demand that *all* the available knowledge be mustered for crises, or at least be on call. The man in jail, or with an abscessed tooth, will accept any reasonably competent practitioner, but he would prefer the highest level of skill he can command. A departmental chairman may have to accept lesser talents in his competition with other universities, but he would prefer to obtain the best physicist possible. Even if intermediate-level medical occupations, or similar ones within any of the professions, were to develop, the society would continue to recognize the highest level of the profession as responsible for *all* of the available knowledge.

Moreover, to the extent that some part of the professional's knowledge becomes so routine that it can be mastered and applied by a secondary occupation with much less training, such ancillary occupations do develop, but they are harnessed to facilitate the work of the professional. They are given what Everett C. Hughes calls the "dirty work," the tedious, less interesting, preparatory, or cleaning-up tasks—ranging from preparing the patient for the X-ray machine to educating the junior college student who has little chance of entering a university. Often, indeed, such helping jobs are even defined legally as subordinate, in that men in them are not permitted to practice except under professional supervision.

It seems likely, then, that one cannot assert that a profession is simply a type of occupation that requires its students to learn some knowledge in the form of codified, abstract principles.[17] In fact its members must acquire a good bit *more* knowledge than other workers, so that a lengthy education is needed, not only in a *practicum* but in book learning.

Another hypothesis may be presented from these notions: at any given phase of development of professionalism in a society, the successful aspirant occupations must demand that their trainees learn about as much as the trainees in the recognized professions. The nineteenth century dentist, architect, or engineer had to learn less than the accepted professions of their day and enjoyed a correspondingly lesser rank. The physician, granted, knew much less than the modern physician but did have to learn more (much of it incorrect) than most other occupations. After the American Revolution, the intellectual demands on U.S. lawyers were lowered, and the profession suffered a corresponding loss of standing.

It is interesting, and perhaps significant in this connection, that all four of the oldest professions in Western society have maintained their high knowledge standing since the Middle Ages and have not been displaced by the new knowledge of the Renaissance and modern eras. Of the four (law, medicine, clergy, and university teaching) only medicine was scientifically technical in content when it arose, and even it always had (as it still has) a large element of human relations in its practice and principles. What one must say, rather, is that in fact these four constituted the highest intellectual levels to be achieved at that time. They required the longest study and the closest supervision by teachers over the acquisition of knowledge. To this extent they attracted the ablest of students and commanded most respect. In important ways to be noted in a moment, they remain the core of a sub-class of professions that differ from others.

The contrasting cases of librarianship and dentistry illustrate the importance of the knowledge base. The latter has certainly achieved a professional status in our generation, and I have asserted that librarianship will not achieve it.[18] It is only recently that dentistry began seriously to build adequate scientific foundations both for general practice and for the specialties within dentistry. Correlative with this change has occurred a rise in income as well as in prestige. It was always possible to develop the general biological knowledge on which modern dentistry increasingly rests, but dental problems were not defined as important enough to require that much investment in research.

It is an amusing quirk of fate, too, that dentistry is the only one of the medical occupations to achieve professional standing without being taken over by medicine. The ancillary medical techniques such as anesthesiology or radiology became medical specialties, and thus still under the jurisdiction of medicine, when their knowledge base became sufficient to justify independent professional life. Dentistry, on the other hand, achieved its body of knowledge as late as the past generation, after the relationship between the two occupations, medicine and dentistry, had become relatively crystallized, i.e., the physicians considered the dentists not to be worth incorporation because of their low ethical standards and their merely artisan skills.

By contrast, though individual librarians have been learned, and librarians in general are as dedicated to knowledge as they are committed to service, the public is not convinced that there is a basic science of librarianship: the skill is thought to be only clerical or administrative. The university librarian's most significant reference group is the university professor, who believes his mastery of his own field is superior to that of the librarian, as is his knowledge of related areas. Nor does the average professor have the experience of being saved from a serious difficulty by the scientific knowledge of the librarian.[19] Moreover, there has been little research and thus little accumulation of knowledge relative to the central professional task of librarianship, the organization and codification of library materials and the development of principles concerning the retrieval of that information.

The school teacher (especially in the primary schools) has a similar relationship to her knowledge base, which is not so much the curriculum content—most adults believe that they could master that after a short period of study—but the technique and principles of pedagogy. This content is, however, relatively small in amount and shallow intellectually. More important, because the crucial matter here is the interaction of public and occupation, even in the area of teaching techniques the teacher is not thought to be a final arbiter. Most college-educated Americans believe they understand such techniques about as well as the average teacher. Nor does it seem likely that the body of pedagogic knowledge that is the teacher's area of prime responsibility will grow much over the next generation.

Nevertheless, perhaps all occupations depend on general natural principles, and these can be discovered. Consequently, one can speculate that every occupation may claim that to understand his task fully, the recruit must study all of the relevant general knowledge. Claiming such a deeper knowledge base, any occupation could then demand a higher prestige ranking. For example, the electrician would have to be an electrical engineer, learning the most advanced physical principles of electricity. It is at least true that as new knowledge accumulates, the occupation may have to change its training practices somewhat. The captain of a modern passenger liner and the international airlines pilot must engage in the formal study of general scientific knowledge as well as learn their practical applications.

The crucial point seems to be the claim of the occupation to the most highly developed body of knowledge in the relevant field, i.e., who is in possession of that body of knowledge. In medicine, it is the physicians themselves, together with men working in the basic biological sciences; in law, it is the lawyers themselves and law professors who are working on the analyses of cases; in engineering, it is the engineers themselves, together with men working in the basic physical sciences. By contrast, even the skilled worker in the occupations of electrician, plumber, TV repairman, and so on have no immediate contact with the sources of their knowledge, or those who develop it, nor has the ship's captain or the airline pilot. The society, in effect, gives the authority of knowledge to the professions as the centers of knowledge from which the knowledge used by subordinate occupations will flow.

A further complexity in this relationship to knowledge may be brought out. Granted that one need not be a sanitary engineer in order to do plumbing or an electrical engineer in order to wire a house, this additional knowledge would certainly not at all be a handicap. If all waiters had to obtain advanced research training in social science and the organic chemistry of foods, they would not on that account do a less adequate job. Against this possibility, however, is the unwillingness of the society to invest great sums in either the development of such formal schools and scientific knowledge, or to pay the much higher incomes that would be necessary to balance the added cost of that investment.

This judgment as to the worth of developing an extensive body of scientific knowledge applies to most occupations. Conceivably, extensive research could be devoted to the tasks of almost any occupation, so that it would be both the master of a body of abstract principles and the source from which additional knowledge would come. Ultimately such research and accumulation depend, however, upon how much support the society is willing to give for the additional knowledge, and how much it will pay for services with such a base.

The key element in this continuing set of decisions is whether the society believes it suffers great costs because members of an occupation do not have sufficient knowledge. Greater investments in research and training will be made only if people feel that important negative consequences follow from the lack of a great knowledge base in the work of, say, typists, nurses, chauffeurs, or teachers. Doubtless, too, potentially positive consequences will count. If the society will not support such an accumulation, the occupation will not become the master of such a highly developed body of principles as is necessary for acceptance as a profession.

Management, whether in school administration, business and manufacturing, or philanthropy, is especially interesting in this context because a considerable body of scientific knowledge can be organized that would be applicable to its problems. Because corporations do calculate costs and even pay for research, many studies have actually aimed at discovering general principles of management, most of them in sociology or psychology.[20] However, not only the society, but managers themselves, believe that success or failure is not dependent on having been trained in these principles and that a good manager can be an intuitive master without knowing them at all.

The medical occupations illustrate a related principle, that it is the profession which is to be the *judge* of valid knowledge. The case is interesting because medicine deals with problems that are of great concern to everyone, so that precision of control, however expensive, is thought never to be sufficient. As a consequence, the society is willing to pour large amounts of personnel and money into research. However, this added knowledge becomes a base only for new specialties within the medical profession, not for independent medical professions in anesthesiology, pathology,[21] pharmacy, nursing or midwifery. The physician remains the judge of valid knowledge and the added data for greater precision are put into his hands, not those of the nurse or pharmacist. The latter two retain a watchdog function, but the society judges their knowledge and their right of judgment to be ancillary.

As any profession accumulates knowledge, perhaps a larger part of its knowledge comes to be developed by men essentially outside the profession, i.e., by specialists in the sub-sciences.[22] At the same time, more practitioners *within* the profession become researchers as well.

Power relations also determine which occupations develop and control the knowledge base. A sufficiently large clientele will hire quacks to permit them to continue existence if laws are not enforced, and correspondingly, some individuals will give money to quacks to "develop their knowledge." Especially in the realms of health and mental disease, almost any kind of research program can obtain *some* support. The established profession, however, retains control over the crucial junctures at which knowledge is transmitted to the next generation or required in examinations. As a consequence, the "knowledge" developed by such aberrant research activities is likely to have a relatively short life.

Who Are the Relevant Groups?

Even if the aspirant occupation moves somewhat toward the development of as much knowledge as is considered adequate for professional standing in a given society, it cannot easily persuade other related occupations of its new achievements. The most closely related occupations have more to lose by such a concession and are also more likely to be able to affect the standing of the occupation with the general public. In a mass market and a growing economy, some part of the public may grant the new claims, but general recognition will likely not occur unless allied occupations also concede them, even if grudgingly, and thus validate them to a larger public.

To implement their own skepticism, the established profession often has legal as well as informal powers. Previously we noted this relationship in discussing the blocked position of the pharmacists, who are, as Adam Smith pointed out long ago, "physicians to the poor at all times, and to the rich whenever the distress and danger is not great." The legal and social controls in the hands of physicians would render profitless any attempt by pharmacists to reorganize greatly the areas of their knowledge. The librarian is not blocked legally from independence, but his most important reference and validating group—university professors—is not likely to alter its judgment of the knowledge base of librarianship.

Public relations and advertising, like management, both have access to a considerable body of social science knowledge, but all three are viewed by the general public as well as by their most relevant reference groups—other businessmen and social scientists—as possessing or needing little more than concrete experience to guide their solutions. In addition, of course, their solutions are thought to be primarily determined by reference to profit, not the needs of the client.

In contrast with these instances are the power and evaluative relations among social work, psychiatry, and clinical psychology.[23] For the past generation, social work has moved steadily toward acceptance as a profession. It has done so primarily because training standards have risen substantially, and its knowledge base has widened and deepened. Not only have social work schools utilized the newest scientific knowledge from sociology, psychology, and psychiatry, but they have also been carrying out research programs of their own.

Rising in evaluation because they are in effect offering more on the prestige market, social workers have also been favored by having no strongly entrenched opposition. One consequence is that at this time it is likely that most of the psychotherapy in this country is being done by social workers, not by psychiatrists or clinical psychologists. Social workers have seen most of their clients in settings where no psychiatrist directly supervised their work. Most social workers have been women, who have not fought hard against the claims to control made by psychiatrists, who, in turn, have consequently organized few counteractions or bothered to set up a pattern of surveillance. Surely of equal importance in the failure to establish legal controls is the fact that the people whom social workers help are not likely to be potential clients of psychiatrists; psychiatrists, therefore, have had little economic stake in a system of legal controls. Now, however, it seems likely that psychiatrists could not regain this control even if they tried to do so.

Clinical psychology overlaps with both social work and psychiatry, and here again it developed in a context in which the medical specialty could not effectively withhold recognition or legally block it from independence. Clinical psychology developed as an offshoot from a firmly-established professional status, that of university professor and researcher. It could claim some respect from related occupations and the society for its general scientific base, psychology, and for its new scientific findings in a specialty. This battle has been relatively strong, but because clinical psychology enjoyed both an independent organizational position and its own body of applicable learning, it could command full professional recognition in a short time.

Autonomy, Service, and Knowledge

Occupations, like people, claim the right of autonomy and usually fail to get it. Professional autonomy— in a bureaucratic era, this means having one's behavior judged by colleague peers, not outsiders—is a derivative trait and is based on both the mastery of a knowledge field and commitment to the ideal of service. Clearly, an occupation cannot claim independence unless it also asserts that no related occupation possesses superior knowledge of its tasks. However, the autonomy cannot be granted without trust, and members of the society are therefore not willing to concede autonomy unless they are persuaded that the profession can and will control the work of its members in the interest of their clients. Finally, even if the body of knowledge is thought to be adequate, and the aspiring profession proclaims the ideal of service, members of the society will not grant autonomy unless it is persuaded that the occupation *must* be trusted if it is to do its work properly.

Indeed, this last requirement is what sets apart one sub-category, which we call *person* professions, from the rest—a group which is closer in many respects to the older established ones. Moreover, as we urged at the beginning of this paper, in an apparently professionalizing occupational structure, this important sub-group is *not* growing at a rapid rate. In this narrower sense, then, the occupations and the society are not moving much toward professionalization.

Within this set of dependent relations or tensions among autonomy, service, and knowledge, there are three extreme outcomes which aspiring professions try to guard against, but over which they have little control: (a) the occupation may achieve some cohesion, but expend this greater strength in merely improving incomes with little concern about the ideal of service; (b) the occupation may, as its knowledge base grows, simply split into numerous sub-associations, so that little cohesion develops; and (c) because the occupation can be supervised by a bureaucracy and the *substance of its work* requires little autonomy, it is simply absorbed into high-level bureaucratic positions. All three outcomes, of course, undermine the claim to trust and autonomy that is one basis of professionalism.

The first outcome, cohesion with self-seeking, is perhaps best exemplified in the labor unions or the medieval guilds, although all professional associations engage in this to some extent. Any operative code of ethics can be read either as a set of protections for the client or a coolly executed plan for serving the ends of the profession. For example, competition is frowned upon, as is the exposure of fellow incompetents; advertising is forbidden, even if the professional's skill *is* superior; prices should not be lowered; and so on. Any relatively cohesive group is likely to arrange for its best interests to some extent if it is permitted to do so. The principle of cohesion and brotherhood in the profession tempts the organization to ignore the societal mandate under which it receives privileges but imposes self-controls.

Nevertheless, this possibility of cohesion only for the purpose of self-seeking seems not to have occurred in the major occupations seeking professional status. The sporadic efforts of some engineers to develop unions during the 1950s were not successful. Of course, some high level occupations with little claim to professional rank have been able to obtain considerable financial and other concessions from their employers or the society when economic conditions favored such concessions. We noted earlier one dramatic case, that of the Mississippi River steamboat pilot, whose knowledge requirements were immense, though never abstract, and who was able to command a high income in the 1850s. Similarly, the International Airline Pilots' Association has been able to command incomes at the average of professionals. The pilots' cohesion has been high and so is their technical training. No one claims that they should have autonomy any more than a truck driver or a steamship captain. They serve the needs of their employer for hire, and indeed passengers would be somewhat alarmed if they thought that such matters as destinations, speeds, altitudes, or fares were to be decided independently by the pilots who direct their planes.

The second extreme outcome is that the aspiring profession or occupation fails to develop any substantial cohesion, and instead splinters into many sub-groups. This occurs especially in the engineering fields, where in spite of a considerable amount of energy and money devoted to organization, the pattern of splitting into specialty associations (exhibited in the earliest periods of professional engineering associations in the nineteenth century) continues apace. In these fields, the operative code of ethics is likely to be the ethic of science, although the paper code follows closely the usual professional codes.

The rapid growth of knowledge and its organization into

specialties encourages each sub-group to focus on its own interests, while members in the broader profession do not believe that they lose much by their lack of cohesion. The typical client (usually a corporation) can measure or have measured to a considerable extent the competence and performance of the engineer, so that the client is in relatively little danger of being exploited; but, as a corollary, the engineer—or any person whose training lies in similar areas—can do as well in the market without the monopoly that a cohesive professional association claims. Engineering associations have not succeeded in maintaining a monopoly over their fields, and indeed many practicing engineers do not bother to obtain state licenses.

This second type of outcome of the tension among autonomy, service, and knowledge overlaps with a third, perhaps the most characteristic professionalizing pattern of this epoch, the absorption of high level occupations and aspiring professions into a bureaucracy, largely because the substance of their work requires little autonomy. Educational and philanthropic administration,[24] librarianship, the engineering specialties, scientists in industry, school teaching, advertising and public relations—all are likely to work in a bureaucracy and to have their work supervised or guided by non-professional bureaucrats or laymen.

The factor of bureaucracy is not the key element here. Indeed, professionals have *typically* worked in bureaucracies. Clergymen and university professors always did. Medical men and lawyers did when they were in orders. True, the bar left the Church in the thirteenth century, and the physician–cleric by the end of the Renaissance, but a high percentage of both now work in bureaucracies. A military structure is a bureaucracy. The crucial difference, then, is not whether members of a profession work within a bureaucracy, but whether *they* (clergymen, military, university professors, physicians, lawyers) or *fellow professionals* (social work) *control* its essential work.

The certified public accountant also works within a bureaucracy, though of course he may instead be chief of a bureaucratic organization. When, however, he is engaged in his most important work, i.e., the tasks for which he is *certified*—dealing with fiscal matters which he then certifies to the public—he is subject not only to the bureaucracy but also to the outside society as well. In that work, he must meet the standards of fellow professionals, not merely the commands of his bureaucracy. Indeed, he may be held legally responsible for certain derelictions of duty in accounting, even though he has been carrying out the orders of a bureaucratic superior.

If professionals, not laymen, judge each other's work even in a bureaucracy, cohesion is likely. Cohesion is needed, for without it the profession as a collectivity is not strong enough to impose acceptable controls of its own. If it cannot impose such controls, the society will not grant autonomy to the profession. Each of these relations is dependent on the others. Without such controls, the occupation cannot protect its own members, and thus will have little cohesion. Thus, as noted previously, the cohesion of engineering specialty occupations has been relatively weak, because competence can be measured more accurately than in other fields, and as a consequence the engineer can succeed in his field without belonging to an association. The profession must also be able to protect its members, even against public attack, when they live by the code.

The correlation of both autonomy and protection in librarianship may be strikingly seen in the fact that not only do librarians avoid controversy in their communities by failing to purchase books which might arouse antagonisms, but a higher percentage of the members of the American Library Association than of nonmembers do so.[25] Their cohesion is so low as to guarantee them no protection against the public, even when in the long run their best professional decisions and ideals would be to the advantage of the society.

Autonomy and Vulnerability

In this analysis we have emphasized what we believe to be a

crucial *structural* element that is operative in this set of relationships, that the claim to autonomy or trust loses its point unless the client or society can *in fact* be *harmed* because of unethical or incompetent work by the practitioner; and because of the substance of the problem certain professionals cannot do their work unless they are *able to do harm*. That is, the professional *has* to be trusted if he is to do his work.

Let us consider the first point separately. How high do the stakes have to be for the society to judge that controls, whether imposed by the society or the profession itself, are necessary? Veterinary medicine is a doubtful but interesting case. At present, the level of training and knowledge required for veterinary medicine may be as high as that for several other professional occupations, but very likely the society will continue to decide that the stakes are not high enough in this case to grant professional recognition and autonomy in return for professional control over unethical or poor performance.[26]

Note, too, that the stakes cannot be very high if the aspiring occupation does not have a sufficient command of knowledge and skill to *be* dangerous in its incompetence. Marital counseling falls into the general group of therapies, and thus the stakes seem to be high. The counselors' work is largely not under anyone else's supervision. However, most people feel that the marital counselors do not know enough to be harmful when they fail to perform well. Those occupations that are somewhat closer to this emerging profession, with its knowledge base resting primarily on sociology and psychology and for the most part growing from the organizational activities of university professors, feel differently.[27] Much of their therapeutic work is psychiatric and psychodynamic, so that the elite of the occupation seeks to impose stricter codes of performance, before state governments do.

At present, certainly, the stakes may not be high simply because most who go to marital counselors have marriages with a low chance of survival, and thus have little to lose. However, the knowledge base and therapeutic skills of marital counselors will develop further, and tighter professional controls are likely to be imposed by the occupation itself.

The image of the librarian is primarily deprecatory, not threatening: he is thought to be able to help, but not to harm. In the public view, there is little reason to give the librarian any autonomy or trust, because he can do his job perfectly well without it. At only one point is he viewed as threatening —the selection of books—and that matter is taken out of his hands with respect to nearly all doubtful cases.

Person Professions

Most of the newer aspiring or recognized professions are technical–scientific or managerial; an industrializing society is also professionalizing in that sense, at least. However, the four great traditional professions are different in important structural elements from them, and we shall explore those distinctions now, keeping always in mind, of course, that each of these traits must be viewed as a *dimension* or continuum, so that a given occupation may be high or low with respect to it.

The crucial difference, we have urged, is whether the substance of the task *requires* trust, and therefore autonomy, and therefore some cohesion through which the occupation can in fact impose ethical controls on its members.

In the prototypical case, medicine, this difference has been analyzed at length many times.[28] The physician cannot diagnose and cure his patient without making him vulnerable. He must probe, examine, and question in any direction his own judgment dictates, deciding independently the needs of his patient. Neither the patient nor the society would permit outsiders to witness these procedures or to supervise them. The patient permits the physician to engage in explorations he would not permit to even a spouse, and these, in turn, are not limited much even by custom.[29]

If we place the various professions along this continuum— the extent to which the client *must* allow the professional to know intimate and possibly damaging secrets about his life if the task is to be performed adequately—a fairly clear ranking emerges, and some complex structural implications can be seen. At one extreme are the psychotherapies, and medicine generally. Next would be the confessional clergy, and then law. Following those would be university teaching and, somewhat marginally, architecture for private clients. Because both the military and certified public accountancy have *corporate* clients, they fall at about the same point along this continuum. Beyond them is the wide range of managerial and then the technical–scientific occupations.

To grasp the structural implications of this distinction it is necessary to see that some *part* of the work of even the most humane professions does *not* have the attribute of trust. Thus, the real client of the pathologist is another physician, not a patient, and this is especially so when he reports to the doctor or the hospital staff about why the patient really died. (Under the latter circumstances, he is in a position of trust with respect to his examination of that physician's work, and some of the same structural patterns are observable.)[30] The ophthalmologist in his simpler tasks of determining prescriptions for glasses develops a much less intimate relationship with his patient, but a much more emotional relationship emerges in his role as an ophthalmological surgeon. The radiologist hardly sees his patient, while at the other extreme the patterns to be noted are accentuated in the medical specialties of psychiatry, internal medicine, and surgery. The surgeon may have relatively less interaction with patients but the emotionality of the patient is high.

In a parallel vein, some distinctly non-professional jobs share a few of these traits—but not all, because they have little authority from a knowledge base—e.g., personal servants, executive secretaries, masseurs, geishas, and the like. Within a profession, too, this difference may be observed in styles of practice, e.g., some architects believe the professional should explore intimately their clients' family life in order to design the kind of home needed.

Toward the *person* end of the continuum, several structural patterns are more common. One is that clients are more likely to become emotionally involved with their professionals, e.g. the probability of a transference relationship is higher, because the client feels more vulnerable. Second, the danger is greater that the professional will be tempted to exploit his clients, because they are more likely to be faithful believers. Consequently, a set of norms for appropriate client–professional relations becomes part of the professional's working code of ethics. Moreover, he takes some time to *teach* these norms to his *clients*. Indeed, fellow professionals will judge him partly on the basis of how effectively he keeps his clients under control. Some of these norms are: the professional should not become emotionally attached to his client; he should not give any special favors to one which may disadvantage another; he should rate his client's needs as primary, and should not even be seduced by the client's description of his own needs into following procedures that run against his real needs; he should keep the relationship within the limits of the task to be done; and so on.

Because client–professional relations in this sub-category of professions are more likely to become emotional than in others, and their clients feel more vulnerable, these professions are more likely to be socially *salient*: they are universally known, unlike technical-scientific specialties; they figure in novels; stereotypes are created about them; they are more definitely recognized as distinct occupations.

In a parallel fashion, these professions and the men in them are more likely to live in a swirl of gossip and ambivalence. It is difficult, for example, to end a group conversation that starts with one person's account of "my doctor. . . ." The university professor is the intellectual glory of his country, but in the United States he is also the long-haired fool, as well as the dangerous dreamer. Indeed, I would offer the hypothesis that the more closely a professional's life style approximates the ideal of his profession, the greater the amount of ambivalent gossip generated about him, within the circles that know him.

The client's vulnerability stems from both his exposure under diagnosis and the lesser technical control that the professions at the human end of this continuum enjoy over their problems. All patients die; half of the law cases are lost, as are half of most battles. Many students do not learn much, even when professors do their best. Psychiatric patients terminate therapy eventually, and psychotherapists (like parents) have a touching faith that their patients have improved, but this outcome is often debatable.[31] And how many sinners have clergymen really saved from eternal damnation?

One of the important structural consequences of this is that in these professions more than others the inept can be more easily protected.[32] Indeed, if clients are treated well as human beings, they are less likely ever to question the competence of their professionals.[33] In any event, as we have already noted, the structural fact is that there are no easily available techniques by which the client can test his professional's competence.[34]

Because the client cannot measure performance accurately and is vulnerable, and the profession itself has less technical control over its own problems, the only point at which assurance can be created is the *commitment* of the profession and the professional to the needs of the client whether private or corporate. Because essential behaviors may not be observable to clients or the society, and sometimes not even to colleagues, the internal controls on the professional must be stronger, as must colleague controls when internal controls weaken. One consequence of this structural relation is that ethical problems loom larger and are more frequent in the professional lives of occupations at the *person* extreme of the continuum.

Although we have not exhausted the implications of this great dimension, we must consider the theoretical problem we glossed over in the last paragraph. We have essentially said that ethical controls are stronger because they must be. But to invoke "need" or "must," even in a nonevaluative sense, expresses a touching faith that sociologists can no longer afford. Societies, like people, "need" a great many things they will not get. At best, if a social structure "needs" something, that will mean no more than that opportunities will be seized if they appear, not that opportunities will in fact appear.

My own view, which I emphasize is essentially unprovable at this phase of theoretical exploration, is that this relation is a *corporate bargain*. The profession is given a mandate to obtain potentially dangerous information about its clients because in fact there is no option: the client otherwise cannot be adequately helped. For three of the four traditional professions, society also imposes a restriction, i.e., the clergyman, lawyer, and medical man are not permitted to disclose professional secrets. As part of that bargain, in exchange for a considerable freedom in obtaining possibly threatening data and for the mandate to practice, the profession itself proclaims its intention of preventing its members from exploiting its clients. For example, it enlarges and specifies still further the restrictions on professional secrets, establishes control systems, and may censure or even expel members for unethical behavior. By contrast, toward the technical–scientific end of the continuum, cases of ethical violations are only rarely the subject of discussion in professional councils.

Such a corporate bargain cannot be made or carried out unless the profession is cohesive enough to be able to impose such controls. Specifically, this means that it must be able to organize practice in such a fashion that the more ethical practitioners are, in general, more successful than the less ethical men.[35] Exceptional cases do occur—in academic life, the professor who takes over the work of a brilliant student, the researcher who fudges his data a bit or who alters his conclusions to fit the wishes of an employer, the teacher who exploits the emotions of his students, and the like—but it is notable that such cases arouse considerable moral indignation. They are not simply treated as incompetence or as violations of an ordinary commercial agreement. In academic life, as in other professions, most cases do not become officially known, but the informal network of judgment does operate in all of them.

We cannot treat at length the conditions under which this kind of cohesion is generated, but a brief comment is necessary beyond our earlier discussion. First, the group feels the need of some kind of protection, i.e., precisely because its professional work creates so much emotion, it is also vulnerable. Second, group cohesion usually grows, as well, from a set of shared experiences that other members of the society do not have: one further structural consequence is that some part of professional training is likely to be a type of apprenticeship. For the clergy, medicine, and the military, where perhaps the differences in shared experience are greater, the apprenticeship contains a period in which the trainee essentially lives apart from the rest of the society.[36] The closest similarity is psycho-therapy, where the most highly valued training includes a long period of very personal apprenticeship, usually a didactic analysis of some type.[37] Third, both as students and as professionals, men in these more vulnerable occupations see one another in informal social interaction more than men in other occupations. Their success is more dependent on each other's judgments.[38] Indeed, because precise measurement is difficult, the professional will have much less validation of his competence from his visible mastery of the problem itself, and therefore must get it in interaction with his peers.

A further consequence of these relations is that men in these professions are less likely to abandon their *métier*, and are more likely to say that they would choose the same profession if they were young and faced that decision again.

A few additional relationships may be stated in a more laconic form, since by now the underlying social dynamics are somewhat clearer:

A. The greater the need for the professional to know about his client's private world, the greater is the amount of social interaction between client and professional, and the higher the possibility of intensity of emotional involvement between the two; and the greater is this possibility or intensity,

> 1. The more *explicit* are the ethical codes, both formal and informal, in specifying appropriate relations between client and professional;
> 2. The more explicit and stronger are the prohibitions on accepting close relatives or friends as clients;

3. The more heavily do status variables (age, sex, ethnic membership) count in professional–client relations;

4. The greater is the possibility of (a) using the client's emotions as a means in the solution of his problem, or (b) exploiting him through his emotional involvements;

5. The more likely it is that legislatures consider possible resolutions or laws relating to the profession.

B. The greater the technical control of the profession over its variables, and the greater the precision of its calculations, the less need there is to obtain intimate data about the client in order to solve the problem; and,

1. The more closely does the client–professional relationship approximate a contractual one, with a specification of price and definite results as part of the agreement;

2. The less will be the personal authority of the professional, and the more likely is his advice to be of the form, "if you do so and so, these will be the results," rather than "you must do so and so";

3. The more likely it is that clients will demand proofs of competence, and the less likely that they will demand proofs of devotion to their interests;

4. The less the professional needs the client's confidence in order to do his best work;

5. The less important will be the problems of communication between client and professional, or the difficulties of learning "how to be a client";

6. The less frequently will failure in a case be rationalized or explained away in personal or unique terms ("This was the judge's first case"; "You misunderstood my exposition of the theorem"; "After the operation he did not seem to want to live.")

From the foregoing analysis, it seems clear that a considerable number of consequences hinge on this crucial variable of trust which distinguishes the *person* professions from the rest.

Academics, The Military, and Certified Public Accountancy

It should be emphasized that we are distinguishing a category of professions, and that doubtless over time other occupations will arise, especially of the healing type, which will take on these traits. Thus, we are not so much describing a few concrete occupations as a set of relationships.

However, three of these occupations do not exhibit so obviously as the others all the relations we have described. Let us consider them briefly. Two have a corporate client: the career officer serves the nation, and the certified public accountant serves (usually) a corporation. The third, the university professor, is ambiguous, because it is not clear whether he has a corporate client (the society or the university) or an individual one. Many humanists argue that the client *ought* to be the student, but some might assert that the professor has no client at all.

The first two cases are at least conceptually clear, and most of the relations we have outlined do apply wherever the proposition is not altered beyond recognition by the insertion of "nation" or "corporation" instead of "person." The military must inquire deeply into many weaknesses and strengths of the nation (production, morale, age structures, sedition, political agitation), and indeed their knowledge is potentially dangerous to the nation. Professional socialization is isolated and intense.

The temptation of exploiting the nation's vulnerability must be guarded against by an ethic that emphasizes the ideal of service, even to the point of death, and of course history is also replete with violations of this ideal. The military is both glorified and feared. Because of its cohesion and its successful assertion of autonomy within its peculiar *métier*, its incompetents are more easily protected. Proofs of devotion and loyalty are valued highly, status variables (age, ethnic membership, class) count heavily, and outsider-laymen do not often try to test the skill of the insider-professional.

Thus, where it makes sense at all to apply these general propositions to a profession with a corporate client, most seem to hold. We would expect them to be observable in certified public accountancy, as noted earlier, only at the junctures where the crucial variable we are analyzing is relatively high, i.e., not in the ordinary work of bookkeeping, but only at those points where the professional must enter into the corporate secrets of a firm, diagnose and analyze its internal and external circumstances and actions, and bear the responsibility—*certify*—to outsiders, such as stockholders, law courts, appraisers, buyers, or the society at large, for an accurate statement.

Because, on the other hand, the substance of the certified public accountant's task falls somewhat closer to the technical-scientific end of the continuum than that of the older professions, we would expect that all the relations we have presented would be much weaker. For the present, however, these assertions remain hypotheses not descriptions, as they may apply to certified public accountancy.

Precisely because the temptation to analyze the academic at length is strong, I shall stifle it, and instead simply locate the problem. Academics are accustomed to eliminating the professor from discussions of the client–professional relationship, not because they believe the university or the society is the client, but because they feel they serve the cause of learning, not an individual person (as the priest serves God, not merely his parishioner) and because the student does not pay professors directly. Moreover, academics do not think of themselves as having a code of ethics, because for the most part theirs is the ethic of science and scholarship, which they have so fully absorbed that they do not see it as a set of rules, but as a set of norms which are relatively unquestioned. Indeed, only when they begin to see ambiguities in the ethic, as occurs in the social sciences in modern research on human beings, do university men consider whether they ought to have an explicit code, forgetting that they already follow a set of ethical rules.

Professors are also likely to think of the recurring emotionality (both love and hate) in their relations with students—and the gossip about themselves—as adventitious and unique, rather than as a structural trait of the occupation. Academics use their authority and these emotional relations in order to guide the student toward his best future, and professors feel they have the responsibility to help define their students' ends for them, rather than simply to carry out the students' wishes or serve student-defined goals. If an academic recruit is talented, but exploitative or unethical, his colleagues not only press him to reform, but will refuse to recommend him to others if he persists in his violations.

In short, with respect to most of the relations outlined, the academic fits rather well, but the professor typically does not see them as organized structures, as common conditions, but as individual decisions and commitments. On only one major trait does this pattern fail, that of organizational cohesion, but this is compensated for to a considerable extent by the frequency of interaction among academics, and the informal exchange of information and judgments.

Conclusion

It is not possible to summarize adequately this complex analysis, but its main lines of progression can be stated briefly. Concerned with the general process of professionalization within the society and within individual aspiring occupations, I have noted the two traits that generate all the other characteristics that are considered typical of the established professions. These two, the knowledge base and the ideal of service, were specified in considerable detail, so as to lay bare their major aspects and dimensions. Much of this paper was devoted to analyzing why some aspiring occupations have risen, and others have been unable to rise: because in their transactions with the society or other relevant occupations, what they offered on (mainly) the prestige market in these two major areas was viewed as sufficient or not. Among the occupations analyzed by reference to these generating traits, and the transactions concerning them, are social work, veterinary medicine, the military, architecture, clinical psychology, marital counseling, advertising, educational administration, the management of business and philanthropy, and Mississippi River steamboat pilots.

But though the outcomes of these transactions—these bargains between an aspiring occupation and the society or relevant other occupations—do determine both the larger structure of modern occupations and the social acceptance of an occupation as a profession, we have analyzed at length a further variable that cuts *across* these two main generating variables: the substance of the problem itself. We have noted that the four great established professions of the clergy, medicine, university teaching, and the law retained a number of traits that have to do with the *substance* of their problem, rather than simply with how high they are ranked. Specifically, I suggest that a category of occupations is set apart by a primary variable, upon which a considerable number of structural consequences hinge: whether the professional must symbolically or literally "get inside the client," become privy to his personal world, in order to solve the problem that is the mandate of the profession.

I have examined at length the close sociological dependence of these structural consequences on this variable, and have analyzed their varying form in several professions. I have analyzed to what extent these hypotheses may be correctly applied to two professions that have a corporate client, but which must nevertheless obtain what is in effect "classified knowledge" in order to serve the needs of the client. I have noted the points at which the academic profession exhibits the social patterns I have outlined, although the individual professor may not see these as structures, but as individual and unique decisions and attitudes.

Finally, it is clear that this last sub-category of professions, whose core is the four great, traditional *person* professions, has not expanded much to include many new professions, in contrast with the higher-level managerial and scientific-technical professions and semi-professions. In this much narrower sense, then, it is not entirely clear that the industrial occupational structure of the society is generally professionalizing. Relatively few professions are arising that require trust and autonomy and that can obtain it through transactions with the society.

Notes

1. Here, I am using what I consider the major control systems in social action (power, money, prestige, and friendship–civility) without further theoretical elaboration. A forthcoming monograph will analyze their operations. Here, I am omitting a fifth control system, qualitatively different, that of information–expertise. However, in the present paper, I am not using these terms in any esoteric senses that require conceptual explication.

2. For one version of this view, see W. J. Goode, "A Theory of Role Strain," in *American Sociological Review*, 25 (August, 1960), 483–96. As I understand Homans and Blau, both seem to believe that values and norms are created within such transactions among individuals. In my view, the fact that pre-existing evaluations determine the worth of what is exchanged is crucial to an analysis of exchanges. See George C. Homans, *Social Behavior* (New York: Harcourt, 1961); and Peter M. Blau, *Exchange and Power* (New York: Wiley, 1964).

3. Vernon K. Dibble (in "Occupations and Ideologies," in *American Journal of Sociology*, 67 [September, 1962], 229–41) argues that a high ranking occupation can more easily persuade others that its ideology is acceptable.

4. At a minimum, a substantial percentage of the men in high places came from modest origins, though of course if a society is composed *mainly* of peasants, it is not numerically possible for a high percentage of that stratum to rise to the top. For comparative figures, see Robert M. Marsh, *The Mandarins* (New York: Free Press, 1961), and W. J. Goode, "Family and Mobility," in *Class, Status, and Power*, ed. Reinhard Bendix and Seymour M. Lipset (New York: Free Press, 1966), pp. 582–601.

5. "There are some very agreeable and beautiful talents . . . of which the exercise for the sake of gain is considered . . . as a sort of public prostitution. . . . The exorbitant rewards of players, opera-singers, opera-dancers, etc. are founded upon those two principles; the rarity and beauty of the talents and the discredit of employing them in this manner." Adam Smith, *An Inquiry into the Nature and Causes of the Wealth of Nations* (New York: Modern Library, 1937), p. 107.

6. It is likely that Twain was a victim of the usual exaggeration of occupational prestige among practitioners. He was proud of his skill. It is unlikely that pilots were generally ranked among the upper class of the Old South, which included large plantation owners, great merchants or factors, and successful professionals. See Wilbert E. Moore and Robin M. Williams, "Stratification in the Anti-Bellum South," in *American Sociological Review*, 7 (June, 1942), 343–51.

7. Although A. M. Carr-Saunders and P. A. Wilson do not use this concept, their historical inquiry into a wide range of aspiring occupations, *The Professions* (Oxford: Clarendon, 1933), clearly aims at establishing such a sequence. T. A. Caplow presents a sequence of four steps in *The Sociology of Work* (Minneapolis: University of Minnesota, 1954), pp. 139–40.

8. These are presented in Harold Wilensky, "The Professionalization of Everyone?" in *American Journal of Sociology*, 70 (September, 1964), 142–46.

9. Carr-Saunders and Wilson (*op. cit.*, pp. 284–318) summarize them, but also use them throughout their historical descriptions. William J. Goode, Robert K. Merton, and Mary Jean Huntington,

in *The Professions in Modern Society* (New York: Russell Sage Foundation, 1956, mimeo), Chapter 1, present a tabulation from many sources. Ernest Greenwood, in "The Attributes of a Profession," in *Social Work*, 2 (July, 1957), 44–55, presents such a list. Similar statements will be found in Goode, "Community Within a Community: The Professions," in *American Sociological Review*, 22 (April, 1957), 194–200; and Goode, "Encroachment, Charlatanism, and the Emerging Profession: Psychology, Sociology, and Medicine," in *American Sociological Review*, 25 (December, 1960), 903–4.

10. See Goode, "Encroachment . . . ," pp. 903–4, and Wilensky, *op. cit.*, p. 138.

11. For the reciprocal process by which a monopoly over a valued service supports the standing of an occupation in the prestige market, see Dibble, *op. cit.*, pp. 236–37.

12. Perhaps it should be emphasized that we are referring to the social worker, who has undergone professional training which culminates in the M.S.W. or the doctorate in social work. By contrast, the welfare or case worker in urban departments of welfare is much less likely to have been trained in a formal curriculum, and of course does not fall into this category.

13. I have analyzed this case more extensively in "The Librarian: From Occupation to Profession?" in *The Library Quarterly*, 31 (October, 1961), 306–20.

14. In these analyses, I am largely omitting the manipulations within power markets. I view them as ultimately important, but largely derivative. A professionalizing occupation is more likely to gain power through its success on the prestige and economic markets, rather than the reverse.

15. For the interaction of autonomy, discipline, and knowledge, see W. J. Goode, "Encroachment, Charlatanism, and the Emerging Profession," pp. 910–14, where references are made to various attempts to measure the usefulness of psychotherapy.

16. In these rebuttals we are concerned only with the relation of the occupation to the highest levels of relevant knowledge. A different kind of refutation is that in many instances no medicine is still worse than bad medicine. Therefore, the less trained person should not be allowed to practice independently.

17. Separate from the *amount* of knowledge an occupation needs to learn is its abstractness, as Amitai Etzioni has reminded me, although this problem does not often figure in arguments about professional standing. Even when many concrete facts are missing in a problem, command over an abstract framework may yield productive (if tentative) solutions; at a minimum, it suggests ways of deducing which facts are important, and how to get them.

18. Goode, "The Librarian . . . ."

19. See the extended analysis of these points in William J. Goode, "The Librarian . . . ," pp. 311ff., as well as Arthur M. McNally, "The Dynamics of Securing Academic Status," in Robert B. Downs, *The Status of American College and University Librarians,* ACRL Monograph No. 22 (Chicago: American Library Association, 1958), p. 3.

20. See, for example, *The Handbook of Organizations,* ed. James G. March (Chicago: Rand-McNally, 1965).

21. Note, however, the threat of independence in this area. See Harry P. Smith, "Clinical Pathology: Its Creators and Its Practitioners," in *American Journal of Clinical Pathology,* 31 (April, 1959), 283–92, and *Preliminary Report of the Committee on Professional Qualifications for the Practice of Laboratory Medicine* (College of American Pathologists; August, 1959).

22. Thus, very likely most basic medical research is done by biochemists, physiologists, and even physicists, but a far higher proportion of physicians are also engaged in research than were so engaged in 1900 or 1850.

23. For further details, see Goode, "Encroachment, Charlatanism. . . ." See also Alvin Zander, Arthur Cohen, Ezra Statland, and collaborators, "Average Attitudes of One Professional Group Toward Another," in *Professionalization,* ed. H. M. Vollmer and D. L. Mills (Englewood Cliffs, N.J.: Prentice-Hall, 1966), pp. 237ff.

24. For an analysis of the problems in maintaining autonomy of the *foundation,* see Richard Colvard, "Foundations and Professions: The Organizational Defense of Autonomy," in *Administrative Science Quarterly,* 6 (September, 1961), 167–84.

25. Marjorie Fiske, *Book Selection and Censorship* (Berkeley: U. of

California, 1959), pp. 11ff. and 52–71; and Robert D. Leigh, *The Public Library in the United States* (New York: Columbia U.P., 1950), pp. 120–1.

26. Perhaps all occupations approaching professional status try to control, and assert their claim to autonomy. In a formalized type of society such as ours, both actions may be ignored and the state may impose its own controls. Note the very high stakes involved in transportation. Here, however, the failure is first of all either incompetence or carelessness—*not*, self-interest—and whatever the cause of the failure it is likely that the practitioner himself (railroad engineer, bus driver, airline pilot, steamship captain) will physically suffer when he has an accident. One basic control is built into the environment itself.

27. For some of those attitudes, see Richard K. Kerckhoff, "Interest Group Reactions to the Profession of Marriage Counseling," in *Sociology and Sociological Research,* 39 (January-February, 1955), 178–93.

28. See the extended analysis in Talcott Parsons, *The Social System* (New York: Free Press, 1951), Chapter 10.

29. Note that though this is not recent, in various times and places in the past the physician was *not* allowed to examine so thoroughly, especially when the patient was a woman; but so intimate a probing was not thought to be—and, with the knowledge of the time, was not in fact—useful or necessary.

30. For a fuller analysis, see Fred E. Katz, *Autonomy and Organization* (New York: Random House, 1968), esp. Chapters 4–6.

31. See the attempts at measurement of outcome, noted in Goode, "Encroachment, Charlatanism . . . ," p. 912.

32. More extended analysis may be found in Goode, "The Protection of the Inept," in *American Sociological Review,* 32 (February, 1967), 5–19.

33. For example, malpractice suits are much less likely, even when poor medical procedures have been followed, if the physician has convinced his patient that he has been solicitous, warm, and so on.

34. As many departmental chairmen in the humanities and social sciences have learned to their sorrow, it is dangerous to fire a man whom colleagues agree is incompetent if he has good relations with his students.

35. The best recent analysis of the variables that affect ethical conformity is Jerome S. Carlin, *Lawyers' Ethics* (New York: Russell Sage Foundation, 1966).

36. Analyses of this socialization may be found in Morris Janowitz, *The Professional Soldier* (New York: Free Press, 1960), Chapter 7; *The Student-Physician,* ed. Robert K. Merton, George G. Reader, and Patricia L. Kendall (Cambridge: Harvard U.P., 1957); and Howard S. Becker, Blanche Geer, *et al., Boys in White* (Chicago: U. of Chicago, 1961).

37. A measure of "occupational community" that embodies both friendship patterns and formal organization is used in a study of lawyers, professors, and engineers in H. Wilensky and J. Ladinsky, "From Religious Community to Occupational Group: Structural Assimilation among Professors, Lawyers, and Engineers," in *American Sociological Review,* 32 (August, 1967), 541–61. Professors have a higher index rating than lawyers or engineers, whose training period is shorter.

38. In Wilensky (*op. cit.,* p. 152), professors, lawyers, and engineers were asked whose judgment they thought should count most in the evaluation of their work. Eighty-one per cent of the professors ranked their colleagues foremost, 51 per cent of lawyers, and 18 per cent of engineers.

Index